Springer Series on Cultural Computing

More information about this series at http://www.springer.com/series/10481

Nelson Zagalo • Pedro Branco

Editors

Creativity in the Digital Age

Editors
Nelson Zagalo
University of Minho
Department of Communication Sciences
Portugal

Pedro Branco
University of Minho
Department of Information Systems
Portugal

ISSN 2195-9056   ISSN 2195-9064   (electronic)
Springer Series on Cultural Computing
ISBN 978-1-4471-7247-5   ISBN 978-1-4471-6681-8   (eBook)
DOI 10.1007/978-1-4471-6681-8

Springer London Heidelberg New York Dordrecht
© Springer-Verlag London 2015
Softcover reprint of the hardcover 1st edition 2015

Printed on acid-free paper

Springer-Verlag London Ltd. is part of Springer Science+Business Media (www.springer.com)

Preface

The drive for creating this book originated from teaching and researching in this field. As education practitioners we felt the lack of consolidated knowledge, which made us improvise new paths year after year. As researchers we believe that novel technologies require in-depth discussion within diverse fields of human knowledge to consolidate definitions, approaches and methodologies. This led us to invite a group of colleagues to edit a book on Digital Creativity.

The work to arrive here took 3 years, from submitting our intention to Springer to delivery of the full manuscript. The topic was relevant, and we found many researchers interested in participating in the book, in bringing their expertise to make the subject more understandable. However during the first attempt to edit a preview of the book we found that half of the contributions were not concerned with the core topic. Even among scholars the topic was not clear, giving rise to very different ideas, mostly related to misconceptions around the idea of creativity. We then requested another set of contributions, on very specific topics within Digital Creativity. All this said and done, we must say that we are very pleased with what we have achieved with this process.

We unveil this part of the process because it delves into the main point of the domain of Digital Creativity (DC). We live in a time where creativity is a buzzword; it represents for many, the salvation from "darkest times". Words like creativity, creative or creation pop up almost anywhere, not only in the business world, but also in academia. Having these experiences is good because it gives strength to the subject, but at the same time, it brings a lot of other things unrelated to the matter. So what happened with our first attempt to edit this book is what has happened during the last few years whenever people tried to put together projects related with creativity.

We want to trace from here a concrete line about what DC is not, because for what it is, you should read the book. Firstly, DC is not the same as "creativity support tools", tools to make people more creative. Secondly, DC is not tools to serve only the media industries. And thirdly, DC is not the "saint saviour" of capitalist economies. Even if DC can address these topics, in the long run, none of these matters are central to them. DC is mainly concerned with matters of self-realisation and self-discovery, the central concern are the human needs of expression. DC is concerned with opening new dimensions and help human beings to flourish.

As we have identified, addressing knowledge in depth on the domain of DC represented a significant enterprise with many challenges that had to be addressed consistently at many levels, starting with the multidisciplinary approach that needed interdisciplinary and transdisciplinary values. To achieve workable definitions we had to bring together researchers from many different knowledge areas, such as: computer science, design, communication, engineering, arts, philosophy, psychology, pedagogy, media, linguistics, literature, electronic, film, games, music and marketing. The scope of background knowledge for DC is large but the discussion is concerned with a very specific set of objectives.

To achieve the objectives the book is divided into four parts: Fundamentals of Digital Creativity; Expressive Processes; Co-creation and Collaboration; Makers and Players. The idea is to present different fronts of DC, starting with a first defining part, setting the general approach and main definitions. It is followed by a more generic part, which opens the scope of possibilities and domains for the expression through DC. The second half of the book is confined to strict dimensions of our definitions, thus discussing co-creation, collaboration and making aspects.

Part one begins with our chapter to define our vision of creative technologies, central to the domain of DC, talking about possible impacts and effects we expect they will have in the future. We have also requested the help of David Gauntlett, who has been working with the topic for the past decade, helping to connect cultural dots between industrial and information revolutions. Our colleagues from Auckland University, (responsible for one of the first bachelor's degree on Creative Technologies) Andy M. Connor, Stefan Marks and Charles Walker in their chapter give us a flavour of the difficulties behind creating a University degree that is multidisciplinary, to go beyond theorisation, and achieve production of material artefacts.

In the second part, Expressive Processes, our intention was to open up the areas for which DC can be relevant. It is easy to understand that with that in mind, we could arrive at a very large part, or even make an entire book on these ramifications; we decided therefore to have only three chapters. The first one by Stefano Gualeni is dedicated to expand DC through philosophy, using the expressivity of digital technologies to make complex ideas simple and cognitively easy to grasp. In the second chapter, Maria Soto-Sanfield works on the ways these technologies empower human narrativisation, which cognitively is the way through which we make meaning of our worlds. The third chapter, was reversed, because instead of going out, we brought in, approaching the field of ubiquitous music to bring its knowledge on the socially distributed nature of creative activity, into the modelling of DC.

In part three, Co-creation and Collaboration, we start with a more delimited discussion of very specific topics of DC. In the first chapter, our colleagues from Georgia Tech discuss the new opportunities made possible by having computers at our side, as colleagues for creation, and discuss a new realm of research, which will be very relevant for the future of DC. The collaboration with computers is followed by a presentation of the results of studies with children in collaborative communities, which identifies a set of logics, models and approaches, which are highly relevant for the building of DC. The third chapter presents an analysis on the co-creative methods used by LEGO to maintain its relevance in the twenty-first century, which helps us to better understand how DC has already impacted real-world business, and its changing communication paradigms. To close this part, we bring an analysis of the crowdfunding platforms, its achievements but mainly its communicative traits, identifying relevant approaches for the DC communities.

In the last part, Makers and Players, we open the discussion around the maker movement, with Josh and Karen Tannenbaum speculating about the future of the movement grounded in scenarios from Sci-fi literature. This speculation gives place to empiria in the next chapter, where colleagues present different technologies built and validated within creative communities, discussing maker approaches and potential new paths for the DC implementation. The final chapter of this part closes the book with a discussion around one of the most defining topics of the appearance of DC, the vocational training and how it affects motivation, engagement and the passion of learners.

In closing, we as editors would like to thank and congratulate the entire group of researchers, educators and practitioners that made possible the building of this book. Also we would like to thank Springer for being open to publish a book on such a novel, and still undefined, area.

Portugal   Nelson Zagalo
January, 2015   Pedro Branco

Contents

Contributors

Simone Bekk Karlsruhe Institute of Technology, Institute of Vocational and General Education, Karlsruhe, Germany

Vlada Botoric Department of Aesthetics and Communication, Aarhus University, Aarhus, Denmark

Pedro Branco Department of Information Systems, University of Minho, Portugal

Andy M. Connor Colab, Auckland University of Technology, Auckland, New Zealand

Sara Cortés Department of Philology, Communication and Information, University of Alcalá, Madrid, Spain

Leandro Costalonga Federal University of Espirito Santo, Vitória, Brazil

Clara Coutinho Institute of Education, University of Minho, Braga, Portugal

Nicholas Davis School of Interactive Computing, Georgia Institute of Technology, Atlanta, GA, USA

Maria Helena de Lima Federal University of Rio Grande do Sul, Porto Alegre, Brazil

María Ruth García-Pernía Department of Philology, Communication and Information, University of Alcalá, Madrid, Spain

David Gauntlett Faculty of Media, Arts and Design, University of Westminster, London, UK

Gloria Gómez-Diago Department of Communication Sciences II, Universidad Rey Juan Carlos, Madrid, Spain

Stefano Gualeni Institute of Digital Games, University of Malta, Msida, Malta

Chih-Pin Hsiao College of Architecture, Georgia Institute of Technology, Atlanta, GA, USA

Marcelo Johann Federal University of Rio Grande do Sul, Porto Alegre, Brazil

Damián Keller NAP, Federal University of Acre, Rio Branco, Acre, Brazil

Pilar Lacasa Department of Philology, Communication and Information, University of Alcalá, Madrid, Spain

Victor Lazzarini National University of Ireland, Maynooth, Ireland

Brian Magerko School of Interactive Computing, Georgia Institute of Technology, Atlanta, GA, USA

Stefan Marks Colab, Auckland University of Technology, Auckland, New Zealand

Nuno Otero Linnaeus University, Kalmar, Sweden

Marcelo Soares Pimenta Federal University of Rio Grande do Sul, Porto Alegre, Brazil

Yanna Popova Department of Cognitive Science, Case Western Reserve University, Cleveland, OH, USA

Daniela Reimann Karlsruhe Institute of Technology, Institute of Vocational and General Education, Karlsruhe, Germany

María T. Soto-Sanfiel Department of Audiovisual Communication and Advertising, Universitat Autònoma de Barcelona, Barcelona, Spain

Cristina Sylla Centre for Child Studies, University of Minho, Braga, Portugal

Joshua G. Tanenbaum Department of Informatics, Donald Bren School of Information and Computer Sciences, University of California-Irvine, Irvine, CA, USA

Karen Tanenbaum Department of Informatics, Donald Bren School of Information and Computer Sciences, University of California-Irvine, Irvine, CA, USA

Charles Walker Colab, Auckland University of Technology, Auckland, New Zealand

Nelson Zagalo Department of Communication Sciences, University of Minho, Braga, Portugal

Part I
Fundamentals of Digital Creativity

Chapter 1
The Creative Revolution That Is Changing the World

Nelson Zagalo and Pedro Branco

1.1 Introduction

Since the dawn of humanity, we have developed creative technologies, tools that would support externally expressed creations, as ink, carving tools, or sounding objects. Creative technologies have always been the basis for human expressivity: to sustain self-realization, to raise self-esteem, to increase community bonds, and to create a better society. Also understanding technology as "anything useful invented by a mind" (Kelly 2010) encompasses an idea of humanity inextricable from technology. Technology sorts solutions for problems, rises our adaptability, and functions as a second skin between the world and ourselves, as an "extended body of ideas" (Kelly 2010:44). It is part of our culture and of our evolution and is responsible for what we are today.

Nevertheless, in the last 30 years, the development and convergence of a series of technologies has lead to new phenomena. The online sharing of knowledge, ideas, and content and the arrival of new accessible technological tools for creation have enabled many more people to create and express themselves through digital media, leading to massive amounts of rich media content creation by the curious hobbyist all the way to the artists and professionals. So much professional and amateur content is online that you can learn anything just by searching video tutorials, *instructables*, and discussion forums: someone has tried it, someone has tested it, and someone has explained it.

N. Zagalo (✉)
Department of Communication Sciences, University of Minho,
4710-057 Braga, Portugal
e-mail: nzagalo@gmail.com

P. Branco
Department of Information Systems, University of Minho, Portugal
e-mail: pbranco@dsi.uminho.pt

© Springer-Verlag London 2015
N. Zagalo, P. Branco (eds.), *Creativity in the Digital Age*,
Springer Series on Cultural Computing, DOI 10.1007/978-1-4471-6681-8_1

We then believe that there is a new cultural movement taking shape. This movement is providing a "voice" through which anyone can express to everyone whatever their imagination can create, democratizing innovation and creativity like never before. At the core of this emerging cultural movement are digital technologies that enable the access to sophisticated tools for rich media content creation, sharing of ideas, discussion, and distribution.

An example of such phenomenon is the Star Wars fan film awards. Fans submit entries to that contest, showcasing their ability and acknowledging their appreciation for the Star Wars saga. What used to be completely out of range technically and economically for nonprofessionals, and would signify a massive and expensive effort of a movie studio to produce, has now become possible for dedicated hobbyists to produce sophisticated computer animations.

That and many other examples of entertainment content is distributed, commented on, shared, and reshared over social networks, shaping new ways of what we do for leisure. Increasingly more people are turning off the television and tuning to Facebook to watch what others are saying, commenting on, and following and what is being linked on YouTube, Vimeo, and Blogs.

The more we express ourselves, the more we tend to sense ourselves. We believe that new creative technologies are forming the ground for the next great cultural movement giving voice to user's wishes to express inner feelings, ideas, and visions; transforming; and giving shape to whatever imagination can generate. We believe that the future of technology will be largely determined by end users who will design, build, and share their own worlds, and creative technologies will inspire and support this shaping process.

Not all roses. A recent documentary by David Dworsky, "PausePressPlay" (2011), discusses how the digital revolution of the last decade has unleashed people's creativity and talent, but at some point it questions the dark sides, asking if this is not the end of our cultural industry. Seemingly apocalyptic it raises concerns for our reflection; Andrew Keen shot one of the first rocks, with "The Cult of the Amateur: How Today's Internet Is Killing Our Culture" (2007), which was pursued by Jaron Lanier with "You Are Not A Gadget: A Manifesto" (2010) and "Who Owns The Future?" (2013) and then by Evgeny Morozov with "The Net Delusion: The Dark Side of Internet Freedom" (2012) and "To Save Everything, Click Here: Technology, Solutionism, and the Urge to Fix Problems that Don't Exist" (2013). We understand that there are problems, as there are always with all transformations; our goal here is not to cleanse and paint a one-colour landscape, but we simply chose to focus our analyses on the creative production side, leaving outside the reception transformation. We acknowledge that this will change culture as we know it, raising new drawbacks; however, we cannot forget the new real possibilities all these changes represent for human creativity and all the impact it can have in human life.

In the next sections we will argue that while there have been incredible creative individuals in our history, in fact many more may never have discovered their area of intervention to express their creativity, maybe the technology to allow them to shine never came across. We will look at the events in recent history and the technological developments that brought to the very edge a new cultural movement. We continue to reflect on what makes a particular technology support this creative revolution movement.

1.2 The Motivation

The creation process is enclosed within us, and because of that has always existed since we exist. Boyd (2009) refers to the need, this urge to express through creation, as "cognitive play" behaviour, a "set of activities designed to engage human attention through their appeal to our preference for inferentially rich and therefore patterned information" (p. 86). The patterned information is key. Humans, among higher primates, prefer regular, symmetrical, and/or rhythmic patterns (Gazzaniga 2008:215). In space and time we sense beauty in "the rule of order over randomness, of pattern over chaos" (Weiss 1955:286). Edward Purcell (cited by Gould 1992) said we have "avidity for pattern" for information forming arrangements that can stimulate in us deep and varied inferences. The functionality of this patterned world and ideas serve to stimulate mind flexibility and with that lead human activity "for engendering creativity, for producing options not confined by the here and now or the immediate and given" (Boyd 2009:87).

Classical views of creativity from Sternberg to Csíkszentmihályi define creativity as something extraordinary, difficult to achieve, and at reach for only a small group of individuals. Csíkszentmihályi (1997:8) states that

> creativity results from the interaction of a system composed of three elements: a culture that contains symbolic rules, a person who brings novelty into the symbolic domain, and a field of experts who recognise and validate the innovation.

The idea is then to produce something never seen before, something outstanding from all previous manifestations. We're talking about symbolical works like the ones created by Michelangelo and Caravaggio, Galileo and Copernic, Mozart and Beethoven, Borges and Pessoa, or Méliès and Eisenstein. These are people who have created a new, from grasp, who have opened up new ways to express, to think, and to imagine the domain itself – works that have been admired, recognized, and validated by peers as truly creative.

Albeit we accept these individuals can have attained levels of performance that outpace the great majority of common individuals, we agree with Gauntlett (2011) when he says that this is a very reductionist perspective of creativity as a human activity. We believe that all humans are creative, and this is central to our quest in this work.

Humans are strongly creative; the main problem most of us have is the lack of opportunities to find the right domain to express our inner ideas and exteriorize them through creative productions. Robinson (2010) defines this finding for the right domain as encountering "the element", the activity in which we feel comfortable enough, in which our passion opens path to go beyond own limitations. Gardner

(1983) has been talking about this for long, demystifying the idea that for people to be brilliant they need to follow narrow and specific literacy scholarly paths. Gardner defined human's performance within eight domains: "spatial, linguistic, logical-mathematical, bodily-kinaesthetic, musical, interpersonal, intrapersonal, and naturalistic".

School as we know it today still lives in the industrial revolution period. The need for a massification of societal behaviours and habits has developed large man-ufactories that we now call schools. In this environment teachers have no time to look for singular abilities in each student; they fight most of their time to communicate the conventional knowledge and to achieve uniform "positive" results. Students are taught to conform to norms and rules of the majority eliminating the possibility to spot unusual manifestations, thus blocking expressive potential.

We believe it is our responsibility to fight to eliminate this misconception on human normalized capabilities and to help strongly diminish the lack of opportunities of our students to manifest self-expression. Our answer is a new cultural movement we call creative technologies, technologies that enable common people to express themselves. People who had no opportunities to learn how to read musical scores, to learn how to program a computer, and to learn how to sing, paint, dance, film, perform, and design are now given through these new creative technologies new modes to participate, collaborate, and share learning processes which will liberate creativity.

Obviously these persons, beginning new activities, will not produce outstanding works immediately. The goal is not to outperform, but to find the right element, the vocational attitude. The aim is to free people to express, to let them exteriorize their inner feelings though different creative possibilities. We believe that in opening and bringing closer the entire set of creative domains, embedded in participatory culture, we'll be able to explore more fully human potential, because this impulse to create together, helped by creative technologies, will be serving directly two of the most important elements – socialization and self-realization – in the human quest for happiness (Sheldon and Lyubomirsky 2004).

1.3   Cultural State of the Art

The domain of creative technologies has been approached by other topics here and there, like the domain of the "creativity support tools" well supported by Shneiderman et al. (2005), as with all the most recent discussions on participatory culture subjects like the Web 2.0, the user-generated content, the collaboration tools, or the social networks and social media.

Shneidermans' (1987, 1999, 2002) work has always been around the enhancing of human-computer interaction, through the easing of user interfaces; with that he has been looking for ways to improve the access to technologies by more and more people with as less digital literacy as possible. In 2005 he organized the workshop, "Creativity Support Tools" (CST) (Shneiderman et al. 2005) sponsored by the National Science Foundation.

This workshop intention was stated to have the aim "to develop improved software and user interfaces that empower users to be more productive and more innovative", which shows a bias from creativity into the production processes and task-oriented software. And this bias becomes even clearer when they state the users "include software and other engineers, diverse scientists, product and graphic designers, architects, and many others". Thus the CST was for people already producing and creating; the goal was not to enhance inner creativity but to enhance the production daily processes – creativity tools that facilitate their daily tasks, in part to free their minds for other tasks, possibly more creative tasks.

With creative technologies the goal is not to facilitate workflows; however, it can have that effect, but to facilitate the creative act, to make it happen – to open new "windows" for expression, using digital technologies. Here we agree with the CST report stating that creativity increases with available technologies:

> the capacity of individuals to be creative grows as the software tools spread to diverse disciplines. The first generation of business software such as spreadsheets, database management, email, and web services changed the face of industry and created a global marketplace. The impact of improved software tools is also clearly visible in filmmaking, digital photography, video editing, and music composition. The next generation of these tools will have an even stronger impact as the number of users grows dramatically from few million to a few billion people. (Shneiderman et al. 2005:7)

But needless to say that albeit creative technologies are being spread across the globe, the goal is not to create a "global marketplace" in the sense of creating mass customers, because it goes against the idea of a "few billion people" creating. This was well stated in the "long tail" definition by Anderson (2006) on the changes going on in the cultural markets and more recently well illustrated by Godin (2011) where he defends the shrinking of mass markets, and emergence of thousands of new niche markets, totally in accordance with Anderson "long tail" vision.

Another point from the report where we disagree is on the subject of "creativity enhancement" defended by the report as the main quest. The idea that supports creative technologies is not grounded within the concept of enhancement, but of discovery. Tools are not supposed to improve the person's capabilities, but to help the person to find their own creative unique skills, to output them to the world. As Kelly (2010:350) said,

> if we fail to enlarge the possibilities for other people we diminish them, and that is unforgivable. Enlarging the scope of creativity for others, then, is an obligation. We enlarge others by enlarging the possibilities of the technium – by developing more technology and more convivial expressions of it. (..) can you imagine how poor our world would be if Bach had been born 1,000 years before the Flemish invented the technology of the harpsichord? Or if Mozart had preceded the technologies of piano and symphony? How vacant our collective imaginations would be if Vincent van Gogh had arrived 5,000 years before we invented cheap oil paint?

In this sense creative technologies have as their main goal the task of facilitating creation by general people, to allow general people to self-discover the best of themselves that they can give back to the community.

On the other side of the literary spectrum, we have the debate on the subject of participatory culture. Jenkins has been talking about the changes in the culture of content creation for so long (1992), moving from mainstream media content to artworks produced by amateurs, for example, the gigantic fan base for Star Wars, or Star Trek, which takes communities to produce amateur films, comics, clothes, and toys.

Also more recently Jenkins was responsible for the white paper on participatory culture (2009) funded by the MacArthur program on "Building the new field of digital media and learning". Here Jenkins talks about the shift occurring with culture that have been produced by some to serve the masses, into culture produced by all to serve all, and the new approaches we need to take into account in schools. The discussion focuses around the idea that media literacy taught from the analytical and critical perspective only is not enough and that kids should be also taught about the creative dimensions and learn the skills to express themselves and communicate with all others.

Creative technologies strongly defend this perspective, the need to open up the teaching subjects, allowing different domains to enter schools. Thus new technologies being created are aimed at novices, people with no special knowledge, which sits very well with children at school.

The idea of moving from all-to-one to all-to-all is directly connected with the idea of democratization of knowledge, shortcutting through creative authorities. Gauntlet (2011:49) compares the democratization allowed by the open-source software movement in the 1990s of the twentieth century, with the one developed by the Arts and Crafts Movement in the nineteenth century by William Morris inspired by the writings of John Ruskin. Both movements were responsible for the appearance of subsequent movements that we now label as "do it yourself" (DIY). The DIY creations appear as the basis for the communication all-to-all, engendering a culture of doing things on your own. The DIY emerges because the community, in the sense they support creation and sharing processes, allows creators and also because of the intrinsic pleasure they get from doing, creating, and being recognized by the community, which grants self-esteem. Compensation doesn't come in economic form but as social reward in the form of community acknowledgement.

On this movement to a participatory culture, Shirky (2010:28) reflected about the mode in which it happens, dividing the process in three dimensions: "the means", "the motives", and "the opportunities". Shirky defends that we can have access to a cognitive surplus if we enjoy the free time we have participating and collaborating with others. The day has 24 h, 8 h to work and 8 h to sleep, and we still have 8 h free. The "means" appear with the collaboration with people connected through digital technologies. The collaboration makes it possible to create artworks that are not possible for one person living in isolation. The "motives" surge with the realization of higher-quality works through this connection and admired by the connections.

Finally "opportunities" appear when people connect with technologies that not only allow them to share, participate, and collaborate but also enable them to express their intrinsic creative desires. This simple tripartite process explains the basics for the launching of any new creative technology, as a necessity to open up new opportunities for people to create and express self-talents and to answer to the means generated by the participatory culture and the motivation people feel to get involved in the process.

The digital participatory culture developed in recent years has been also responsible for changes occurring in the funding of creative projects, albeit economic views such as the *long tail* (Anderson 2006) were insufficient to convince editors and producers to give a green light to risky projects. Thus in 2009 a completely new idea emerged among the social creative turbulence online, bringing the charity values into play and creating a crowd funding social software for creative work. *Kickstarter* is only one of these systems that allow any person to pledge for his future work on journalism, music, film, games, or even a start-up company. The production here is reversed: consumers pay before consuming; they pay to see, hear, or play; but they also pay to strengthen creative community values. No more editors, people communicate directly, people share problems and share needs, and people exchange knowledge and help each other. This is the final frontier, where authors meet receivers and interact for real and where all can be authors and consumers at the same time.

1.4   Technological State of the Art

At the beginning of the 1980s, the first home computers appeared, the microcomputers ZX Spectrum, BBC Microcomputer, and Commodore 64. Using these microprocessors (which only had 8 bits, 16 Kb of RAM, no hard drive, and as support to exchange content the old magnetic cassettes) changed the world of communication, playing, and creation. In order to create games or applications, people needed to know how to code BASIC, but BASIC couldn't serve the graphical needs of games, so it would demand assembler skills, which is difficult for people with little or no programming skills. What then happened was truly dignifying and representative of the power of the communities and their sharing values. Some of programmers created software packages that would help nonprogrammers to create their games. Packages like *The Quill* (1983) by Howards Gilbert, *Games Designer* (1983) by Quicksilva, and *Graphic Adventure Creator* (1985) by Incentive allowed people with creative ideas for games to be able to create them. Although it was not of the same quality of a program totally created from scratch in assembler, it was possible for anyone to prototype and demonstrate his or her visions. These tools came with what we call one of the fundamental basics of creative technologies, embedded knowledge. Users were able to create new projects because tools were embedded with knowledge from programmers in the form of editors, behaviours, and other structures.

These developments contributed to the creation of a new business model that we call today "authoring software" – software that takes users by the hand in the process of integrating multiple types of media with almost no programming, applications like *Hypercard, Hypermedia, Macromedia Director, Adobe Flash*, or the new HTML5 editors. All these packages transfer knowledge from specialists to nonspecialists in usable and comprehensible forms; hence all these authoring tools belong to the creative technologies domain.

In 2007 the authors of this chapter released the application *Emotion Wizard*, a prototype that allows users with no skills in the design of virtual worlds to very quickly and easily set up the mood of 3d environments (Zagalo and Torres 2008). In the same year the MIT group, Lifelong Kindergarten, using the mantra "Showing the Seeds for a More Creative Society", delivered the visual programming language, called *Scratch*. They wanted to permit nonskilled users, the children, to create "from scratch" their "own interactive stories, animations, games, music, and art",[1] in synthesis, to express themselves, giving external form to inner, private, and individual imagined worlds.

Scratch visual metaphors have been so successful that in 2010 Google used it to create *Google App Inventor*,[2] a tool allowing anyone to create their own software applications for the Android OS. And again in 2011 another company created *StencylWorks*,[3] a game engine to permit anyone to create games, making use of a programming layer based in Scratch and working upon Actionscript 3.0.

In parallel to the "authoring software" evolution, back in the 1980s appeared another community movement, grounded in mass collaboration that came to be defined as the GNU Project. Created by Richard Stallman from MIT in 1983, it was a response to all corporate software. The goal was to liberate creativity by granting free access to the code to improve software and free to redistribute it to anyone. Free software emerged as a leading force for computer communities all over the world. The concept created a movement, which opened the digital arena for totally freedom and creation – liberation from the "not do," from the copyright infringements, and from the corporations laws impeding consumers creativity. The free software movement then merged in 1998 into the movement on open source.

In 2002 the open-source movement, typically restricted to the computer science communities, expanded to receive creators with no digital skills, Web 2.0 emerged, the term RIA (Rich Internet Applications) was coined,[4] and the first Creative Commons licenses were released.[5] This larger group was in the first phase much more concentrated on sharing activities; the creation was limited to productions with text (e.g. blogs), maybe because most of the initial tools where not yet open to other possibilities.

---

[1] Scratch information can be gathered at http://info.scratch.mit.edu/About_Scratch

[2] For more information on the tool, visit http://appinventor.googlelabs.com/about/

[3] For more on StencylWorks, visit http://www.stencyl.com/stencylworks/overview/

[4] Jeremy Allaire, 2002, Macromedia Flash MX – A next-generation rich client, Macromedia White Paper, http://download.macromedia.com/pub/flash/whitepapers/richclient.pdf

[5] On the history of Creative Commons, visit http://creativecommons.org/about/history/

2005 saw the real impact of having an open-source spirit working for the larger online communities, producing more and more free tools[6] that would allow people with low technical skills to create. That's when the concept of user-generated content (UGC) appeared, and free distribution gained allies with the birth of YouTube. During 2005, discussions started among the game community for the necessity of player-generated content (PGC) in order to respond to the high-content demand of the next-generation consoles (PS3 and Xbox360). Companies were afraid of being unable to deliver the detailed content permitted by these new generation consoles. Will Wright, creator of *Sims*, appeared in the front line with *Spore*, an evolutionary game with in depth layers of AI, the so-called "procedurally generated content".[7] Wright's goal was to develop an intelligent world, which would be able to interact with the creative desires of the players. With a bunch of editors within the game, players would become creators "from scratch",[8] of their own worlds, their own games.

Then during the second half of the decade, new Web 2.0 tools started to appear. Albeit existing authoring multimedia tools, and networks for sharing and distribution, there were still limits to the creative process in the sense that past the facilitation of sharing with the world and facilitation of programming you still needed to bring into play all the assets you wanted to integrate (text, images, audio, animation, and video). Thus you still needed literacy on the creation of the assets. Consequently a lot of Web 2.0 tools started to develop their interest in providing technology with knowledge embedded in order to suppress this lack of literacy – tools like *Mindmeister* for idea organization, *Picasa* for photo editing, *Sumo Paint* for illustration, *ComicSketch* for comics, *SketchUp* for 3d, *GoAnimate* for animation, *Animata* for real-time animation, *Animoto* and *Masher* for video, *Audiotool* for music, or *Creaza Audio Editor* for sound.[9] All these creative tools allowed for the creation process within collaborative settings, and build for community sharing. Most of them used databases of media elements, mostly built by other creators online, in order to ease the creative work. These new creative tools were opening new dimensions for the facilitation of creation by general people and at the same time making possible self-discovery.

---

[6] At the moment we can find hundreds of free online tools available on the Web, tools that serve media as text, photography, music, video, and games. Examples can be found at http://www.go2web20.net

[7] Game Developers Conference of 2005 was a rich gathering of discussions on the subject of procedural content. Will Wright conference on "The Future of Content" marked that year. Read more at http://www.gamasutra.com/gdc2005/features/20050315/postcard-diamante.htm

[8] idem.

[9] All these tools can be accessed online and free. Sumo Paint can be explored at http://www.sumo-paint.com, ComicSketch can be explored at http://mainada.net/comicssketch, GoAnimate can be tested at http://goanimate.com, Animata at http://animata.kibu.hu, Animoto can be accessed at http://animoto.com, SketchUp at http://www.sketchup.com, Masher at http://www.masher.com, Audiotool can be used at http://www.audiotool.com, Audio editor can be accessed at http://www.creazaeducation.com/audioeditor, and Mindmeister can be accessed at http://www.mindmeister.com

This discussion however goes beyond virtual worlds and digital assets; between 2005 and 2008, physical and low cost devices for all were a dream coming true, thanks to Arduino[10] and RepRap.[11] People from all over the world, with little to no resources, would be able to create artefacts that until that moment would necessitate highly expensive machines only available to the biggest world corporations. All these new technologies have opened up complete new hands-on possibilities and, together with the social networks, have been crucial in creating community ties, to increase collaboration and participation, opening space for more elaborative creative technologies allowing in depth collaborative creation.

1.5 Traits of Creative Technologies

As we have seen from both previous points, cultural and technological, creative technologies are strongly grounded in two ideas: facilitation for everyone and creation within environments of collaboration and participation. But these technologies still need to guarantee that they will be able to attract people willing to create, because as Robinson (2010) and Csíkszentmihályi (1990) said, to engender creativity we need to be able to evoke passion and fun. Both emotions play an essential role in pushing levels of self-motivation, dedication, and perseverance in the pursuing of original creation. Having fun while playing (Brown 2010) with creative technologies and finding new passions will guarantee the success of these new tools.

One example that encompasses all these ideas is *Scratch*. Its approach to visual programming was able to embed programming knowledge into visual elements, in a very easy approach. The embedded knowledge permitted users to enter the world of programming and discover own interest in the beauty of logics without effort. But *Scratch* was not the first tool to put programming in a visual and embedded form; then why all this success? We believe that great deal of the success was achieved, thanks to the *Scratch* community, which was designed with participatory culture in mind. Hence, the easiest way to publish work created in *Scratch* is through the *Scratch* website, but more interesting than this is the openness of *Scratch* projects in their library. Anyone in the community can download and open any project in the Scratch library. This means that any person in the community can use code made by others and assets created by others. This means that whenever someone doesn't know how to code something, they just need to go to the library and look for an example matching his interests. If someone doesn't know how to draw, or how to create sounds, they can use them from other artworks in the library. Scratch is a creative technology in all senses, because it not only makes it easier through embedded knowledge but also through sharing knowledge. Due to the tool being free plus

---

[10] For more details on the building of Arduino, watch the "Arduino The Documentary" (2010) at http://arduinothedocumentary.org

[11] RepRap is a concept defined as the replicating rapid prototype, a 3D printer, developed by Adrian Bowyer. More about the project at http://reprap.org

the content in the projects, this defines a community built, on social recognition, and not on moneymaking. Finally all this together creates the perfect fun environment for people to create, share, learn, and discover their own creative motivation.

Another recent example of a creative technology is *Minecraft* developed by Markus Persson in 2009 and initially given free to players. *Minecraft* is generally defined as a game, but it's much more than that. Like LEGO it allows any person to build any world, without having any previous skill or technical knowledge. The building has been greatly simplified by using a visual approach made of cubes only, like LEGO pieces, and a basic Boolean logic circuitry. Similarly to *Scratch* it is possible to create animated and interactive digital artefacts that can be experienced by the community. Different from LEGO, the entire community is online and can visit projects and worlds made by others in the moment. Not only can users enjoy these worlds, but they can also learn how to give shape to new ideas. The community also shares packages of textures for the building or skins for the characters, helping people to constantly raise the level of quality of their creations.

These two examples show us that any tool, the simpler it is, need to convince people to persevere in performing, in order to be rewarded. Also looking at Scratch or *Minecraft*, we can easily understand that beyond the immediate labels of being a tool or being a game, the most important feature we can emphasize in them compared with other tools and other games is the fact that both can be defined as toys.

Toys define objects designed for the act of play. Toys categorize any kind of artefact that allows people to interact with, not necessarily with a purpose, but able to reward the interaction or simply stimulate fun. Together with these aspects, another high interest in toys comes from the fact that they serve learning purposes. Consequently, the mixing of fun and learning helps toys rise to the condition of objects that easily activates engagement in players, which is essential to maintain perseverance of the use.

Adding to this, we should also say that *Minecraft* could easily be defined as a tool, because beyond permitting people to play in-world, the world can serve the purpose of simulation, or the creation of scenarios for video and pictures. Tools are designed to facilitate actions to be performed, to help the process of creation or deconstruction. Contrary to toys that are normally the objective itself, at the end of our actions, tools serve more as a means to attain something else. The object itself is not engaging, but it can transform the activity being performed in a more appealing one. Being able to perform our task well using a tool, the process to master that tool can be highly rewarding.

Finally we can also say that Scratch beyond being a tool is immensely used as a game, more even if we think about the open community galleries, and social reward systems, that prize achievements done with the tool. Hence a game defines a set of rules commonly designed within an artefact with the purpose to engage players in the activity. Games are designed to captivate completely the attention of the players and normally reward the attention with sensations of fun, like toys do. Also performing tasks in games well, being able to master the game rules, can be highly rewarding as with tools. On the other hand games are very different from toys in the nature of purpose, because there's always an objective for any action performed.

The game also differs from the tool in that the game is the end itself and doesn't serve as a means to attain anything outside the boundaries of itself. In this sense, Scratch is really a game, because most of the creations built within Scratch don't serve to be used outside that domain, even the project files are not exportable to any other model.

All this said, we should state that the three main traits that make a technology become creative is the ability to respond to the needs of being a toy, a game, and a tool. Creative technologies should then be able to:

– Elicit attractiveness and easy interaction, like a toy.
– Engage, motivate, and maintain concentration while pushing for mastery, as games do.
– Serve a purpose, like help, guide, connect, or facilitate the attaining of an objec-tive, as a tool.

1.6 Conclusions

An increasingly wider set of technological tools are emerging and enabling new ways for a democratic creation. These tools are accessible and available to anyone and forming the new mechanisms for self-expression, for communicating points of view, or for raising one's attention. Examples range from viral videos to interactive artworks, but looking below the surface reveals new modes of learning and enjoying life.

These new technologies are opening horizons for new creative demographics. On one hand, facilitating creation by general people, through the embedding of knowledge, and pushing motivation for perseverance from the natural will to self-discovery in each person and, on the other hand, pushing for a participatory culture made of content generated by all – creating a culture that is open and free, built on the values of community and social reconnaissance against financial retributions.

Finally, these new tools are being shaped within a tripartite conception of func-tionality, that of being at the same time a toy, a tool, and a game. This conception is the guarantee to create technologies that will motivate people to struggle for the self-discovery in search of their inner creation desires.

References

Anderson C (2006) The long tail: why the future of business is selling less of more. Hyperion, New York
Boyd B (2009) On the origin of stories. Harvard Press, Cambridge, MA
Brown S (2010) Play how it shapes the brain, opens the imagination, and invigorates the soul. Avery – Penguin Group, New York
Csikszentmihalyi M (1990) Flow: the psychology of optimal experience. Harper & Row, New York

Csíkszentmihályi M (1997) Creativity: flow and the psychology of discovery and invention. Harper Perennial, New York

Dworsky D (2011) PausePressPlay. http://www.presspauseplay.com/

Gardner H (1983) Frames of mind: the theory of multiple intelligences. Basic Books, New York

Gauntlett D (2011) Making is connecting: the social meaning of creativity, from DIY and knitting to YouTube and Web 2.0. Polity Press, Cambridge

Gazzaniga MS (2008) Human: the science behind what makes us unique. HarperCollins, New York

Godin S (2011) We are all weird: the myth of mass and the end of compliance. The Domino Project, USA, www.thedominoproject.com

Gould SJ (1992) Bully for brontosaurus: further reflections in natural history. 1991. Reprint. Penguin, London

Jenkins H (1992) Textual poachers: television fans and participatory culture. Routledge, New York

Jenkins H (2009) Confronting the challenges of participatory culture: media education for the 21st century, MacArthur. MIT Press, Cambridge, MA

Keen A (2007) The cult of the amateur: how today's internet is killing our culture. Crown Business, London

Kelly K (2010) What technology wants. Viking Adult, New York

Lanier J (2010) You are not a gadget: a manifesto. Knopf, New York

Lanier J (2013) Who owns the future? Simon & Schuster, New York

Morozov E (2012) The net delusion: the dark side of internet freedom. PublicAffairs, New York

Morozov E (2013) To save everything, click here: technology, solutionism, and the urge to fix problems that don't exist. Penguin, London

Robinson K (2010) The element: how finding your passion changes everything. Viking Adult, New York

Sheldon KM, Lyubomirsky S (2004) Achieving sustainable new happiness: prospects, practices, and prescriptions. In: Linley A, Joseph S (eds) Positive psychology in practice. Wiley, Hoboken, pp 127–145

Shirky C (2010) Cognitive surplus: creativity and generosity in a connected age. The Penguin Press, New York. ISBN 9781594202537

Shneiderman B (1987) Designing the user interface: strategies for effective human-computer interaction, 1st edn. Addison-Wesley, Reading. ISBN 0-321-26978-0

Shneiderman B (1999) Readings in information visualization: using vision to think. With Card SK, Mackinlay JD. Morgan Kaufmann, San Francisco. ISBN 1-55860-533-9

Shneiderman B (2002) Leonardo's laptop: human needs and the new computing technologies. MIT Press, Cambridge, MA. ISBN 0-262-69299-6

Shneiderman B, Fischer G, Czerwinski M, Resnick M, Myers B et al (2005) Creativity support tools: report from A U.S. National Science Foundation Sponsored Workshop, Washington, DC, 13–14 June 2005. http://www.cs.umd.edu/hcil/CST/

Weiss P (1955) Beauty and the beast: life and the rule of order. Sci Mon 81(December):286–299

Zagalo N, Torres A (2008) Character emotion experience in virtual environments. Vis Comput Int J Comput Grap 24(11):981–986, ISSN: 0178-2789, Springer

Chapter 2
The Internet Is Ancient, Small Steps Are Important, and Four Other Theses About Making Things in a Digital World

David Gauntlett

2.1 Introduction

Human beings have been creative, and made things, for many thousands of years. Indeed, the evidence suggests that the first human tools were made almost two million years ago (Donald 2001). Digital technologies and the internet have not initiated creativity, therefore, but they have certainly given creative practices a boost, by enabling several things to be achieved much more simply and quickly: connections between people, distribution of material, conversations about it, collaborations, and opportunities to build on the work of others.

Therefore I would say that the internet is certainly empowering for people who like to make things, share ideas, and learn together. The six theses which I will discuss in this chapter all concern different dimensions of that strength. Before we get going, though, I'd like to directly address how self-conscious one can feel in saying such a thing.

There is, unmistakably, a fundamental divide between those who say positive things about the value of the internet for culture and society and those who are broadly critical or negative. If you read things published in this area, you can't really miss it. The pessimistic ones – which includes a majority of the academic writers – clearly take pride in their 'critical' position, as if they have been really clever to avoid being brainwashed by the pro-internet propaganda (whatever that is), and like to give the impression that their position is risky and iconoclastic, even though it is the most common one in academic circles and the most populist in terms of academic professional kudos. Whilst there is a valuable social role to be occupied by the critic who can observe that 'the emperor has no clothes',[1] I believe that there

---

[1] If you are a stranger to this cultural reference, see https://en.wikipedia.org/wiki/The_Emperor's_New_Clothes

D. Gauntlett (✉)
Faculty of Media, Arts and Design, University of Westminster, London, UK
e-mail: d.gauntlett@westminster.ac.uk

© Springer-Verlag London 2015
N. Zagalo, P. Branco (eds.), *Creativity in the Digital Age*,
Springer Series on Cultural Computing, DOI 10.1007/978-1-4471-6681-8_2

should still be an expectation that constructive alternatives can be offered. Some critics have made excellent points – Evgeny Morozov has shown that an online presence can make activists more liable to identification and persecution, for instance (Morozov 2011), and has punctured the weirder parts of Silicon Valley 'solutionism' (Morozov 2013). Jaron Lanier (2010) makes persuasive points against the Facebook-style 'template identity' and certain ideas of collective creativity (although Lanier perhaps does not belong in the 'pessimistic' camp anyway, as he is only raising cautionary notes about the development of a creative online life, which he potentially still believes in). Other critics have fewer ideas of their own and are content to make fun of everyday people's genuine creative efforts (Miller 2009; Curran et al. 2012). These writers suggest that the shift where citizens become media creators, rather than mere consumers, is a waste of time – which I find rather shocking (Gauntlett 2013).

The present book – the book you are reading now, of which this is a chapter – is clearly on the optimistic side of the fence. The blurb sent to me by the editors says things like: 'This [online] movement is providing a "voice" through which anyone can express to everyone whatever their imagination can create, democratizing innovation and creativity like never before'. The pessimists like to shoot down this kind of statement as recklessly giddy – and indeed the terms 'anyone' and 'everyone' here are ill-advised – but this optimistic stance is at least preferable to the grim elitism of those who seem to wish we could go back to a world where professional people made professional media which professional researchers knew how to deal with.

The 'critical' scholars implicitly sneer at those of us who try to be more constructive and optimistic. Their working assumption is that they are the ones blessed with the intelligence to see through the 'hype' about possible uses of the internet. (This ignores the fact that they are often engaged in a different kind of 'hype', which is – even less helpfully – in praise of themselves.) As a father of young children, I couldn't live with myself if I merely stood around moaning about things. It's certainly true that the dominant internet companies are not angelic and may have regrettable ways of working, but to dismiss the potential of what people can do online because particular providers are problematic is like saying that people shouldn't have footwear because some sneaker companies use sweatshops.

In spite of all this discord, I think that it is possible to make some strong positive statements about qualities of the internet which it is difficult to disagree with. I present six of them here. Several of them are pragmatic 'X is better than Y' statements which I would hope are pretty irrefutable. Let's see.

2.2 The Statements

1. The internet is ancient (*in other words*: the internet has affordances which connect with ancient, great aspects of humanity).

2. A world with lots of interesting, creative things is always better than a world which offers a small number of popular, smartly finished things.
3. People doing things because they want to is always better than people watching things because they are there.
4. The distribution and funding possibilities of the internet are better than the traditional models.
5. Small steps into a changed world are better than no steps.
6. The digital internet is good, but hands-on physical things are good too.

2.2.1 The Internet Is Ancient (In Other Words: The Internet Has Affordances Which Connect with Ancient, Great Aspects of Humanity)

The internet, and the World Wide Web which was built on top of it, are powerful tools for humanity, and connect with ancient ways of doing things. The internet enables humanity to get back onto the track which had been the main story for centuries, where we at least *try* to develop bonds and communities and exchange things largely at a manageable, social level. The industrialism of the late nineteenth and the twentieth centuries, and the broadcast mass media model of communications which peaked in the twentieth century, destroyed this sense of collective engagement with a one-size-fits-all, have-what-you're-given, service-the-masses model. Having gone off down that path – a path associated with political passivity and environmental destruction – it was hard to see a way back. But the internet offers a way of exchanging communications, and goods and services, which is much more like the previous model but on a bigger, broader, and international scale. A lot of it is about *conversation*, but the conversations can happen on a vastly bigger canvas than before. Nevertheless, the conversations can retain focus, because any one conversation is only there for those who want to participate, there are no limits to the number of conversations, and anyone not interested in a conversation can just ignore it – indeed, would not even be aware of it.

Of course, this view is simplistic and romantic in all directions – both overly romantic about the past and the present and crudely dismissive of the twentieth century bit in the middle. Nevertheless, I think it represents a sketch of something genuine – and part of the evidence in its favour is the enthusiasm with which people over the world, from all walks of life, have adopted online communications. The internet could have remained a forum for exchange of information amongst scientists, geeks, and government and military organisations, whilst the majority of people stuck with the mass-market (or even relatively niche) television and movie formats that had already established their popularity. This did not happen.

This argument may also seem to be compromised by the fact that, as has been observed, there are certain internet-based businesses that can be accused of profiting from everyone else's creativity. However, those companies are not necessary or inevitable for what the internet can do. We could also note that the human capacity for greed is also well documented in ancient texts.

In a 2012 essay about online social networks, Daniel Miller argues that networks such as Facebook offer the possibility of communities which offer 'something much closer to older traditions of anthropological study of social relations such as kinship studies' (Miller 2012: 147). Facebook itself has many dubious qualities and is not the best expression of online-social-networking potential, but nevertheless, you can see his point:

> Instead of focusing on [social networking sites] as the vanguard of the new, and the rapidity of its global reach [– or on the idea that they represent a trend towards individualism –] it may well be that [social networking sites] are so quickly accepted in places such as Indonesia and Turkey because their main impact is to redress some of the isolating and individualizing impacts of other new technologies and allow people to return to certain kinds of intense and interwoven forms of social relationship that they otherwise feared were being lost. (Miller 2012: 148)

The internet certainly offers the possibility of building social connections, with or without Facebook, and importantly enables people to share ideas through these networks. There is a popular idea of the internet as a platform for an open, sharing culture, where ideas are made available for others to build upon. Over time, of course, some aspects of this open sharing have been closed down and/or replaced by more modern systems aligned with today's conventional ideas of intellectual property, copyright, and ownership. Nevertheless – or perhaps *because* of this – there remains a strong interest in the idea of the commons, a shared space where things are made available for use by others, of which Wikipedia is a strong and popular example. The Creative Commons licensing system offers creators the opportunity to make their work available with specific prescriptions, for example, that the creator should be credited. The 'commons' model connects – indeed, is based upon – ancient notions of communal public space, although the self-serving regimes of the rich and powerful, as well as the casual selfishness of individuals, have historically meant that a thriving commons is difficult to sustain (Hardin 1968). A digital commons is different, of course, as digital resources can be copied and used without depleting and damaging the stock available to everyone else.

The commons is about having free access to resources, so that people can share and build together. This is a valuable dimension of culture. It does not necessarily follow, however, that everything online must be free. In everyday life, we are able to comprehend a library and a bookshop, side by side, without thinking that one cancels out the other, and it is unfair to assume that only the malign or greedy would seek to charge money for things online. For example, Jaron Lanier offers a sensible defence of the right of an artist to make a living by selling their work directly online (2010, 2013). The kind of transaction that Lanier suggests is more like an ancient market, or bazaar, where the producers of diverse goods sell them directly to people – presenting and selling them across their own stall. This kind of trade is much more convivial, and good for the producer, than the twentieth century idea that we should be able to get everything via one 'supermarket'.

I also like to think that between the poles of the open (free) and the closed (paid for), there might be a compromise position which is known as: reasonably open (inexpensive). When the artist or producer has cut out the 'middle person' such as a publisher, they can make the same amount of money by charging far less for the product, as in the argument for 'Latte-priced ebooks' (Dunleavy 2012; Gauntlett 2012) which suggests that books can both be cheap for readers and still provide a modest return for their authors.

The internet, then, forms the basis for a new set of technologies, which enable people to converse, exchange, share, and trade in ways which are closer to ancient and traditional ways of interacting than the monolithic technologies of the previous century, such as television and supermarkets. Even when conducted via proprietary platforms (such as Google services, Pinterest, or Etsy) – which they often are, but don't have to be – these exchanges are still much more healthy than the one-way, mass-market kinds of product and communication that had otherwise become the norm.

2.2.2   A World with Lots of Interesting, Creative Things Is Always Better than a World Which Offers a Small Number of Popular, Smartly Finished Things

The slightly longer formulation of this is: 'An ocean of interesting, creative things, regardless of their professionalism or audience size, is always better than a small box of popular, smartly finished things'. Let me explain.

Way back in 2006, Chris Anderson published *The Long Tail*, which became a successful and much-cited analysis of one of the big differences that the internet makes. 'The long tail', you may recall, refers to the kind of graph where the vertical axis represents popularity (measured as number of readers, or viewers, or sales) and the horizontal axis represents a row of particular items (such as specific books, songs, videos, blog posts, or whatever). When these items are sorted by popularity, there is typically a peak of popular items on the left – that's the 'hits' – and then the graph quickly curves down and along to an apparently infinite number of little-loved, not-very-popular items bobbling along the bottom of the graph – which is the long tail.

Much of Anderson's book was concerned with highlighting the striking difference in what you can sell when you're not limited to shelf space in a physical shop. So whilst a physical bookshop might offer, say, 20,000 titles – all the current best-sellers, some classics, and a scattering of everything else – an online bookshop could have literally millions of titles on sale. Apple's iTunes did the same for music, Netflix for movies, and so on. Anderson highlighted the fact that although any single item in the long tail was apparently not-very-successful – in physical shop terms, it was *literally* a waste of space – when all these long tail items were taken together, they added up to a huge market. The demand for obscure and back-catalogue music, films, or books is such that these non-hits (or at least, not *current* hits) represent 'a market as big as, if not bigger than, the hits themselves' (2007: 8).

Sold as a 'business' book, *The Long Tail* left readers with the memorable insight that in the new digital economy, businesses could cater to fans of all kinds of things and still make a profit. Whilst it would still be good to have big successes, the emphasis would shift from a focus solely on mass-market, 'lowest common denominator' hits to a broader and rational support for making available *anything* that someone, somewhere, might want, because that business was as good as any other kind of business.

This was all interesting and, at the time, a revolutionary observation (although, as Anderson acknowledges, it was basically the insight that Jeff Bezos of Amazon had had a decade earlier). But perhaps the most important *cultural* point of *The Long Tail* was lost on most readers at the time – including me.

What *now* seems really striking is that you can forget about big media altogether. The point is not 'the long tail is also quite interesting'. The point is that the long tail is *everything* that is most interesting – it's genuinely rich and interesting and wonderful. The things with big audiences aren't the successful siblings of everything else – they're in a different category. But they're not in a *better* category.

One of the errors made by critics such as Natalie Fenton (2012) is to look at online media through a traditional media lens, where size of audience is a key measure of significance. Comparing the online presence of established media brands, such as CNN and the BBC, with home-made sites made by amateur enthusiasts in their spare time, Fenton unsurprisingly finds that the former have much bigger audiences (pp. 134–5). Rather more surprisingly, she concludes from this that self-made media is a waste of time, made by deluded narcissists (I paraphrase, but that *is* what she says – see Fenton 2012: 135). Even if we ignore that extreme misanthropic view, the old-media lens nevertheless tells us that a typical article on the BBC website, read by a million people, is important, whereas a number of blogs that are only read by 500 people each are basically irrelevant.

But what, we might ask, if there are lots of these blogs – what if there are 10,000 of them? The old-media lens says, 10,000 times nothing is still nothing – they're still irrelevant, they're just too small. However, if we take a more contemporary view, where small pebbles can add up to something significant alongside the big boulders (to borrow a metaphor from Leadbeater 2008), the 10,000 blogs read by only 500 people have an 'audience' – to use a now-clumsy term – that add up to five million people, five times our example BBC number. In terms of which *single* source has the most power, clearly the BBC wins. But in terms of a diverse and interesting hubbub, the BBC can't compete. And if you look on the production side – who made the thing and the difference it made in *their* own lives – in the BBC case you are likely to have two or three employees who have contributed to the production of a webpage, because it is their job to do so – in terms of human engagement and excitement, that's pretty close to nothing. Compare that with the 10,000 people who are so engaged with a subject, so passionate about it, that they have bothered to create a diverse array of original content about it, and that's really powerful in itself before we have even started to think about the 'audience'.

So the really key thing about the 'long tail' is not exactly about the size of markets, but rather that it describes an ocean of independent amateur activity that's as *big* as (or bigger than) the produce of the mainstream and professional brands – and richer as well as wider, with a thousand independent ideas for every one professional message. This is why a world with lots of interesting creative things is always better than a world which offers a small number of popular smartly finished things. The implication of critics such as Fenton (2012) is that the wealth of interesting creative things are, at best, a distraction from the important arena of professional products with larger audiences, where we should, presumably, focus our demands for better and more critical media content (or something). But the implication that you can't trust ordinary people to do good things themselves, or that it's pointless because nobody is listening, is unreasonably nihilistic. The ocean of independent amateur activity is where the interesting and powerful stuff is to be found.

2.2.3   People Doing Things Because They Want to Is Always Better than People Watching Things Because They Are There

After *Making is Connecting* was published in spring 2011, I did a number of talks about it in different places, enlivened by a swooshy Prezi presentation with some pictures and a few words which sought to remind me of central points from the book that I wanted to highlight. I was about half way through this 'tour' when it suddenly struck me that I should add a bit in the middle which summarised the spirit of so much of what the book was saying: the words '*because we want to*'.[2] People creating music videos for YouTube, or making puppets by hand, or writing a blog about environmental politics, or setting up a free library on a street corner – all of these are people doing stuff just *because they want to*.

This is obvious, but important, in part because it relates to the category error made by critics when they talk about the exploitation of digital labour. The exploitation of labour is a useful Marxist concept which – in simple terms – describes the situation where someone does work, which they wouldn't be doing if they weren't doing it for the money, but their employer sells the product of this work on for *more* money and keeps the difference. This is exploitation in the straightforward technical sense – the employer 'exploits' the difference between cost x (the amount they have to pay a worker to get them to do the work) and cost y (the amount they can sell the fruits of that work for) – and it may well also feel like exploitation in the negative personal sense – where the worker feels frustrated and miserable at this shoddy situation.

Most amateur making is not at all like this, because it is done by people 'because we want to': because they have a message or meaning that they wish to share with

---

[2] Unintentionally influenced, perhaps, by the 1999 Billie Piper #1 pop hit of the same name.

others and a desire to make their mark on the world in some way. Therefore, their effort is not 'labour' at all in the Marxist sense, and so they cannot be 'exploited' in the manner of a supermarket employee. Nevertheless, of course, the vast amounts of online creative work produced in this way *are* exploited, en masse, to make a profit for the companies that host them – but this is an exploitation of aggregated content, rather than of individual workers, because they are not *working* in that sense.

The desire of people making things because they want to is much better understood as part of a human need to shape our environment to our own needs and preferences (Illich 1973), as part of a resistance to being positioned as a consumer (Gauntlett 2011), and as a central plank of human happiness – as economist Richard Layard says, summarising piles of data on human activities and satisfactions: 'Prod any happy person and you will find a project' (Layard 2006: 73).

This self-motivated activity is not *brought about* by the internet, but the ways in which the internet enables people to share creative things, and have conversations around them, work as a significant boost to amateur creativity (Gauntlett et al. 2012). This helps to foster an environment which is more about being a maker and a thinker, less about being an 'audience' and a consumer, and this can only be a good thing.

2.2.4   The Distribution and Funding Possibilities of the Internet Are Better than the Traditional Models

As a word, 'distribution' doesn't sound like something to get excited about. But distribution is just a word for how we get stuff to people, and, as suggested above, the internet is an incredibly efficient way of getting stuff to people – anything you can transport digitally anyway: brilliant for songs, videos, or stories, although not so good for actual cats or bananas. The delightfulness of this efficiency is especially noticeable to anyone who has tried to distribute physical publications or products themselves (Gauntlett 2000: 13).

For things that can be conveyed digitally, such as texts, videos, poems, pictures, and songs, we now have remarkably simple tools for getting them out and about. There is still the big problem of getting people to look at your stuff. That's not to be underestimated – but it's not the killer blow that some critics (Fenton 2012, again, and others) seem to think it is. The online world offers many ways of drawing attention to your interesting stuff, and building networks around it, or having communities talk about it.

In terms of how creative work is funded or can be financially supported and then exchanged, first of all, we should acknowledge that it's nice that much of this can just be done for free. You can make your own animation, video, song, or blog post in your 'spare time', and it doesn't really cost anything. That's wonderful. (Admittedly there are some costs of equipment and internet access, but these are costs which have *already* been borne by a substantial proportion of the population in developed countries.) Second, we should acknowledge that we might imagine a post-capitalist vision of our society, which may enable all kinds of collectively supported creative activity with no cost to the individual (and no profit made by companies putting adverts on it), but we won't spend time on that here because frankly it's not going to materialise any time soon. So then third, it's interesting to look at the disruptive ways of funding larger-scale creative projects which are emerging within the present system – notably the crowdfunding platforms such as Kickstarter and Indiegogo.

Indiegogo was launched in 2008; Kickstarter came along a year later, with a then-unique all-or-nothing model which seemed to make quality outputs more likely: if a project couldn't raise its desired total within a set period (normally 30 or 60 days), then it wouldn't be funded at all and no money would change hands. Kickstarter has gathered media attention for certain high-profile fundraises – such as the creators of cult TV series *Veronica Mars* hitting their target of $2 million for a movie version in 10 h, in March 2013 (and raising $5.7 million over their 30 day period)[3] – but the founders of the site are keen to emphasise that it is primarily a community for small-scale artists and projects. Interviewed in *Fast Company* magazine (Chafkin 2013), Kickstarter co-founder Yancey Strickler suggests that, unlike Indiegogo which will more or less accept any project, Kickstarter is a more carefully curated enterprise:

> The thing is, if [blockbuster movie director] Michael Bay came along and wanted to do a Kickstarter we'd probably tell him, please don't. I would never want to scare the girl who wants to do a $500 lithography project, 'cause that's why we started this thing. We think we have a moral obligation to her.

The makers of *Indie Game: The Movie* (2012) offer an interesting account of their Kickstarter-funded production, and DIY approach to movie distribution, in a series of blog posts (as well as showing in some cinemas, the film was available DRM-free from their own website, and to download from platforms such as iTunes, and was the first to be distributed via the video game platform, Steam).[4] They discuss how they were inspired by Louis C.K., a stand-up comic who took a commercial risk by releasing his stand-up show *Live at the Beacon Theater* (2011) as an inexpensive, DRM-free download from his own website. As he explained in a blog post 4 days after its release (Szekely 2011):

> The experiment was: if I put out a brand new standup special at a drastically low price ($5 [£3.25, €3.75]) and make it as easy as possible to buy, download and enjoy, free of any restrictions, will everyone just go and steal it? Will they pay for it? And how much money can be made by an individual in this manner?

---

[3] The *Veronica Mars Movie Project* page on Kickstarter: http://www.kickstarter.com/projects/559914737/the-veronica-mars-movie-project. Actor and director Zach Braff was inspired by this and raised $3.1 million for his feature film *Wish I Was Here* a month later (http://www.kickstarter.com/projects/1869987317/wish-i-was-here-1). Spike Lee also launched a fundraising effort in July 2013, raising $1.4 million for his next film project (http://www.kickstarter.com/projects/spikelee/the-newest-hottest-spike-lee-joint).

[4] See all details at http://www.indiegamethemovie.com/news/2012/10/31/indie-game-the-movie-the-case-study.html

The success of this DIY release (which took $1 million in 12 days[5]) seemed to establish an impressive precedent: however, a sensible amateur might think, 'well that worked for the already-established comedian, Louis C.K. – but I'm not Louis C.K.'. In a blog post entitled 'We're not Louis C.K. – and you can be too!',[6] the makers of *Indie Game: The Movie* discuss this reservation, from the standpoint that they managed to have a successful DIY-released movie without already being well-known movie makers. As they point out: 'Even Louis C.K. wasn't "Louis C.K." until he was "Louis C.K."'. Nevertheless, they note that they, like him, did work very hard, establishing their skills and their contacts over a number of years, building up the position which would enable their eventual success. So, on the one hand, it is obviously the case that not everyone can spontaneously generate a big DIY hit. But it *is* the case that new online platforms enable crowdfunding and DIY distribution opportunities which help talented and dedicated people to break through without having to gain the support of others already embedded in mainstream media businesses.[7]

Of course, the potential of online crowdfunding goes beyond individual creators wishing to realise their publishing or film projects. A really notable tool that was made possible by Kickstarter is MaKey MaKey, 'An Invention Kit for Everyone', which enables children and adults to use everyday objects as input devices for a computer, and so use food, cutlery, or pets as interfaces for the internet. A popular

---

[5] Details at https://buy.louisck.net/news/a-statement-from-louis-c-k and https://buy.louisck.net/news/another-statement-from-louis-c-k

[6] See http://www.indiegamethemovie.com/news/2012/11/19/were-not-louis-ck.html

[7] A simple way of thinking about the economics of this kind of thing was offered by Kevin Kelly in 2008, in a blog post entitled '1,000 True Fans'. Kelly suggests that a creator 'needs to acquire only 1,000 True Fans to make a living'. A 'True Fan' is defined as 'someone who will purchase anything and everything you produce'. Kelly explains:

> Assume conservatively that your True Fans will each spend one day's wages per year in support of what you do. That 'one-day-wage' is an average, because of course your truest fans will spend a lot more than that. Let's peg that per diem each True Fan spends at $100 per year. If you have 1,000 fans that sums up to $100,000 per year, which minus some modest expenses, is a living for most folks.

This sounds promising, although in subsequent posts ('The Reality of Depending on True Fans' and 'The Case Against 1,000 True Fans') Kelly had to admit that for artists bumping along at this level of success, with no security and a rather continuous need to generate products or ticket sales to avoid the drift into poverty, this is an uncomfortable existence. Conversely, as one commenter said:

> In the old environment most musicians weren't making any money anyway or had debts to the record companies. And they did not have control over rights [to their own work]. At least some things have changed for the better now. ('Max', 11 May 2010)

Certainly, a lot of comments on these posts referred to the pleasure of *control* over an artistic career, and 'making a living' from it, with a meaningful connection to some people who love the work, even if the artist is not having big hits.

example is the 'banana piano', a music keyboard made from a row of bananas.[8] Furthermore, as Matthew Hollow (2013: 70) notes, platforms such as Kickstarter can support community-focused social projects as well:

> For civil society activists and others concerned with local welfare issues, the emergence of these new [crowdfunding platforms] has been hugely significant: It has opened up a new source of funding when governments and businesses around the world are cutting back on their spending as a result of the on-going financial crisis. [As well as artists and film-makers, a] number of local civic initiatives also have received substantial backing from funders on online [crowdfunding platforms]. For instance, when... Kickstarter launched in the UK in October 2012, the first project to successfully reach its funding goal was a student-led architecture project to design a new pavilion for a park owned by The National Trust conservation charity.

This section was entitled 'The distribution and funding possibilities of the internet are better than the traditional models'. In this kind of case, of course, the 'traditional models' – decent state funding for civic services and amenities – could well be preferable (although the crowdfunded solutions offer a working alternative where otherwise there is none). For individual people, though – or amateur groups, or an innovative duo, say – the Kickstarter model is a powerful new way of making things happen where otherwise they simply wouldn't happen.

2.2.5   Small Steps into a Changed World Are Better than No Steps

In the second thesis, we have already discussed the value of having a vibrant culture of 'interesting, creative things, regardless of their professionalism or audience size' – where the value was in terms of the array of cultural items available to people in the world. This fifth thesis emphasises the value of making things, no matter how small, for an audience, no matter how small, for the creators *themselves*. My research for *Making is Connecting* (2011) and for other reports (Gauntlett et al. 2011, 2012; Gauntlett and Thomsen 2013) has clarified for me the significance of people taking a step, however small, into the world of making, and the sharing of that making.

Making things is not a rare or elite activity, of course. Everyone makes things: as children, when creative activity is common, and as adults, when preparing a meal, or setting up a new home, or fixing something in an inventive way. But the act of consciously making something as a maker, and deliberately offering it to be seen by others, may be slightly different. In a talk called 'Six Amazing Things About

---

[8] MaKey MaKey is described on its Kickstarter page as 'a simple Invention Kit for Beginners and Experts doing art, engineering, and everything inbetween', and in June 2012, the project exceeded its fundraising target by 2,272 % (with $568,106 pledged against a mere $25,000 goal). See http://www.kickstarter.com/projects/joylabs/makey-makey-an-invention-kit-for-everyone   and   http://www.makeymakey.com

Making' that I presented with Mitch Resnick of MIT at the Fourth World Maker Faire in New York, September 2013, I said[9]:

> When you are a maker yourself – when you make something and put it into the world – I think that this changes your relationship to the world, to your environment, the people around you, and the stuff in the world.
>
> "Often we're expected to be participating in the world, but essentially using stuff made by other people, and consuming stuff – or being active fans of – things made by other people."
>
> When you make things yourself, you break that expectation. You step into the world more actively. I think it's about taking a step. It doesn't matter what you've made, whether it's as good or effective or neat as something made by someone else or made by a company. Just the fact is, you've made a thing and put it into the world. So you're making your mark, and you've taken that active step. You're making a difference. It's fine if it's a tiny difference or if it's only noticed by one person. It's the step you've made. It's a great step.

The psychotherapist Nossrat Peseschkian notes that the search for meaning in life is always 'a path of small steps'. This leads, he says, to a common paradox, 'that we must strive for something that we already carry within us' (1985: xi) – but it is only unlocked through a process of taking a small step, and developing confidence and stability, before taking the next.

The importance of small steps into a changed world is also a notion suggested by the phrase 'the personal is political', popular in feminist movements since the late 1960s, and sometimes attributed to Carol Hanisch or Shulamith Firestone.[10] 'The personal is political' highlights the obvious but often overlooked fact that real change begins in homes, and workplaces, in the terrain of everyday life; that slogans or manifestos are empty if not backed up by efforts, however modest, to change one's actual practices. The notion also reminds us that such personal changes are not trivial, but are crucial, and are the bedrock of everything else. Better to be the person who tries to make ethical changes in everyday life, even if those choices only affect one or two people, than to be the one who broadcasts political messages of fairness and equality to a large audience but who is not fair and ethical in everyday life.

Therefore, 'small steps into a changed world are better than no steps': in terms of 'X is better than Y' arguments, this one is so easily defended that it might seem pointless. But small steps are easily derided by those who imagine that they are concerned with bigger things. The surly critics that I noted in the introduction to this chapter may dismiss the significance of little actions, preferring to call instead for vast changes to the social structure. But lots of little things can add up to something very big indeed. When lots of people take the step into being active makers and sharers, it alters the character of that group previously thought of as the 'masses' –

---

[9] This quotation is from the notes I made in advance, rather than what was actually said. The video of the talk can be seen at: http://fora.tv/2013/09/22/six_amazing_things_about_making

[10] Discussion of the origins of the phrase can be found at http://womenshistory.about.com/od/feminism/a/consciousness_raising.htm

or the 'audience' – and moves us from a world of 'reception' to one of creativity, exchange, inspiration, and conversation.

2.2.6 The Digital Internet Is Good, but Hands-on Physical Things Are Good Too

The excitement about the internet's capacity to distribute material, build networks, and make connections can at times lead to a sense that human creativity only really found its feet in the mid-1990s. Of course, that is obviously far from being the case, as was noted at the very start of this chapter. It is surely preferable to see continuity between today's creative practices and those of earlier times and continuity between what people do in the digital realm and what they do in the physical world.

Services that make connections between the 'virtual' and 'real' worlds have turned out to be offering something that people want. As Dougald Hine (2009) has noted, the entirely virtual world of Second Life was somewhat popular in the mid-2000s, but never quite took off, because most people didn't really dream of swapping their physical existence for a cyberspace avatar.[11] Meanwhile, much simpler technologies, such as Twitter and Meetup.com, which enable people to build quite straightforward conversations and relationships with people whom they might actually have met or can plan to meet, have been more successful. Hine was a co-founder of the School of Everything, which connects people who want to learn something with people who want to share their knowledge. Hine sees the School of Everything 'as part of a larger shift in the way people are using the web, away from spending more and more of our lives in front of screens, towards making things happen in the real world' (Hine 2008).

The rise of craft and maker communities (Levine and Heimerl 2008; Gauntlett 2011) offers a clear example – or rather a vast and diverse *range* of examples – of people who like to do 'real world' things but whose activity has been given a substantial boost by the opportunity to connect, organise, share ideas, and inspire each other online. There is much evidence of this. A study of online DIY community participants by Stacey Kuznetsov and Eric Paulos (2010) obtained 2,600 responses to an online survey about their motivations and practices (which means it was a self-selected sample of enthusiasts, of course, but 2,600 is a remarkable number of people willing to share their experiences).[12] The responses indicated a strong ethos of 'open sharing, learning, and creativity' rather than desire for profit or self-promotion. Over 90 % of respondents said that they participated in DIY communities by posting questions, comments, and answers. They did this frequently and diligently: almost half of the participants responded to others' questions, and posted comments

---

[11] This bit about Dougald Hine and the School of Everything is a summary of some material that previously appeared in Gauntlett (2011).

[12] This bit about the Kuznetsov and Paulos study draws on an account of the study that I first wrote in Gauntlett et al. (2012).

or questions, on a daily or weekly basis. The online interactions did not remain purely 'virtual', with one third of the respondents attending in-person meetings and over a quarter presenting their work in person at least several times a year. The other respondents used the internet to inspire and share their real-world making activities, even if they were not meeting up with other people in person.

The question of how to meaningfully connect digital and physical tools and experiences has been central to my work with the LEGO Group and the LEGO Foundation (Ackermann et al. 2009, Ackermann et al. 2010; Gauntlett et al. 2011, 2012; Gauntlett and Thomsen 2013). This research concerns broad trends in learning, play, and creativity, although it has an obvious starting point in the fact the LEGO bricks themselves offer an engaging hands-on experience which is not easily mirrored in the digital world. (For sure, for well over a decade, there have been several computer programs, games, and online tools which simulate LEGO building, but the experience is not really the same as picking up a 'random' selection of LEGO pieces and putting them together.)

In *Systematic Creativity in the Digital Realm* (Ackermann et al. 2010), we highlighted ways in which play forms a bridge between the virtual and physical worlds. Most striking of these was 'one reality' – the sense in which the notion of two worlds dissolves – and there is a seamless shift between things experienced as physical and those experienced as digital. These connections could be strengthened by stories and storytelling, as well as other meaningful people and shared interests (p. 77). In *The Future of Play* (Gauntlett et al. 2011), we prescribed an 'expanded playfield' in which there would be more room for free play, exploration, and tinkering; an expansion of adult play, in both home and work contexts; and a blending of digital and physical tools (pp. 71–73). The role for an organisation such as LEGO would be in co-creating collaborative 'ecosystems', helping enthusiasts to connect with others and build things together, without the company getting in the way (p. 69). The subsequent study, *The Future of Learning* (Gauntlett et al. 2012), developed these themes in the area of education, offering a vision where digital tools are used to weave together and magnify real-world learning experiences and to add a valuable layer of social interaction and creative inspiration. Most recently, *Cultures of Creativity* (Gauntlett and Thomsen 2013) suggested that creative tools should be available in everyday life which would support people to shift from the role of 'consumer' to that of 'designer' – facilitated by what Gerhard Fischer describes as 'a shift from consumer cultures, specialized in producing finished artifacts to be consumed passively, to cultures of participation, in which all people are provided with the means to participate and to contribute actively in personally meaningful problems' (2013: 76). These tools are likely to make use of the internet's affordances for social connection and inspiration.

Above all, this integration of online and physical practices of making, exploring, and sharing can be seen as an archetype of 'open design', the movement persuasively advocated in the book *Open Design Now* (Van Abel et al. 2011). Open design, as the name suggests, describes a participatory sphere of sharing, exchange, and collaboration across a broad range of design processes. To some extent, *Open Design Now* is reasonably keen to preserve a role for the professional designer –

albeit in a rich, collaborative relationship with 'everyone' (a term used on the back cover, which seems preferable) or with 'users' (as in the chapter by Stappers et al. 2011, which seems to preserve some of the sense of 'us and them'). After the back cover has asserted that 'We have entered the era of design by everyone', it goes on to say: 'And the good news is: this is the best thing ever for professional designers'. This may be the case, but I would say that one of the most interesting dimensions of open design is the shift from a world where 'design' is something done by professionals, who are consulted by their clients, to a world where 'design' is the process where people work together – sharing ideas and inspiration, both online and offline – to create better things, processes, or networks. Indeed you could say that one of the most significant impacts of the internet on culture and society was this broadening and opening up of creative practices – not just that creative materials, tools, and conversations are now more accessible but rather that they become more central to everyday life, break down old hierarchies, and help to build a world where everyone is more creatively engaged.

2.3   Conclusion

This chapter began by noting an academic resistance to the view that the internet may have changed anything for the better and then set out six ways in which the internet *has* changed things for the better, in the sphere of people making and communicating. (Of course, the impact of the internet has actually reached many more areas than those mentioned here, with substantial shifts in the conduct of politics, protest, economics, news, entertainment, and war, to name but a few.) When saying that 'the internet' can have changed something, it is always important to stress that the internet – a vast bundle of non-sentient cables and processors – couldn't have done this on its own. We are really talking about how people use technologies, for particular purposes of their own designs. Transformations take place within, and as part of, social relationships and everyday life. It can be easy to be negative and take a cynical stance to changes associated with new technologies and new businesses, but this is insufficient and usually rather self-serving. As I hope the six theses here have shown, there are clear reasons to be positive about the role that online connections can make in people's lives – especially when integrated with everyday physical experience. And small steps can lead into a new world, which is less about consumption and more about conviviality, conversation, and creativity.

References

Ackermann E, Gauntlett D, Weckstrom C (2009) Defining systematic creativity. LEGO Learning Institute, Billund

Ackermann E, Gauntlett D, Wolbers T, Weckstrom C (2010) Defining systematic creativity in the digital realm. LEGO Learning Institute, Billund

Chafkin M (2013) True to its roots: why Kickstarter won't sell. Fast Company, April 2013, http://www.fastcompany.com/3006694/where-are-they-now/true-to-its-roots-why-kickstarter-wont-sell

Curran J, Fenton N, Freedman D (2012) Misunderstanding the internet. Routledge, Abingdon

Donald M (2001) A mind so rare: the evolution of human consciousness. W. W. Norton, New York

Dunleavy P (2012) Ebooks herald the second coming of books in university social science. 6 May 2012. http://blogs.lse.ac.uk/lsereviewofbooks/2012/05/06/ebooks-herald-the-second-coming-of-books-in-university-social-science/

Fenton N (2012) The internet and social networking. In: James C, Fenton N, Freedman D (eds) Misunderstanding the Internet. Routledge, Abingdon

Fischer G (2013) Social creativity and cultures of participation: bringing cultures of creativity alive. The LEGO Foundation, Billund. Available from: http://www.legofoundation.com/en-us/research-and-learning/foundation-research/cultures-of-creativity/

Gauntlett D (2000) Web studies: a user's guide. In: Gauntlett D (ed) Web.studies: rewiring media studies for the digital age. Arnold, London

Gauntlett D (2011) Making is connecting: the social meaning of creativity, from DIY and knitting to YouTube and Web 2.0. Polity, Cambridge

Gauntlett D (2012) A tale of two books: an experiment in cutting out the middlepeople with Kindle self-publishing. 28 May 2012. http://blogs.lse.ac.uk/impactofsocialsciences/2012/05/28/tale-two-books/

Gauntlett D (2013) Creativity and digital innovation. In: Youngs G (ed) Digital world: connectivity, creativity and rights. Routledge, Abingdon

Gauntlett D, Thomsen BS (2013) Cultures of creativity. LEGO Foundation, Billund. Available from: http://www.legofoundation.com/en-us/research-and-learning/foundation-research/cultures-of-creativity/

Gauntlett D, Ackermann E, Whitebread D, Wolbers T, Weckstrom C (2011) The future of play: defining the role and value of play in the 21st century. LEGO Learning Institute, Billund

Gauntlett D, Ackermann E, Whitebread D, Wolbers T, Weckstrom C, Thomsen BS (2012) The future of learning. LEGO Learning Institute, Billund

Hardin G (1968) The tragedy of the commons. Science 162(3859): 1243–1248. Available from: http://www.sciencemag.org/content/162/3859/1243.full

Hine D (2008) The "Why Don't You?" Web. 1 December 2008. http://schoolofeverything.com/blog/why-dont-you-web

Hine D (2009) How not to predict the future (or why Second Life is like video calling). 27 April 2009. http://otherexcuses.blogspot.com/2009/04/how-not-to-predict-future-or-why-second.html

Hollow M (2013) Crowdfunding and civic society in Europe: a profitable partnership?. Open Citizsh. 4(1):68–73. http://www.opencitizenship.eu/ojs/index.php/opencitizenship/article/view/80/73

Illich I (1973) Tools for conviviality. Calder & Boyars, London

Kelly K (2008) 1,000 true fans. The Technium [blog]. 8 March 2008. http://kk.org/thetechnium/archives/2008/03/1000_true_fans.php

Kuznetsov S, Paulos E (2010) Rise of the expert amateur: DIY projects, communities, and cultures. Paper presented at the 6th Nordic conference on human-computer interaction, October 2010. Available at http://www.staceyk.org/hci/KuznetsovDIY.pdf

Lanier J (2010) You are not a gadget: a manifesto. Allen Lane, London

Lanier J (2013) Who owns the future? Allen Lane, London

Layard R (2006) Happiness: lessons from a new science. Penguin, London

Leadbeater C (2008) We think: mass innovation not mass production. Profile Books, London

Levine F, Heimerl C (eds) (2008) Handmade nation: the rise of DIY, art, craft and design. Princeton Architectural Press, New York

Miller T (2009) Cybertarians of the world unite: you have nothing to lose but your tubes! In: Snickars P, Vonderau P (eds) The YouTube reader. National Library of Sweden, Stockholm

Miller D (2012) Social networking sites. In: Horst HA, Miller D (eds) Digital anthropology. Berg, London

Morozov E (2011) The net delusion: how not to liberate the world. Allen Lane, London

Morozov E (2013) To save everything, click here: technology, solutionism, and the urge to fix problems that don't exist. Allen Lane, London

Peseschkian N (1985) In search of meaning: a psychotherapy of small steps. Springer, Heidelberg

Stappers PJ, Visser FS, Kistemaker S (2011) Creation & co: user participation in design. In: Van Abel B, Evers L, Klaassen R, Troxler P (eds) Open design now: why design cannot remain exclusive. BIS Publishers, Amsterdam

Szekely L (2011) A statement from Louis C.K. 13 December 2011. https://buy.louisck.net/news/a-statement-from-louis-c-k

Van Abel B, Evers L, Klaassen R, Troxler P (2011) Open design now: why design cannot remain exclusive. BIS Publishers, Amsterdam

Chapter 3
Creating Creative Technologists: Playing With(in) Education

Andy M. Connor, Stefan Marks, and Charles Walker

3.1 Introduction

The Bachelor of Creative Technologies (BCT) degree is offered by Colab, a unique academic unit at Auckland University of Technology. The unit is a research-teaching nexus or 'collaboratory' at the intersection of four existing schools (Art and Design, Communications and Media Studies, Computer and Mathematical Sciences and Engineering) in the Faculty of Design and Creative Technologies. The goal of Colab is to develop new experimental alliances, research collaborations and learning experiences across these overlapping disciplines. Its researchers, students and stakeholders are encouraged to imagine, construct and navigate rapidly changing social, economic, technological and career environments.

The BCT is seen as a key enabler of this goal. The flexible and experimental project-organised curriculum draws on philosophical notions of play, community and interaction to promote divergent thinking and to break, blur or transcend normative disciplinary boundaries (Huizinga 2000). In this context, we use the term Creative Technologies as to refer to a multiplicity of design, communication, computing, engineering, entertainment and manufacturing media, employed to produce ideas, intellectual property and artefacts that characterise the outputs of emerging occupations and professions operating across a wide range of entrepreneurial creative industries contexts.

Whilst the degree embodies this definition, at another level it also represents a vehicle for the authors' ongoing search for creative, hypothesis-driven or inquiry-based learning methodologies that address Boyer and Mitgang's impassioned call for

a new educational language … driven by the conviction that the standards used to evaluate performance should be organized not so much around blocks of knowledge … as around

A.M. Connor (✉) • S. Marks • C. Walker
Colab, Auckland University of Technology, Auckland, New Zealand
e-mail: andrew.connor@aut.ac.nz; stefan.marks@aut.ac.nz; charles.walker@aut.ac.nz

© Springer-Verlag London 2015   35
N. Zagalo, P. Branco (eds.), *Creativity in the Digital Age*,
Springer Series on Cultural Computing, DOI 10.1007/978-1-4471-6681-8_3

modes of thinking: the discovery, integration, application and sharing of knowledge. (Boyer and Mitgang 1996)

However, the main weakness of Boyer and Mitgang's thesis is that it is pitched at the level of educational metatheory, leaving individual development, motivations and relationships amongst people in real learning environments relatively unexamined. In designing the BCT curriculum, we sought to develop new 'modes of thinking' that shift the traditional focus from teaching by transmission to a more socialised engagement with learning through creativity, collaboration and play. More specifically, we came to identify a playful approach to 'discovering, integrating, applying and sharing' different kinds of knowledge – whether theoretical, technical, intuitive, practical, emotional or organisational – within cross-disciplinary learning environments. Whilst there is an emphasis on playfulness as an approach to create curious learners, this is balanced through a combination of structured and semi-structured learning. The first year of the degree purposefully selects students from different backgrounds and introduces basic programming, electronics, digital media and artistic practices in parallel to guided projects that integrate this knowledge across the diverse student body. This pattern is modelled throughout the degree, with the expectation that skills and knowledge developed in more formal components will be integrated into the studio projects undertaken.

We adopt an approach that embeds the spirit of play as defined by Millar (1968) who argues that play is characterised as the shifting of the frame of activity from one domain to another; in particular the concept of play shifts activities from 'reality' to a new 'play-specific space-time' with its own protocols. We also consider the definition of play given by Gordon and Esbjörn-Hargens (2007) who expand this to include playfulness, the attitude that shakes off constraints and enables any activity to become play. The removing of such constraints allows students to learn in the play-specific space-time in a free and explorative manner, before then translating the knowledge and skills back to reality.

The ability to think and act outside of everyday constraints is pivotal in the development of Creative Technologists, who are required to find solutions to problems in a given reality and may find these solutions through a process of projecting their knowledge into a unique space through a similar shift from reality.

3.2 The Spectrum of Play(fulness)

Play has historically been a considerable focus of research in terms of understanding early education and childhood development, particularly as a means of developing creativity (Vygotsky 1967; Russ 1998). Russ argues that 'Play skills and creative abilities help lay the foundation for a child's cognitive and emotional functioning and for a happy and meaningful adult life' (Russ 2003), yet this begs the question why the focus on play in early childhood education is not continued into secondary and post-secondary education.

Rice who has considered the role of play in post-secondary education suggests that 'playful learning can be effective in motivating and improving student engagement, promoting creative thinking towards learning and developing approaches towards multi-disciplinary learning' (Rice 2009). Rice also observes that a playful approach towards learning and knowledge can facilitate ontological change within students. Such change is pivotal in assisting students to transcend normative disciplinary boundaries and reach their full potential as creative practitioners. As such, the adoption of play as a learning approach in combination with the development of a safe space that encourages risk-taking and exploration is core to the pedagogical foundations of the degree.

Whilst less attention has been paid to playfulness in adults, it is recognised to exist. For example, adults have been known to evidence playful behaviour even when they are engaged in practical or serious activities (Bologh 1976) as well as in the workplace (Csikszentmihalyi and LeFevre 1989). This perhaps indicates that such activities might be accomplished quite playfully at times (Bowman 1987). Caldwell (2003) argues that lifelong play is a means of continuing transformation, and Göncü and Perone (2005) have found that play and improvisation amongst adult learners foster community as a result of developing dialogue, trust, reciprocity, sharing and negotiation.

Play, creativity and community are linked through the common ground of divergent thinking, a process that generates a variety of ideas and associations to a given problem. There is a variety of research evidence that suggests that play facilitates both divergent thinking and creativity (Russ 2003), both of which are considered to be of considerable importance in the development of Creative Technologists. Our approach to implementing a playful educational paradigm also draws on an understanding of cognitive development. Again, much of the research in this field draws on childhood development which has emerged as an ongoing area of interest since the work of Piaget (1953). Bruner (1977) argues that a child of any age is capable of understanding complex information and explains how this is possible through the concept of the spiral curriculum. This involves the structuring of information so that complex ideas can be taught at a simplified level first and then revisited at more complex levels later on to lead to children being able to solve problems by themselves. Bruner also proposes that learners construct their own knowledge and do this by organising and categorising information using a coding system (Bruner 1961). Bruner believes that the most effective way to develop a coding system is to discover it rather than being told by the teacher. The concept of discovery learning implies that students construct their own knowledge for themselves. Meyer and Land (2013) also acknowledge that this process of change through learning is also a process of loss, in the sense that gaining new insights on the world may involve a 'loss' of one's old self.

Many authors have proposed different development phases that can be mapped to an ability to process complex information in different ways, typically divided into a number of phases. The full-spectrum model divides the development of an individual into four phases, pre-conventional (prepersonal), conventional (personal), post-conventional (postpersonal) and post-post conventional/transcendent (transpersonal). Cook-Greuter (2000) suggests that approximately 90 % of the adult population function within the first two tiers of development and that current conventional adult development is a linear, rational model of reality through which individuals can achieve abstract or formal operations. Cook-Greuter goes on to suggest that post-conventional 'goes beyond the modern, linear–scientific Western mindset and beyond the conventions of society by starting to question the unconsciously held beliefs, norms and assumptions about reality acquired during socialization and schooling'.

Gordon and Esbjörn-Hargens (2007) provide an insight to the nature of play in terms of such a developmental framework. They describe eight 'play selves' in relation to both a four-tier model of development and the rhetorics of play discussed by Brian Sutton-Smith (1997). This comparison is reproduced in Table 3.1.

For Creative Technologists to be able to create new technological paradigms, they need to be able to function at the postpersonal or transpersonal level. Transpersonal theory argues that these higher levels, which involve experiences of connectedness with phenomena considered outside the boundaries of self, can engender the highest human qualities, including altruism, creativity and intuitive wisdom (Kasprow and Scotton 1999).

Whilst a number of mature students are accepted into the programme each year, the majority of applicants are recent school leavers – many of whom have progressed through high school to obtain the New Zealand National Certificate of Educational Achievement (NCEA) at a sufficient level to gain entrance to university. NCEA is a standards-based system where students accumulate credits on the basis of demonstrating that they have met predefined standards of achievement (Lee and Lee 2001). Critics of the NCEA approach have argued that the standards-based approach has both pedagogical and educational concerns because there is no distinction between academic and vocational subjects in assessment methods, and unit standards do not motivate students to excel and extend themselves (Hall 1997). Proponents of the NCEA approach suggest that NCEA allows students and educators to focus on interpersonal relations, critical thinking skills, self-evaluation, risk-

Table 3.1 Play rhetorics in the developmental model (Gordon and Esbjörn-Hargens 2007)

Developmental stage	Play rhetoric	Play self
Transpersonal	Play as frivolity	Unitive player
		Dynamic player
Postpersonal	Play as self	Complex player
	Play as imagination	Sensitive player
Personal	Play as self	Status player
	Play as progress	Ordered player
	Play as identity	
Prepersonal	Play as power	Aggressive player
	Play as fate	Magical player

taking, individual leadership, teamwork, innovation and creativity (Hellner 2003). Experiential and anecdotal evidence suggest that if anything, the NCEA is variable and produces students with a wide range of capabilities. With that in mind, the educational strategies deployed in the BCT programme focus initially on developing play and playfulness at the prepersonal level as a levelling process to assist all students to learn about multiple perspectives and disciplines, before progressing through different play rhetorics to aim to develop students' full potential.

The transition from high school to university is a significant life change that often results in students feeling out of place and unsure of their own competencies. As a result, the behaviour of students is such that they tend to adopt the magical 'play self' that is characterised by feelings of confusion and anxiety arising from dealing with the complexity of the new environment. Incoming students typically have no sense of their potential or capability, which results in some students undertaking overly optimistic projects, whilst others err on the side of caution.

3.3   The Space of Play

The BCT is, in part, conceived as a creative inquiry-led undergraduate degree with the characteristics of a postgraduate research programme (Connor et al. 2009). We emphasise interactive, project-oriented learning in which students are engaged and active participants. As a result, their learning experience is one of personal transformation that has the potential to produce graduates that function at the postpersonal and transpersonal levels. Team-based project work also enhances opportunities for peer review and co-creation.

At another level, it is the hybrid nature of the learning space in which the BCT is 'played out' that is key to how students engage with the transdisciplinary nature of the emerging Creative Technologies domain. We combine aspects of the artist's studio, the design atelier, the workshop and the laboratory in to a unique active learning space. The first two combine personal inspiration, 'creative freedom' and the specific conditions of creative practice, the lab focuses on the scientific simulation of reality and the workshop is concerned with engineering and the production of the world. Thus the programme encourages students to playfully imagine, model and make connections, relationships or associations between ideas and phenomena under investigation, not to find an answer but rather a starting point or an 'attitude' (Gamper 2012; Koethen 2012). Like 'the arena, the card-table, the magic circle, the temple, the stage, the screen, the tennis court, [and] the court of justice', the learning place can be seen as 'a play-ground, a place where 'special rules obtain', dedicated to the performance of an act apart' (Huizinga 2000).

It is important to emphasise that this 'performance .... apart' does not denote a closed or self-contained system but relies on frequent interaction, intervention or dynamic interplay with the everyday world. Neither does our focus on play undermine the importance of real tools, media and context in human development. Following Piaget, we recognise that 'knowledge is experience that is acquired through interaction with the world, people and things' (Ackermann 2001). We also acknowledge a historical trajectory of collaborative learning spaces, from Dewey's concepts of 'continuity and interaction' (Dewey 1938); Vygotsky's 'active partici- pation in the acquisition of knowledge' (Vygotsky 1978); Wenger's components of 'meaning', 'practice', 'community' and 'identity' (Wenger 2008); and Abbott's (2005) 'ecologies of practice'.

This distance between the everyday world and the world of play does not prevent play from being real but enables it to be real. Like art, play both refers to and dis- tances us from the world at the same time. We play against the world – and with it. Thus, our learning place is both, fake and real, ordinary and artificial, fun and seri- ous (Consalvo 2003). Again, like art, play is a process which exists only as experi- ence. Both activities refer to and distance themselves from the world at the same time. Art is playing against, and with, the world, using material, objects and rela- tions of the world but aiming at a quality beyond it. From this point of view, there must be a distance between learners and the real world, even as they work on real- world problems to bring works into existence, beyond the studio, and into everyday life.

For us, play and learning are connected to each other, but the relationship is not as direct as is sometimes assumed. For educators, this can be challenging. Players can, and do, decide what is play and what is not. Play is most free when it is least staged. External restrictions, aims or even learning outcomes imposed on play can destroy it. Indeed, even those who purport to be in favour of play in education often seem to rely on 'a Mary Poppins type of argument. A spoonful of sugar and the medicine goes down!' (Avedon and Sutton-Smith 1971).

We propose to resolve these apparent contradictions by locating our learning environment in a conceptual third place. It is not a little bit real world and a little bit space apart; it is fully real in the sense that play is real; it is taken seriously whilst the game is being played. The learning environment is an individual place and a collective place. It creates experiences that are visited repeatedly, cyclically, whilst at the same time, no experience is ever the same twice. It is a place people want to reach and a place they want to leave, a real place, a virtual space and a journey.

Students are open to this new playspace. In recent years, the students entering the programme can increasingly be referred to as 'digital natives', a term coined by Prensky (2001) to define the differences between generations in terms of their atti- tudes towards virtual environments and digital tools. As a result, a more blended approach has been developed that utilises traditional studio and classroom methods combined with online discussion and Web 2.0 tools such as blogs, wikis, social networking and learning management tools.

Students are required to use online tools to assist their own learning, starting with the development of a blog in the first year (Connor et al. 2014a) to enhance educa- tion by encouraging reflective practice. Beale (2007) argues that blogging provides advantages in terms of both pedagogical and social perspectives. For example, it has been observed that blogging produces a sense of community amongst the students because they can read and comment on other students' postings. The result is that they can learn from both reflecting on their own experiences and from the insights of their peers. Whilst the role of the blog is primarily to develop a reflective habit, it stealthily introduces processes of collection, selection and critical discernment. Beale (2007) also argues that the fact that students can see the sort of activities done by other students there is transparency in terms of the amount of work that is required as well as the quality of work being produced. Because others can also see their level of activity or inactivity, peer pressure should exert an influence and encourage them to maintain a degree of selectivity in terms of how the students present their work and their reflections.

One of the aspirations of the course is to generate an environment where both student and teacher construct the learning agenda in partnership. A key element of this construction is a continuous dialogue that is achieved through frequent critique sessions (or 'crits'). Questioning is often used to guide student thinking. A particular technique (or style of questioning), gleaned from educational literature (Schoenfeld 1998), is used – the reflective toss. The purpose of the reflective toss is to allow the lecturer to interpret the meaning of a student statement but ensure that the student continues to elaborate their underlying thinking. In such an environment, the traditional transmissive view of education is replaced with one where the role of the lecturer is not to supply information to the students but to guide and facilitate their learning.

The overall goal of the lecturer as facilitator is to move the focus of student learning away from simply remembering facts towards some form of higher learning, such as the understanding of underlying principles. Such a goal is appropriate for a programme that aims to develop graduates with competency at the higher level skills of analysis, synthesis and evaluation associated with postpersonal and transpersonal development. In order to achieve this development, the students in the programme are guided through a range of projects that are designed around different rhetorics of play with a view to guiding students through different stages of personal development.

This playful student-centred learning environment aims to develop the learner's capacity to be self-directed. Given rapid change, the continuous creation of new knowledge, and an ever-widening access to information, we endeavour to let students identify and choose their own challenges; define their own areas of interest; decide on methods, focus and direction; form project teams; formulate research questions; design their own research plan; and develop knowledge of practices in the particular field or area (Cermak-Sassenrath and Walker 2012). All of this is intended to stimulate connective, imaginative and explorative learning. In the absence of fixed or predetermined outcomes, students are challenged to learn, to analyse and to critically discuss their own work and that of others, e.g. by regularly conducting open peer reviews of project work. Learning happens not only through participation, by doing, but also by analysing and critiquing the work of one's peers.

An exhaustive coverage of the projects is impossible; however, the following section highlights a few examples of playful projects.

3.4   Playful Projects

3.4.1   Poetry in Motion

'Poetry in Motion' is an example of a typical first year project that encapsulates a wide range of theoretical and conceptual elements into a unified whole. The project is designed to explicitly embody the concept of play and playfulness whilst implicitly introducing students to a range of design and manufacturing technologies and principles.

The project was inspired by the popular 1960s board game, Mousetrap, in which players cooperate to build a working Rube Goldberg-like mousetrap. Once the mousetrap has been built, players turn against each other and attempt to trap their opponents' mouse-shaped game pieces. In 2006 the game was rereleased with a new design in which there are three mousetraps and completely different mousetrap mechanism and gameplay. The project also references artistic works such as 'The Way Things Go' by Fischli and Weiss or Jean Tingluey's 'Homage to New York' as inspiration. The focus of such works is on the playful and creative sequence of events that trigger each other without any practical purpose in mind. They are mechanisms for mechanism's sake – 'art for art's sake'. They exploit an innate understanding of physics and a fundamental enjoyment of movement and mechanics. The structure and context of the Poetry in Motion project suggest that 'You don't have to be an Engineer to figure it out'.

The overall goal of the Poetry in Motion project is to design and create a chain reaction game using imaginative and interesting combinations of basic mechanical systems. Overall, the project is designed to promote risk-taking as well as achieve a practical appreciation of principles of physics and mechanics. The project is structured in two parts, the first being the creation of a simple mechanical automata that is designed using CAD software and then manufactured by utilising the laser cutters in the faculty fabrication facility. This part of the project ensures that students understand that the practicalities of motion of manufactured parts may differ from simulated motion in the CAD software, often in catastrophic ways with mechanisms failing to operate. One aspect of promoting a playful approach to learning and the taking of risks is being prepared to deal with failure. A 'failed' project is often a successful learning experience, and whilst beyond the scope of this chapter, we embrace the success of learning even when the outcomes of a project may typically be considered a failure (Connor et al. 2014b). Typical mechanical automata are shown below (Fig. 3.1).

Upon completion of the first stage of the project, students are encouraged to let their imaginations run wild in the design and implementation of their chain reaction game, applying what they have learned in terms of how mechanical systems work in practice in combination with their understanding of the importance of social and cooperative play. The outcomes of the project are predictably variable, with some students successfully using the project to extend themselves into other play selves through the process of an experimental approach to developing play. Some sample student projects are shown in Fig. 3.2.

Fig. 3.1 Sample automata

Fig. 3.2 Sample student projects

3.4.2 Synthesis

The first year of the BCT degree is to some extent 'scripted' by tutors to reduce the likelihood of students becoming lost and unproductive. As students progress to the second year of the degree, such defined projects are removed and replaced with one or more thematic concepts that are used to guide student projects without overly constraining content.

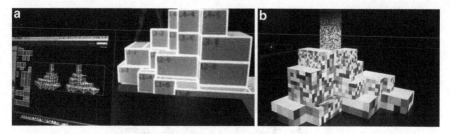

Fig. 3.3 Project mapped installation – 'Synthesis'[1]

'Synthesis' is an interactive installation developed by a group of second year students to encourage an exploration of synthetic and organic growth within a projected environment. Using emerging technologies, Synthesis aims to engage the audience with an artificial system of interactive construction and invites participants to become part of the harmony or imbalance created. Images of the installation during preparation and in the final presentation stage are shown in Fig. 3.3.

Using a process known as projection mapping, Synthesis harnesses a central free-standing geometric sculpture as a canvas. A video feed is mapped and projected onto the many surfaces of the sculpture, inviting audience members to view the installation from 360°, anywhere in the room. Interaction is registered through Kinect sensors, tracking movement and altering the display accordingly.

Developing within the installation is a planar building block-esque formation representing engineered or synthetic construction and an organic movement-based representation which utilises softer, more flowing aesthetics and palettes. Both are linked to the level of audience interaction, synthetic elements relying on interaction for growth and organic elements developing in areas with less interaction.

This particular project is of interest in the context of playful creation and engagement as it marks a milestone in the developmental journey of a team of students who formed the collective agency, Fantail Studios, whilst enrolled in the degree. In terms of the rhetorics of play, this indicated a transition into both play as identity and play as self for the students in the team. This clearly marked the shift into the personal developmental stage which is commonly encountered with students in their second year of study. The team describes their relationship with the installation as:

> As the creators of Synthesis we have a firm personal connection with the ideology of harmony and balance. These key themes were a major influence on the construction of the installation. Although not necessarily goal driven, there is an underlying desire that audience members will explore and observe the way they affect the environment, and the consequences of their interaction. With Synthesis, we hope many personal interpretations are formed, and aim to provide the opportunity for participants to explore the concept of harmony and synthesis for themselves.[2]

---

[1] https://www.youtube.com/watch?v=dYjlZ7HTI_w

[2] http://fantailstudios.co

The stated intent to have no specific goal in terms of the interaction with the installation implies a degree of playfulness and a faith in the ability of the audience to respond in an equally playful way. This suggests that the team is on the cusp of entering the sensitive play self, which emphasises interpersonal connectivity by sharing experiences and acknowledging contextual aspects of play. They are clearly aware of the observer and multiple viewpoints as they suggest their installation raises questions regarding the nature of man and the relationship between humanity and its environment such as 'Where does man fit into nature?' and 'At what point does something become inorganic?' and suggest that Synthesis demonstrates the relationship between organic and synthetic growth and therefore gives form to these questions by implementing an experience that enables the observer to play with that form.

3.4.3 Guerilla Playspaces

Guerilla Playspaces was a semester-long project undertaken by second year students, in partnership with an external civic organisation, the Committee for Auckland (CFA). The group sought to address the aim of the Auckland City Plan to be the 'world's most livable city'. This aim is threatened by the segregation of life between dispersed residential suburbs and the largely commercial districts of the Central Business District (CBD), particularly for certain residential groups such as families and senior citizens. This situation is made worse by Auckland's geography and the challenges of creating a transport system that enables people to move simply and efficiently from the sprawling suburbs to the CBD. As a consequence, many Auckland residents do not identify with the CBD and avoid it if they can. The aim of the project then was to create life, vitality, connection and enjoyment in prominent areas of the CBD where these elements were lacking or not considered possible.

Successful city centres are a melting pot of peoples, cultures and life. They have an energy that is sustaining and regenerative. Despite recent excellent work to improve the quality of the city centre and waterfront spaces, loitering and socialising in the CBD only really occur as a result of organised events or for short bursts as weekend evening revellers fill the bars and clubs.

Jan Gehl, a renowned urban designer once stated 'First life, then spaces, then buildings – the other way around never works'. Despite the creation of some fantastic new spaces in the city as a result of the shared space and other urban design initiatives, the 'life' that would fill these spaces throughout the day is largely missing.

Multiple teams of students worked on this project to develop different concepts for spaces to create opportunities for play that fundamentally alter people's perception of the CBD as a desirable location to live and thrive. The variety of playspaces attests to the diversity of the student cohort and each concept each had a different

Fig. 3.4 Hit the Floor and the Planter Box

Fig. 3.5 The Social Pavlova

level of cohesion and resolve. For example, two subprojects ('Hit the Floor[3]' and 'Planter Box[4]') are relatively unsophisticated in their nature, relying on active and passive interaction of passersby to activate the playspace. The outcomes of these projects are shown in Fig. 3.4.

Meanwhile, another subproject ('Social Pavlova') incorporates audio feedback based on a behavioural algorithm to allow the space to take on a more sublime living nature. The Social Pavlova is shown in Fig. 3.5.

The adaptive nature of the playspace prevents it from being a simple chair or sculpture, and it becomes a living thing within the city. How people interact with it influences how it 'feels', and thus how it responds to others. This connects people together through shared experiences across time, as the interactions of one person will affect the mood of the piece for the next person who encounters it. The piece seeks to both draw people in and push them away depending on how it feels. It mediates this interaction through sound, attempting to influence the behaviour of the people who come across it.

---

[3] https://www.youtube.com/watch?v=obitExGhY7k

[4] https://www.youtube.com/watch?v=t7qWvPxB_9M

The different levels of sophistication and quality of finish in the prototypes are accompanied by a difference in the nature of playfulness exhibited. The less sophisticated projects were developed by groups who very much identified themselves in relation to their peers, a characteristic associated with the ordered play self. The outcomes of these projects have elements of play as imagination, yet the simplistic and deterministic interaction has overtones of the play as fate. In terms of development progress, this suggests that the students individually may be at different stages, some prepersonal, some personal and some postpersonal, and that the tensions that exist between them have implicitly been embedded in the work they produce. The more sophisticated projects, such as the Social Pavlova, have less confusion in terms of classification of the outcomes being clearly associated with the play as imagination rhetoric and the sensitive play self.

When considering both of the previous project examples, Synthesis and Guerrilla Playspaces, it becomes clear that the second year of the degree is a period of development and growth for the students, with many students clearly reaching the personal stage and moving on to the postpersonal stage of development.

3.4.4 *Virtual Reality Wheelchair Simulator*

The Virtual Reality Wheelchair Simulator is a serious game project developed by five students during a second year 'Simulated Environments' paper with the generic topic 'serious games'. At the beginning, students inquired and learned about the topic in general, investigated and developed definitions of 'serious game' and looked at development and educational frameworks around serious games in general. The lectures were short and concise, merely plotting the outline of the area that the students were then asked to fill out, for example by giving seminars about types of serious games, collaborative development of a wiki and group critique sessions. As assessment, the students were required to build a serious game using a topic and implementation platform of their choice. After having gone through some brainstorming, one of the teams came up with the idea of a wheelchair simulator that uses the Oculus Rift for immersion and an actual wheelchair as an input device. With the help of other Colab staff members and their connections and networks, we were able to actually have a wheelchair 'donated' for the project duration, and the game quickly took on form.

Halfway through the semester, the students were given the opportunity to showcase their prototype at Digital Nationz 2013,[5] a public exhibition about new technologies with a specific focus on New Zealand. Although the learning curve for the project was steep and the conference deadline was a few weeks before the submission deadline of the paper, the incentive of the conference showcase motivated the students sufficiently that they were able to deliver a fully functional prototype in

---

[5] http://digitalnationz.com/

time. The response of the audience to the wheelchair simulator was very positive, even resulting in a TV interview.[6]

In their blogs, the students afterwards reflected positively on the challenges of this project that it forced them to deviate from their usual course of more comedic and controversial works and that it was a great confidence boost to see their works being shown in public.[7] Most of the time, this project was approached in a very playful and fun way, but the students were also aware of the serious applications and the market potential of this project.

With respect to the play rhetoric, this project can be categorised as 'play as imagination', clearly demonstrating the postpersonal development stage of the students. The virtual shopping centre within the simulator was deliberately designed to demonstrate everyday frustrations of wheelchair users like stairs, narrow doorways, long meandering ways to places, etc. Therefore, the wheelchair simulator assists the user to expand the sense of identity, putting them into a situation that is different from their normal life, forcing them to see the world from another perspective – literally and metaphorically. The images in Fig. 3.6 show the simulator in use at the Digital Nationz event.

Fig. 3.6 Virtual Reality Wheelchair Simulator at Digital Nationz

[6] http://www.youtube.com/watch?v=0I0p9JU6sJw

[7] http://jarnetcreativetech.tumblr.com/post/65752097677/wheelchair-simulators-and-life

3.4.5   Lost in a Rift

'Lost in a Rift' is a third-year studio project that was designed and implemented by three students. The intent was to extend the amount of sensory information for a virtual environment beyond visual and auditory.[8] Using Arduino and a custom circuitry, they connected a fan and a heat lamp to the computer that run the virtual reality simulation. The students then designed and modelled virtual scenarios with locations and situations that would make the best use of these additional devices. In one scene, the user could feel the wind blowing when they would cross a bridge over a mountain pass. The heat lamp would be activated in a scene where an explosion occurs close to the user or where the sun is shining.

In order to also facilitate a seamless transition from the real world into the virtual world, the starting and ending scene were modelled in a way that resembled the setup of the physical installation, so the user would find himself/herself sitting in a chair in a high-rise building, being able to look out of the windows. Navigation was made simple by merely three buttons for walking forwards and turning left and right, conveniently located on the chair's armrest.

Nothing in this project was predefined by lecturers or course content. The project was born from the students' fascination of virtual reality and latest technologies like the Oculus Rift and a desire to play with such technologies to see what may emerge. Such an approach is common with final year students who learn through a process of making, rather than having a specific goal in mind. From this starting point, the group developed the whole concept, did the necessary background research and kept in close contact to the lecturers who would help them in specific aspects, e.g. game engines, electronics and the aspect of 'presence' (Slater and Wilbur 1997). Some design decisions even happened by accident, e.g. the idea of the heat lamp was born during a feedback session where the lecturer happened to sit in the sun shining through the window during a sunny virtual reality scene. The final environment developed by the students is shown in Fig. 3.7.

As with the previous project, this is very much an example of students adopting the play as self rhetoric, using their projects to explore themselves and their interests. Whilst play as self rhetoric is often applied to solitary activities and hobbies or high-risk phenomena like bungee jumping, there is also an element of play as self-realisation (Henricks 2014) which correlates well with elements of the self, particularly where play is idealised by attention to the desirable experiences of the players – their fun, their relaxation and their escape. In this project, the students truly escaped the confines of a more traditional education by having fun whilst exploring their own interests.

---

[8] http://cargocollective.com/bctyear3catalogue13/Lost-in-a-Rift

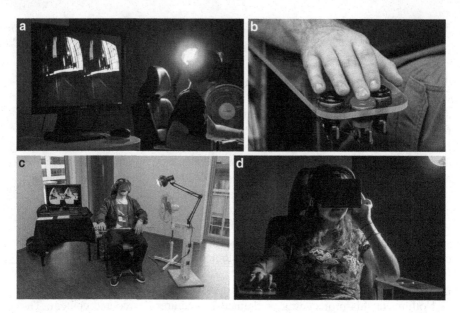

Fig. 3.7 Lost in a Rift

3.4.6 Rabble Room Arcade

'Rabble Room Arcade' is another third-year studio project by two students based on the idea of a 'social playspace' with a focus on 'local video games, tangible interfaces and physical fun' (Gavin et al. 2014). It is an example of a student project that extended beyond a single semester and as such is a case study in sustained inquiry.

In the first semester, the students experimented with the idea of constructing unconventional physical input devices for games, for example, pulleys or handheld tilt sensors. Whilst they focused mainly on providing the input hardware, they started to commission game developers to provide custom mini games tailored for the provided input devices. The students also developed a classification framework for the characteristics of games and the input devices, e.g. 'eight-player one-button'. The second semester was largely dominated by the curation and planning of the final event, the 'Rabble Room Arcade'. Located within the university premises, but open to the public, the event featured eight very different games:

- 'Double Shovel', a game where two players would cooperatively shovel grain into a chute to trigger events like feeding a child or cleaning up a kitchen
- 'Elevator', a two-player competitive game with cranks as input devices that have to be operated as fast as possible to make the game character go up an elevator as fast as possible whilst avoiding virtual objects being thrown at them

- 'Space Octopus Mono', an 8-bit style arcade game where the players control the horizontal position of the spaceship via wooden sliders on wooden rails
- 'Off Da Railz', a game where the player controls a train with a wooden board that has tilt sensors for direction and speed control
- 'CatManDudu', an experimental game controlled by two foot-operated buttons for direction and a toilet chain switch for triggering 'shots'
- 'Eight-player Word Wars', a competitive game for up to eight players that have to form words by 'grabbing' letters that appear on the screen by pushing a single button
- 'Fruit Racers', a four-player competitive game with rotary encoders as input devices to control the direction of fruit on the screen in a race setting
- 'Shadow Showdown', a cooperative game where one or more players have to match silhouettes on the screen by creating silhouettes with their own body/bodies

The event was visited by more than 100 people and also featured on an evening TV show (Fig. 3.8).[9]

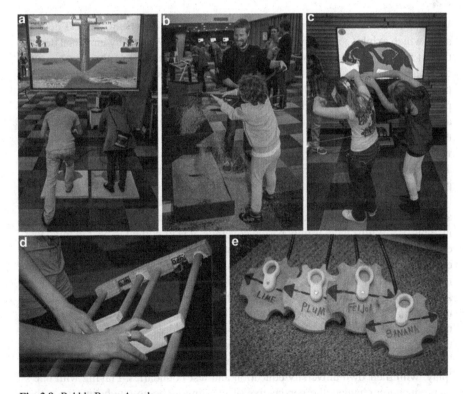

Fig. 3.8 Rabble Room Arcade

---

[9] http://tvnz.co.nz/seven-sharp/future-gaming-video-5624010

More than any other project considered in this chapter, the Rabble Room Arcade project articulates the more developed rhetorics of play. The students are clearly advocating 'play for the sake of play' which would be in line with the expectations of the frivolous play rhetoric. Not only are the students promoting frivolous play but are simultaneously poking fun at the societal norms associated with game culture and utilising their arcade to enhance social interaction and emphasise the physical importance of play. It is clear that the students are attempting to share their view that the world is a place full of potential and paradox and that this can be explored through a shared play experience. This confirms that these students have also adopted more advanced play selves by demonstrating the capability to integrate multimodal and multidimensional elements across contexts in service of humanity, or in this case a social grouping. Such characteristics would tend to be associated with the dynamic player.

3.5   Summary: The State of Play

We have described a representative sample of student projects from the BCT degree, all of which exhibit some degree of play or playfulness. Whilst any universal defini-tion of play or playful behaviour remains elusive, an analysis of the projects sug-gests that as students progress through the degree, the nature and character of their play change. It is important to emphasise here that we do not present play as a purely instrumental approach to learning. Our observations indicate that students are undergoing a developmental journey that extends their creative capabilities and their potential to contribute to society. Such anecdotal evidence is in accordance with other research that suggests that play can contribute to the social capital of adult learners (Gordon and Esbjörn-Hargens 2007; Harris and Daley 2008). Whilst play may seem fanciful, the projects outlined in the previous section can be mapped to the expected characteristics of the graduate profile. A number of generic graduate attributes have been excluded; however, the mapping to relevant attributes is shown in Table 3.2. Whilst there is only partial coverage, it is important to bear in mind that each project only constitutes a single semester of study. Whilst gaps and anomalies exist, the projects at the higher levels of study show the highest degree of achieve-ment in terms of demonstrating the attributes stated in the graduate profile. This suggests that as students develop through the degree that they are more capable of undertaking work of sufficient scale and complexity that demonstrates this achieve-ment. Interestingly, few of the projects discussed address issues of sustainability though many other projects not included do consider this.

Whilst demonstrating achievement is important, we also encourage students to 'play' with their own university education and test boundaries. Playing with one's own education changes the perspective of learning as being taught into an active process driven by one's own interest and curiosity. More specifically, we aim to cre-ate conditions in which students learn to use play, interaction and games to develop both exploratory and performative ways of operating in the university environment.

Table 3.2 Graduate attributes

Graduate attribute	Projects					
	Poetry motion	Synthesis	Playspaces	Wheelchair	Lost in a Rift	Rabble Room Arcade
Work together in transdisciplinary project teams	✓	✓	✓	✓	✓	✓
Embrace multiple creative and technological perspectives	✓	✓	✓	✓	✓	✓
Demonstrate skills of self, colleague and task management	✓	✓	✓	✓	✓	✓
Acquire an astute awareness of the technical and commercial contexts of the creative sector			✓			✓
Work within and between a range of interlinking technological domains		✓	✓	✓	✓	✓
Possess an awareness of new and emerging technologies		✓		✓	✓	
Scan, select and combine technologies suitable for specific projects		✓	✓	✓	✓	✓
Communicate with specialists and stakeholders from diverse disciplines and enterprise levels			✓	✓		✓
Plan, organise and execute collaborative work	✓	✓	✓	✓	✓	✓
Generate ideas, concepts and artefacts encompassing creativity and innovation	✓	✓	✓	✓	✓	✓
Use analytical, synthetic and critical perspectives in the generative process		✓		✓		✓
Produce elegant solutions to problems	✓	✓		✓		✓[a]
Reflect on avenues for future development and improvement				✓		✓
Incorporate a concern for environmental sustainability		✓				
Base new learning and research on the cumulative knowledge gained during and after the course of study	✓	✓	✓	✓	✓	✓

[a]In this example, inefficiency and an unfinished aesthetic were design goals and in this context would be considered elegant, even if objectively they are inelegant

In this sense, playfulness also develops qualities of perception, differentiation and judgement that often transcend limits set by formal and, for some, somewhat artificial or extrinsic curriculum requirements.

Students are encouraged to take individual and collective responsibility for their own learning as an emergent process of experimentation, exploration and discovery. Learning and play are initiated by tutors but realised and managed by students themselves. We suggest that a playful approach affords the freedom for learners to take a greater degree of ownership and control over their own learning. The projects above illustrate how this playful methodology has been applied to learning in the emerging, as yet 'undisciplined', field of Creative Technologies.

The remaining questions relate to the future of the degree and the ongoing nature of play and playfulness in post-secondary education. Whilst this chapter outlines anecdotal evidence to support that play is indeed a useful mechanism in assisting students develop as individuals, there is a pressing need to maintain momentum and keep abreast of a changing educational arena. Whilst post-secondary play has seen little research activity to date, recent publications suggest that there will be a greater focus in the future. For example, in a recently published volume (Tierney et al. 2014), various authors consider the role of games and social media in aspects of post-secondary education such as the need to maintain or increase enrolments, ensuring the transition from school to college is successful and the ongoing question of the role of technology in the classroom to name but a few. Our experiences support the outcomes of the contributors to this volume that whilst play and games can be powerful tools for encouraging students to develop, quality projects, the more important focus is ensuring the ability to develop skills whilst engaging in the game. It is this engagement that is essential in the effective use of games and playful approaches in teaching and learning. In a manner of speaking, educators are faced with a challenge of designing a game that students want to play – the game of learning. In that regard, maintaining playfulness as an educator is as important as promoting playfulness in the students themselves.

References

Abbott A (2005) Linked ecologies: states and universities as environments for professions*. Sociol Theory 23(3):245–274

Ackermann E (2001) Piaget's constructivism, Papert's constructionism: what's the difference. Future Learn Group Publ 5(3):438

Avedon EM, Sutton-Smith B (1971) The study of games. Wiley, New York

Beale R (2007) Blogs, reflective practice and student-centered learning. In: Proceedings of the 21st British HCI Group annual conference on people and computers: HCI…but not as we know it – volume 2 (BCS-HCI '07), Vol. 2. British Computer Society, Swinton, UK, pp 3–6

Bologh RW (1976) On fooling around: a phenomenological analysis of playfulness. Ann Phenomenol Sociol 1:113–125

Bowman JR (1987) Making work play. In: Fine GA (ed) Meaningful play, playful meanings. Human Kinetics, Champaign, pp 61–71

Boyer EL, Mitgang LD (1996) Building community: a new future for architecture education and practice: a special report. Carnegie Foundation, Princeton

Bruner JS (1961) The act of discovery. Harv Educ Rev 31:21–32

Bruner J (1977) The process of education. Harvard University Press, Cambridge, MA

Caldwell C (2003) Adult group play therapy. In: Schaefer CE (ed) Play therapy with adults. Wiley, New York, pp 301–316

Cermak-Sassenrath D, Walker C (2012) S(t)imulating interdisciplinarity. In: Nygaard C, Courtney N, Leigh E (eds) Simulations, games and role play in university education. Libri Publishing, Faringdon, pp 139–149

Connor AM, Buchan J, Petrova K (2009) Bridging the research-practice gap in requirements engineering through effective teaching and peer learning. In: Proceedings of the sixth international conference on information technology: new generations (ITNG 2009), 678,683, 27–29 April 2009, IEEE Computer Society, Washington, DC, USA. doi:10.1109/ITNG.2009.134

Connor AM, Martin M, Joe S (2014a) An extensible framework for automatic knowledge extraction from student blogs. Int J Integr Technol Educ 3(2):9–18

Connor AM et al (2014b) An unexpected journey: experiences of learning through exploration and experimentation. In: DesignEd Asia conference 2014. Honk Kong Design Institute, Hong Kong

Consalvo M (2003) It's no videogame: news commentary and the second gulf war. In: Proceedings of Digital Games Research Association (DiGRA), Utrecht University, Utrecht

Cook-Greuter SR (2000) Mature ego development: a gateway to ego transcendence? J Adult Dev 7(4):227–240

Csikszentmihalyi M, LeFevre J (1989) Optimal experience in work and leisure. J Pers Soc Psychol 56(5):815–822

Dewey J (1938) Experience and education. Collier-MacMillan Canada, Toronto

Gamper M (2012) 'Experimentierkunst' – Geschichte, Themen, Me-tho¬den, Theorien. In: Kreuzer S (ed) Experimente in der Künsten. Transmediale Erkundungen in Literatur, Theater, Film, Musik und bildender Kunst. Transcript, Bielefeld, pp 19–47

Gavin J, Kenobi B, Connor AM (2014) Social play spaces for active community engagement. In: Blackmore K, Nesbitt K, Smith SP (eds) Proceedings of the 2014 conference on Interactive Entertainment (IE 2014). ACM, New York, Article 31, 5pp. doi:10.1145/2677758.2677789

Göncü A, Perone A (2005) Pretend play as a life-span activity. Topoi 24(2):137–147

Gordon G, Esbjörn-Hargens S (2007) Are we having fun yet? An exploration of the transformative power of play. J Humanist Psychol 47(2):198–222

Hall C (1997) The national qualifications framework green paper: what future for the framework. N Z Annu Rev Educ 7:29–57

Harris P, Daley J (2008) Exploring the contribution of play to social capital in institutional adult learning settings. Aust J Adult Learn 48(1):50–70

Hellner J (2003) NCEA: a terrible beauty is born. New Zealand Educ Rev, 6

Henricks TS (2014) Play as self-realization. Am J Play 6(2):190–213

Huizinga J (2000) Homo ludens: a study of the play-element in culture. Routledge, London

Kasprow MC, Scotton BW (1999) A review of transpersonal theory and its application to the practice of psychotherapy. J Psychother Pract Res 8(1):12

Koethen E (2012) Das Experiment des Findens als Verfahrensweise der Kunst. Gemeinsamkeiten mit – und Differenzen zur – Wissenschaft. In: Kreuzer S (ed) Experimente in der Künsten. Transmediale Erkundungen in Literatur, Theater, Film, Musik und bildender Kunst. Transcript, Bielefeld, pp 337–366

Lee H, Lee G (2001) The National Certificate of Educational Achievement (NCEA): "Fragile–handle with care". N Z Annu Rev Educ 10:5–38

Meyer J, Land R (2013) Overcoming barriers to student understanding: threshold concepts and troublesome knowledge. Routledge, London

Millar S (1968) The psychology of play. Penguin, Oxford

Piaget J (1953) The origin of intelligence in the child. Routledge & Paul, London

Prensky M (2001) Digital natives, digital immigrants part 1. Horizon 9(5):1–6

Rice L (2009) Playful learning. J Educ Built Environ 4(2):94–108

Russ SW (1998) Play, creativity, and adaptive functioning: implications for play interventions. J Clin Child Psychol 27(4):469–480

Russ SW (2003) Play and creativity: developmental issues. Scand J Educ Res 47(3):291–303

Schoenfeld AH (1998) Toward a theory of teaching-in-context. Issues Educ 4:1–94

Slater M, Wilbur S (1997) A framework for immersive virtual environments (FIVE): speculations on the role of presence in virtual environments. Presence Teleoperators Virtual Environ 6(6):603–616

Sutton-Smith B (1997) The ambiguity of play. Harvard University Press, Cambridge, MA

Tierney WG et al (2014) Postsecondary play: the role of games and social media in higher education, Tech.edu: a Hopkins series on education and technology. Johns Hopkins University Press, Baltimore

Vygotsky LS (1967) Play and its role in the mental development of the child. J Russ East Eur Psychol 5(3):6–18

Vygotsky LS (1978) Mind in society. Harvard University Press, Cambridge, MA

Wenger E (2008) Communities of practice: learning, meaning, and identity. Cambridge University Press, Cambridge

Part II
Expressive Processes

Chapter 4
Playing with Puzzling Philosophical Problems

Stefano Gualeni

4.1 Introduction

The academic context from which the following essay understands mediation (and from which it presents its claims) is commonly referred to as the 'digital humanities'. By definition, the work of a digital humanist is interdisciplinary, interpretive, experiential and generative (Gold 2012). Offering perspectives and ideas that contribute to the shaping of a 'digital humanism', the present work necessarily involves a degree of *praxis* and implicates 'the creation of new technologies, methodologies, and information systems, as well as in their *détournment*, reinvention, repurposing [...]'.[1]

In this text I will articulate a perspective on virtual worlds as mediators of philosophical thought. From the recognition of digital simulations and videogames as viable instruments to be employed in the crafting and communication of philosophical notions, ideas and frameworks, I will propose an understanding of digital mediation as the context when a new, projective[2] humanism has already begun to arise.

---

[1] The quote corresponding to this footnote is an extract from the online 'Digital Humanities Manifesto 2.0', available online at http://www.humanitiesblast.com/manifesto/Manifesto_V2.pdf, page 6.

In particular, the 'pracademic' efforts discussed in *PLAYING WITH PUZZLING PHILOSOPHICAL PROBLEMS* can be understood as a 'direct engagement in design and development processes that give rise to richer, multidirectional models, genres, iterations of scholarly communication and practice'. (Ibid.)

[2] In Martin Heidegger's 1927 *Being and Time*, the term 'projectivity' (*Entworfenheit* in the original German edition) indicates the way in which a person approaches the world in terms of his or her possibilities of being. Inspired by Heidegger's writings in the field of philosophy of technology as well as by Helmuth Plessner's philosophical anthropology, the present study understands the concept of 'projectivity' as the innate openness of human beings to construct themselves and their

S. Gualeni (✉)
Institute of Digital Games, University of Malta, Msida, Malta
e-mail: stefano.gualeni@gmail.com

© Springer-Verlag London 2015
N. Zagalo, P. Branco (eds.), *Creativity in the Digital Age*,
Springer Series on Cultural Computing, DOI 10.1007/978-1-4471-6681-8_4

As a philosopher who designs videogames and as a game designer who is passionate about philosophy, I develop videogames that overtly pursue the objectives of:

- Making certain philosophical notions playable
- Materializing thought experiments
- Experientially and interactively disclosing worlds[3] that are alternative to the ones human beings can experience in their everyday engagement with the world commonly labelled as 'actual'.

Practical examples of videogames designed with philosophical scopes and themes will be illustrated and dissected in their design and playful interactions in the fourth and fifth sections of this essay.

4.2 Problematizing Play

In this section, I will articulate a perspective on why the virtual worlds that are disclosed by digital simulations and videogames (see note 3) can be considered to be practicable ways of communicating philosophical notions.

When discussing the various effects of digital mediation on culture and its growing involvement in social as well as artistic practices, it is not uncommon to observe that contemporary academic discourses gravitate around the unique affordances of computers. In other words, when we discuss the digital medium, we tend to talk about how its specific ways of granting access to information 'classify the world for us, sequence it, frame it, enlarge it, reduce it, colour it, argue a case for what the world is like' (Postman 2005, 10). Both the potential for artistic expression and the cultural relevance of digital mediation are understood as derivations of the specific ways in which computers disclose interactive experiences. According to this perspective, the cultural meaning of interactive digital media content cannot be understood as simply emerging from *decoding* of such content – as was the case for traditional forms of mediation such as textuality – but also from acting within mediated content: from 'doing'.

---

world with the intercession of technical artefacts. Borrowing the words of Robert Musil, 'projectivity' is 'a conscious utopianism that does not shrink from reality but sees it as a project, something yet to be invented'. (Musil 1996, 11) This position derives from a fundamental standpoint which understands technology as the materialization of the innate tendency of human beings for overcoming their physical, perceptual and communicative limitations.

[3] The understanding of what a 'world' is proposed by this essay was inspired by Heidegger's existential phenomenology. I understand a 'world' as an interrelated set of beings and relationships among beings that are stably perceivable and persistently intelligible within a certain spatial-temporal context. This interpretation permits to establish a clear distinction between the experiences of virtual worlds and the less stable and accessible ones of dreams and hallucinations. In line with this definition of what a 'world' is, I propose to understand simulations as mediators that grant an interactive access to worlds.

Approaches to the design and academic understanding of virtual worlds that primarily focus on their affording some forms of 'doing' are common. From the artistic perspective on game design commonly referred to as 'proceduralism', for example, the ways in which games allow for the emergence of meaningful interactive experiences have their foundation in the logical structuring of their interactivity: the game mechanics. For the 'proceduralists' games disclose to their players what are effectively artificial worlds. Such virtual worlds are mechanically devised by game designers and are considered capable of establishing unequivocal, interactive relationships with their 'players'. In other words, for the 'proceduralists', digital simulations and videogames can engender predictable effects on the cognition and the behaviour of the players. This is the ideological foundation upon which games (and videogames and more generally any kinds of interactive simulations) can be understood as viable media for delivering information, funneling behaviour, and effectively function as persuasive technologies. From a similar perspective, Miguel Sicart observed, in his 2011 article 'Against Procedurality', that the allure of 'proceduralism' 'comes from its quasi-scientific discourse, from its efficient, postmodern argument that ties technology, systems and reason together, justifying the existence of games as a serious medium for expression' (Sicart 2011).

The outlined 'proceduralist' understanding of 'play' can be criticized (and indeed was criticized) on the basis of its depicting an incomplete and impoverishing picture of what must instead be recognized as a very fundamental and irreducible activity (Sicart 2011). According to the detractors of 'proceduralism', in fact, a valid and thorough understanding of 'play' is ought to be embraced in all its complexity, ambiguity and expressivity. The 'proceduralist' approach to 'play' restrictively focuses on comprehending and predicting quantifiable and performance-oriented dimensions of 'play'[4] while ignoring the freely creative, ritual, social and transformative ones that Bernie DeKoven identified as its 'myth domain' (DeKoven 2002). In other words, 'proceduralism' is criticized on the basis of its disregard towards ways of engaging with games and their worlds (regardless of their digital, analogue or hybrid substrate) that are informal and not strictly deterministic.

When embracing perspectives on 'play' that are broader and looser than the one outlined above, the job of the game developer cannot be recognized as that of 'designing play' but rather as one that is contributory to 'play' in setting up the stage for it to emerge (Salen and Zimmermann 2003, 168). Abandoning a formal and deterministic understanding of 'play', the figure of the game designer can no longer be associated with that of a divinity capable of creating worlds and controlling the fates of their inhabitants but is rather identifiable with an earthly scenographer who sets up constraints and affordances that will be freely appropriated by the actors (the players) during 'play'. As revelatory examples of this approach, Mary Flanagan utilizes the term 'game' as a synonym for 'play scenario' (2009), and according to Ivan

---

[4] For a more in-depth reflection on the relationship between computer games and instrumental rationality, I recommend reading Paolo Pedercini's blog post titled 'Videogames and the Spirit of Capitalism', available online at http://www.molleindustria.org/blog/videogames-and-the-spirit-of-capitalism

Mosca, game developers supply props to play with 'like engineers supply technologies for flying and therapists supply tools for understanding ourselves' (2013, 19).

In line with the previous observations, philosopher of technology Don Ihde noted that no forms of technical mediation establish a fixed and stable relationship with their users. According to Ihde the effects of any technologies can never be said to be solely determined by the (sometimes clumsily pursued) intentions of the designers, but they are 'multistable': they are always appropriated and interpreted contextually by their users (Ihde 1990). In addition to the general 'multistability' of technology, we also need to keep in mind that unexpected behaviours and effects might arise from unforeseen malfunctions of the technologies that mediate human actions and decisions[5] (Verbeek 2011, 97–99).

The 'multistable' qualities of technology appear to be radicalized in our interactions with virtual worlds, as unexpected behaviours, technical glitches and events that were not anticipated by the designers are commonly experienced occurrences in several playful as well as non-playful computer applications. I believe this to be the case in the worlds of videogames and simulations for two main reasons:

1. The first reason consists in the observation that digital simulations in general (and videogames in particular) are characterized by several forms and levels of interaction that are often intricately overlapping, which tends to afford a certain flexibility and expressiveness in their use. As I argued elsewhere, the autonomy granted to the players often leads to behaviours and interactive possibilities that can potentially subvert and trivialize both the experiential goals and the semiotic meanings originally intended by the designers (Gualeni 2014).
2. The second reason why I claim that virtual worlds are particularly 'multistable' technologies stems from the recognition that both the inner functioning of the worlds and the complex interactions outlined above are dependent on interconnected technological systems. As such, they are susceptible to a vaster spectrum of possible malfunctions and unexpected interactive behaviours than technologies that are applied to the actual world or have more binding mechanical and physical dependencies from it. The amount of erratic and exhilarating videogame glitches that are published daily on video-sharing websites are a testament to the imperfect control that we, as developers, have over the technological instruments that we employ.

An example of the awareness of the particularly penetrating 'multistability' of virtual worlds was voiced in a recent interview for the *New Statesman* by Jason Rohrer – independent author of celebrated experimental videogame titles such as *Passage* (2007) and *The Castle Doctrine* (2013) – and Merritt Kopas, designer and creator of *Lim* (2012), a free, web-based videogame about the tension of trying to meet society's expectations:

---

[5] From this perspective, Marshall McLuhan's gnomic observation according to which 'the medium is the message' (the interpretation according to which the message of any medium or technology is 'the change of scale or pace or pattern that it introduces in human affairs') appears to be particularly accurate (McLuhan 1994, 8).

'I think that systems have a tendency to get away from us', says Kopas. 'We intend to portray or produce one thing, but the systems we're creating seem to resist or reshape our intents.' Even Rohrer, with years of programming experience (this game is his seventeenth), has to take responsibility when things go wrong. 'As a designer, I'm trying to build the tightest system that I can build. I don't want there to be those system leaks which allow bizarre readings and involve the procedural rhetoric effectively falling off the rails and going who knows where.' (The complete interview is available online at http://www.news-tatesman.com/voices/2013/02/political-video-game)

Problematizing the possibility for designing 'play' (i.e. our possibility of deterministically predicting its cognitive effects and controlling the ways in which it will engage the players and change their in-game behaviour) also raises questions concerning the effective persuasive and communicative potential of interactive media. If the possibilities for autonomous agency and self-fashioning in virtual worlds threaten to distort and trivialize the affordances and messages originally set up by the game designers, how could such worlds ever be treated as media of communication? How could a defined meaning ever emerge from contents that are not only infinitely interpretable (as was already the case for text and other traditional media forms) but also infinitely manipulable?

It is my belief that neither the recognition of limitations in the possibility to control messages and experiences in videogame worlds nor the discontents with 'proceduralist' approaches to 'play' should encourage game scholars and game developers to bluntly discard their insights and methods of deterministic approaches. The uncompromising rejection of scientist ways of understanding 'play' (understood both as an activity and as its experiential outcome) is in fact no less impoverishing than the excision of its 'ritual' ones operated by 'procedurality'. What I propose here is, instead, to embrace deterministic approaches for framing 'play' as instruments that are useful and revealing in specific contexts. Perspectives like ludology, 'procedurality' and game user research (GUR) can be usefully employed to uncover some aspects of the functional behaviours of simulation and can be recognized as capable of helping designers and researchers alike to anticipate and control some of the effects that design choices will have on the players. As already observed by Sicart, the deterministic framework offered by the 'proceduralist' approach can be fruitfully applied to analyse single-player videogames that offer limited operative options to their players. Those games are, in fact, already structurally efficient in constraining players' behaviour, allowing them to execute a few specific actions in the restraining ways envisaged by the developers (Sicart 2011). Among the videogame genres that more starkly funnel players' behaviour, we can plausibly enumerate the ones defined by a few player-related mechanics such as puzzle games, simple resource management games, point-and-click adventures, 2-D platform games, hidden object games, etc.

What I am advocating in this section of my essay is that the proverbial baby can be saved from being thrown away together with the dirty bath water by means of a cautious and instrumental use of quantitative methods of approaching 'play' both as game designers and as game researchers. In other words, formal and objective approaches to the analysis of 'play' can be fruitful methods to describe player experience when employed on the background of the awareness that play is a complex and irreducible activity which is deeply rooted in what makes us humans and that its experience can never be completely anticipated and controlled by the game designers or fully captured in questionnaires, interviews or the statistical analysis of data.

4.3 (The Question Concerning) Philosophical Play

In what was discussed until this point, the most deterministically controllable dimensions of the activity of 'play' were recognized as viable contexts to develop and communicate philosophical ideas. To be sure, the possibility for critical design and philosophical 'doing' must also be recognized as latent in each of the ways in which human beings extend and objectify their physical functions, their ideas and their desires via technical artefacts. As already purported by several academics in the fields of philosophy of technology and game studies, all technologies cannot avoid to materialize ideologies as well as fundamental aspects of who we are as human beings (Haraway 1991; Coolen 1992; Flanagan 2009; Dunne and Raby 2013; Gualeni 2013; Yee 2014).

As novel and flexible opportunities for philosophical as well as critical performance, digital simulations and videogames are recognized here as particularly interesting mediators. In the virtual worlds disclosed by those media forms, the 'players' have the opportunity for actively negotiating notions and hypotheses that are materially presented to them. When acting within digital simulations, the user (or player) is actively co-authoring the virtually-materialized philosophical arguments in which the extent of the authorship depends on the game genre, on the quantity of agents involved and, clearly, on the degree of interactive autonomy granted to the 'players' by the developers of the simulation.

The two philosophical videogames that I will discuss in the fourth and fifth sections of this essay were single-player videogames that were explicitly designed to direct the player's behaviour towards simple and non-negotiable objectives and to offer the player very limited operative options. As playful systems aimed at restricting and funnelling the behaviour of the player, those videogames can be considered capable of explaining philosophical notions and articulating arguments in ways that are largely unambiguous.

It must be noted, however, that – at least in line of principle – it is always possible to develop interactive simulations and videogames with philosophical scopes and themes that are less constraining and more expressive than the ones purposefully designed to control 'play' and to materialize a specific set of notions. By definition, acting in worlds that allow for freer and more ambiguous types of agency cannot lead to the emergence of univocal and clear meaning but can still interactively disclose worlds that are alternative to the ones human beings can experience in their everyday engagement with the world commonly labelled as 'actual'. More succinctly stated, all videogames allow their players to experience alternative phenomenologies, but not all videogames can function as communication instruments.

To sum up the core argument of this section, I believe that virtual worlds that are characterized by a few operative options for the users (or player-oriented mechanics) and enforce simple, non-negotiable limitations to their experience are recognized as viable communication tools and can, therefore, be utilized for educational, philosophical and other various rhetorical purposes (propaganda, training, advertisement, etc.). Digital simulations that, instead, embrace a freer and more expressive approach to acting within virtual worlds can provide the contexts for various kinds of experimentation including human-animal interaction, the critical subversion of values, research in behavioural psychology, performativity, etc.

The rest of this essay will only focus on the former, which is to say on articulating an understanding of virtual worlds as mediators and, more specifically, as philosophical instruments. Towards that objective, I will introduce and analyse two videogames with deliberate philosophical scopes and themes that I designed and developed in the past few years.

When proposing computer simulations as viable instruments for the pursuit of philosophical – or more widely intellectual – objectives, a frequently encountered opposing line of reasoning contends that books are (and always will be) necessary and desirable on the basis that words afford the subtlety needed to symbolize and organize complicated arguments. According to the detractors of the philosophical use of simulations and videogames, virtual worlds cannot aspire to achieve the subtlety and clarity of verbal and literal forms of expression. At this point in the development of my argument, I believe it is important to clarify that this essay does not advocate for the abandonment of text in favour of videogames, nor does it advance the claim that computers are (or are ever going to be) the ultimate philosophical media. In my opinion there are, however, no logical reasons why it would be ill-advised to embrace a vaster and more compromising media horizon to develop, test and divulge ideas.

With the objective of explaining why I consider it viable to tackle and disclose philosophical notions, hypotheses and thought experiments through the activity of 'play', I will start by focusing on what I consider to be a fundamental quality that playing and philosophizing have in common. In accordance with continental philosophers such as Michel Foucault or Martin Heidegger, I understand philosophy as a transformative practice. As a transformative practice, philosophy is not defined, in its activity, by the specific ways in which its contents can be mediated (oral, textual, visual, simulational, etc.) but rather by its capability to elicit a certain shift in behaviour or in perspective in a person engaging in it (Rayner 2007). In this sense, 'play' and philosophy can be associated in terms of their transformative effects and purposes. Both 'play' and philosophy are, moreover, traditionally considered as having a fundamental importance in the education of individuals, the establishment of social values as well as the development of culture by and large.

By definition, the capability of engendering a transformative effect is not a quality that can be objectively attributed to an artefact or a piece of work, but it is always associated to the idea of being practically engaged in something, hence the term 'transformative practice'. The activities of painting, writing, designing, playing, sculpting, dancing, philosophizing, exploring, building, etc. can have a transformative effect on the recipient of the experience or the performance in question but can also be a self-fashioning, transformative moment for the philosopher, the artist or the designer engaged in the very crafting of a certain experience, artefact, work or performance (Gualeni 2014). The idea of philosophy as an *autopoietic* practice (i.e. functioning as a self-fashioning practice: an activity that has transformative effects through an on-going critical process) is quite well established in the continental tradition and was recently recuperated by Davis Baird in his 2004 book *Things Knowledge: A Philosophy of Scientific Instruments*. According to Baird, the concept of 'building' (understood as the academic *praxis* of 'doing', of 'constructing things' as a heuristic practice) offers an opportunity

> to correct the discursive and linguistic bias of the humanities. According to this view, we should be open to communicating scholarship through artifacts, whether digital or not. It implies that print is, indeed, ill equipped [sic] to deal with entire classes of knowledge that are presumably germane to humanistic inquiry. (Ramsay and Rockwell in Gold 2012, 78)

Baird's notion of 'building' as an academic practice has also evident affinities with the understanding of 'carpentry' explained by Bogost in his 2012 book *Alien Phenomenology*. Bringing together the perspectives of Graham Harman and Alphonso Lingis, Bogost defined 'carpentry' as the 'practice of constructing artifacts as a philosophical practice' (Bogost 2012, 93). In two aspects, I believe, Baird's academic understanding of 'building' and Bogost's notion of 'carpentry' are analogous to the approach to the mediation of thought that I am proposing in this essay:

1. In their openness towards non-textual options for the structuring and dissemination of philosophical notions and experiments
2. In their vision according to which the very crafting and framing of ideas and world views in any media form is in itself a deeply transformative activity

Far from being a neutral way of exchanging information, writing has cognitive effects that are evident and inevitable and has been the focus of philosophical debate since its first introduction in ancient Greek culture. Analogous to the way videogames might not be suitable for presenting abstract concepts in their full intricacy and subtlety, traditional books can neither give the reader agency nor the possibility to negotiate with the objectified thoughts that they mediate. Apart from the choice of whether to continue reading or not, linear books must in fact be recognized as only allowing – like any other traditional form of mediation – for hermeneutical forms of freedom. In addition to that, I believe it is relevant to observe that books cannot embed dynamic and objective representations of spatial contexts, while digital simulations can materialize spaces accurately and interactively and can also offer the opportunity to explore alternative approaches, courses of action and outcomes.

The embedding of videogames and computer simulations in social practices (philosophy being one of them) might, thus, best be pursued on the basis of the understanding that, as any other form of mediation, they disclose reality in specific ways and that such ways are always inherently both revealing and concealing. New ways of establishing relationships with reality through media necessarily entail a balance between the increase in acuity of certain cognitive functions and the desensitization of others (McLuhan 1994).

4.4 Gua-Le-Ni; or, the Horrendous Parade

The fourth and the fifth sections of this text will focus on the *praxis* of designing virtual worlds and virtual experiences with philosophical scopes and themes. In the pages that follow, I will illustrate and dissect the design of two philosophical videogames:

- *Gua-Le-Ni; or the Horrendous Parade* (*Gua-Le-Ni* from now on) – a commercially released, action-puzzle videogame that I designed and developed in collaboration with the Italian developers *Double Jungle S.a.s.* for the *Apple iPad* and *iPhone* platforms between 2011 and 2012
- *Necessary Evil* – a free, self-reflexive videogame that was developed as a contribution to the panel 'G|A|M|E on Games: the Meta-panel' at the 2013 DiGRA conference in Atlanta, Georgia (USA)

In terms of narrative, the world of *Gua-Le-Ni* takes place somewhere in Great Britain during a fictional reinterpretation of the 'age of discovery'. In *Gua-Le-Ni*, the player is given the role of an aspiring scholar who is instructed by an old, befuddled British zoologist on the finer points of combinatorial taxonomy. On top of a dark, wooden desk lays a fantastic book: a bestiary populated by bizarre, finely drawn paper creatures that allegedly inhabit the 'New World' (see Fig. 4.1). Similar to the combinatorial monsters of head-body-tail books that we might have playfully explored in our childhood and to the creatures described in legends and mythical recounts, the paper beasts of *Gua-Le-Ni* are chimaeras: impossible assemblages of real animal parts. For example, the specimen shown in the next page is a CA-BIT-DOR-STER: a four-module creature with the head of a camel, one body part of a rabbit followed by the midsection a condor and concluded by a lobster's tail.

The combinatorial paper creatures of *Gua-Le-Ni* hectically walk across the illustrations of the bestiary from the right to the left margin of its pages. From the point of view of the player, the main goal of the game is that of recognizing the components of the fantastic creatures and their relative order before the creature manages to completely traverse an illustration and flee from the book (which constitutes the 'game over' condition). Encouraged by the unwieldy mentor, the player pursues this purpose by quickly rotating, moving and spinning toy cubes with pictures of animal parts printed on each face of the cubes. A paper beast is correctly recognized – and thus prevented from escaping the old book it belongs to – when the player manages to match the illustrations on the top faces of the taxonomic cubes with the paper beast currently in play.

Gua-Le-Ni is a single-player videogame consisting of only one fundamental player-oriented game mechanic (a matching mechanic that is accessed by the players

Fig. 4.1 Feeding the beasts in *Gua-Le-Ni* does not only temporarily stop their relentless stamped-ing but can also modify the beasts' composition, quell their acceleration or increase their value in terms of points awarded upon their correct cataloguing

via the manipulation of the toy-cube interface) and a simple, univocal goal: correctly categorizing the animals under a growing time pressure. As such, *Gua-Le-Ni* can be considered to be simple enough in its structure and constraining enough in its inter-active affordances to be suitable for the unambiguous expression of philosophical notions and perspectives.

In the specific terms of its philosophical contents, *Gua-Le-Ni* was inspired by David Hume's philosophical understanding of what a 'complex idea' is as presented in his 1738 book *A Treatise of Human Nature* (book I, part IV, section VI: *On Personal Identity*). In extreme synthesis, according to Hume, most people can be said to possess the mental concept of a Pegasus (Hume 1738). For the Scottish phi-losopher, this is patently due to the fact that it is common for human beings to be exposed to Greek mythology in some form. This is also ostensibly the case in the present century, where the Pegasus can still be encountered in books as well as in modern remediations of its folklore. In general, it is presented as a divine horse that could fly using its legendary eagle wings. In Hume's work, the Pegasus is intro-duced an example of an idea that is not caused by direct, worldly experience but is nevertheless one with which we all have familiarity with. Nobody can, I believe, truthfully claim to have encountered a Pegasus in his or her everyday life, to have ridden, smelled or touched it, and yet the Pegasus is an idea that humans can

Fig. 4.2 A more recent update of the game features a new game mode and additional monstrous parts including those of a human being

fantasize of, discuss, write legends about, etc. As such, according to Hume, the idea of a Pegasus does not fall under the category of simple ideas, which is to say ideas that can be simply caused by immediate sensory 'impressions' of the objects. It must, therefore, be recognized as a complex idea: a mental combination of elements and properties of which the human mind has had previous experience of and eventually creatively reassembles into a new idea (Fig. 4.2).

By means of fantastic beasts of the same combinatorial nature as Hume's *Pegasus*, *Gua-Le-Ni* asks the players to reverse the creative capabilities described in *A Treatise of Human Nature* and use them as logical tools: impossible paper beasts will parade across the screen (the page of the taxonomist's fantastic bestiary) only to be recognized as combinations of parts of existing animals. In other words, *Gua-Le-Ni* is a playful and interactive materialization of the Humean notion of 'complex ideas'. This philosophical objective was openly discussed in several reviews, conferences and interviews about *Gua-Le-Ni*. The Italian independent game developers' community website www.indievault.it, for instance, quoted a passage of a discussion with them about this point. In that occasion I explained that

[i]f one learns how to play the game, one implicitly understood Hume's text, regardless of whether one aspired to do so or not. The player does not need to use her imagination or her interpretative capabilities in accessing those concepts of Hume's precisely because the

game offers that portion of his thought in the form of an objectively present, interactive allegory. (The complete interview is available online at http://www.indievault.it/2011/11/23/gua-le-ni-una-perla-made-in-italy-per-ipad/ – translated from Italian)

As author of *Gua-Le-Ni*, I was responsible for the game design, the game balancing and the direction of the aesthetic and creative content of the game. In this last role, my tasks included the design of the game's narrative, the supervision of the production of music and sound effects and the way in which visual design related to gameplay. The creative goals and the research objectives that I had in mind for this video-ludic project were constitutive for *Gua-Le-Ni* since its inception. The game's design aspirations were pursued by embracing virtual worlds not only as inherent factors of cultural change but also (as elaborated upon earlier in this text) as media that can disclose experiences and information in ways which are alternative to, and in some contexts more desirable than, the abstraction and inflexibility of text. When designing the game, I thought it would have been amusing to question the dominant and largely unquestioned textual framing of the philosophical discourse by presenting my criticism in the form of a (digital) book.

4.5   Necessary Evil

The second philosophical videogame that I will analyse here is titled *Necessary Evil* and – as mentioned before – is a free, self-reflexive videogame that I originally designed as a contribution to 'G|A|M|E on Games: the Meta-panel' at the 2013 DiGRA conference.

The philosophical observation that inspired *Necessary Evil* is the following: the interactive worlds of videogames objectify what is effectively an idealistic perspective on reality. According to a radical version of idealism, in fact, the qualities that we can experientially encounter in objects (regardless of their actual or digitally mediated nature) are not objective properties: it is our experience of these objects – for example, in George Berkeley's subjective idealism – that is responsible for bringing them and their properties into existence as mental contents.

Videogames and their worlds are customarily conceptualized and developed with the design goal of disclosing certain player experiences and to elicit certain emotions through combinations of aesthetic stimuli, interaction, and narration. Similarly, from the specific perspective of software architecture, videogame worlds are technically structured around the player's possibility to perceive them or interact with them. I believe it is revelatory, as an example, to think about the fact that objects in the game world are too far from the player, whose sight is occluded by other objects, or are momentarily irrelevant, for gameplay effectively does not exist as far as the game states are concerned. This approach to the representation of virtual worlds has the functional scope of limiting the amount of calculations that are needed to suitably materialize the game world by a computer. Technically speaking it is a desirable, if not necessary, evil.

Necessary Evil tries to problematize and demystify the unquestioned idealistic structuring of videogames in a playful and interactive fashion. By doing so, it also inevitably ridicules the player-centrism of videogame worlds.[6] In game-design wise, this purpose is principally pursued by having the player control a contributory character: a generic and disposable evil minion. Following established conventions of the games industry, the evil minion is a marginal character who plays a secondary role in the process of another character: the main one. The main character will be a hero (see Fig. 4.4). In *Necessary Evil* and in strident contrast with video-ludic tradition, the hero will be a nonplayer character (NPC).

As mentioned, the player controls a horned minion of evil confined in a dark cellar of sorts (see Fig. 4.3). The minion is deprived of any consequential interactive possibilities with the room. This design decision was meant to make the players experience feeling marginal and to practically reveal to them what a virtual world feels like, once it is designed around someone else's desires and perceptive possibilities. In the one room that the player can experience in *Necessary Evil*, in fact, nothing can be meaningfully interacted with: doors do not open for the player, chests contain nothing and objects in the room are mere theatrical props.

The game world is presented as it only exists to be explored and experienced by the NPC hero. The presence of the playing character (the horned minion) only serves as a challenge to the hero, an obstacle to be overcome to continue on his heroic journey. Once the NPC hero finally kills the little horned monster, he opens the door and leaves the room. At that point, the room and the player creature are swiftly removed from the computer's memory, leaving nothing behind. The de-allocation of the game elements and their disappearance corresponds with the end of the experience for the player.

In relation to what was discussed in the previous sections of this essay, the starkly limited possibilities afforded by the game's interaction as well as its narrative (forcing the players only into one out of two possible ending scenarios) make *Necessary Evil* a suitable experience for the conveyance of explicit philosophical messages or standpoints (Fig. 4.4).

---

[6] I believe it is interesting to observe that, like most games and videogames that take a critical stance, *Necessary Evil* relies on controls, conventions and aesthetics that are already established in the tradition of a particular game genre, in this case the action role-playing videogame one. The deliberate design decision of not pursuing innovation and of relying on convention has the double advantage of:

1. Not having to teach the players how to understand the world and operate in it, allowing them to access the critical message of the game in a more immediate and efficient way
2. Making the subversive, critical aspects of the game more evident by contrast, that is to say, by making them stand out in their being unexpected and unfamiliar over the background of what can largely be considered as already known by the players

For a more thorough discussion focused on the ironic and self-critical dimensions of *Necessary Evil*, I recommend reading my gamasutra.com-featured blog post titled 'Self-reflexive Video Games as Playable Critical Thought', available online at: http://www.gamasutra.com/blogs/StefanoGualeni/20131029/202847/SELFREFLEXIVE_VIDEO_GAMES_AS_PLAYABLE_CRITICAL_THOUGHT.php.

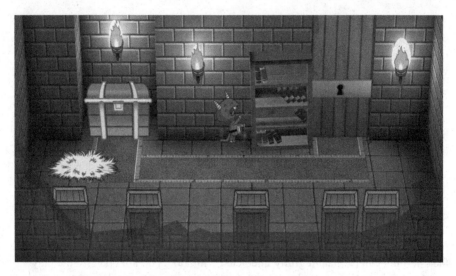

Fig. 4.3 In *Necessary Evil*, the player's interaction with the environment is entirely pointless. The little horned minion of evil controlled by the player cannot meaningfully interact with the room or escape from it

Fig. 4.4 In *Necessary Evil* the hero is an eloquent and relentless nonplayer character whose objective is that of vanquishing evil. He will attack the monstrous player character on sight

4.6   Concluding Remarks

When heavily limiting interactive freedom and expressivity, virtual worlds can materialize notions, simple philosophical concepts, thought experiments, a various array of hypotheses and world views. In disclosing such possibilities, digital mediation is crucially contributing to the rise of a new humanism. Both through my games and in my more conventionally textual academic work, the specific contribution of computer simulations and videogames to the development of contemporary culture can be recognized as twofold:

1. The interactive experiences of virtual worlds are recognized as having the inherent effects of fragmenting, distorting and extending human rationality.
2. Acting in virtual worlds as well as designing such worlds are philosophical practices that can be complementary to – and in certain instances alternative to – traditional forms of mediation of thought.

Facilitated by the increase of computer literacy, the growing accessibility of development tools as well as the progressive diffusion of digital media in social practices, more philosophical questions are bound to specifically arise within virtual worlds. It is also likely that the new generations of philosophers will more and more frequently develop, test and distribute their ideas (new questions and classical philosophical interrogatives alike) in the form of interactive digital media content. In my work, I propose to call this new field of applied philosophy 'augmented ontology'[7] (Gualeni 2013).

To be sure, I am not claiming that digital simulations and videogames are going to be or should be the dominant form of mediation of the twenty-first century. What I am advocating for is, instead, a less intransigent approach to the articulation, the manipulation and the diffusion of ideas, notions and hypotheses. In other words, I am proposing an approach to the development of culture that can, where contextually desirable, hybridize or even substitute traditional media forms with

---

[7] The purpose of 'augmented ontologies' as a philosophical domain is that of understanding the effects of the experiences of virtual worlds on human thought and the potentialities for digitally mediated simulations to serve human beings in 'overcoming' the traditional (predigital) boundaries of human kinds of ontologies. According to the perspectives offered by 'augmented ontologies' and inspired by Heidegger's existential phenomenology, the term 'overcoming' is not understood in the dialectical meaning of the German term *Überwindung* (surpassing) but must be embraced in the nuanced conjunction of two other terms: *Andenken* (rememoration) and *Verwindung* (distortion, twisting, incorporation), 'a going-beyond that is both an acceptance (or 'resignation') and a 'deepening'' (Vattimo 1991, xxvi).

To be sure, what I am claiming here is that even when armed with digital hammers, our projectual efforts cannot ever aspire to break down the operational, intellectual and perceptive walls of our inescapable humanity. Technologies, however, traditionally assisted humanity in making such walls more and more flexible to a point that we could progressively bend them, deform them and increase our room for manoeuvre in thinking about reality and reflecting on ourselves. It is in this sense that virtual worlds are understood in my work as mediators that afford the augmentation of human kinds of ontologies.

simulational ones. The present essay not only upholds this vision but puts it into practice programmatically offering its insights as the complementary combination of text and interactive virtual worlds. *Wanna play?*

References

Bogost I (2012) Alien phenomenology, or, what it's like to be a thing. University of Minnesota Press, Minneapolis

Coolen M (1992) De machine voorbij. Over het zelfbegrip van de mens in het tijdperk van de informatietechniek. Boom, Amsterdam

DeKoven B (2002) The well-played game: a playful path to wholeness. Writers Club Press, Lincoln

Dunne A, Raby F (2013) Speculative everything: design, fiction and social dreaming. The MIT Press, Cambridge, MA

Flanagan M (2009) Critical play: radical game design. The MIT Press, Cambridge, MA

Gold MK (ed) (2012) Debates in the digital humanities. The University of Minnesota Press, Minneapolis

Gualeni S (2013) 'Augmented ontologies; or, how to philosophize with a digital hammer', journal article on Springer's Philos Technol, Edited by Floridi L, 26(2):177–199. ISSN 2210–5433, doi:10.1007/s13347-013-0123-x

Gualeni S (2014) Freer than we think: game design as *Autopoiesis*. Paper published in the proceedings of the 2014 'philosophy of computer games conference', Istanbul, 13–16 November 2014

Haraway D (1991) A cyborg manifesto: science, technology, and socialist-feminism in the late twentieth century. In: Haraway D (ed) Simians, cyborgs and women: the reinvention of nature. Routledge, New York, pp 149–181

Heidegger M (1927) Being and time (trans: Macquarrie J, Robinson E). Harper & Row Publishers Inc., San Francisco (1962)

Hume D (1738) A treatise of human nature. Available online at http://www.gutenberg.org/files/4705/4705-h/4705-h.htm. Accessed on 28 May 2014

Ihde D (1990) Technology and the lifeworld: from garden to earth. Indiana University Press, Bloomington

McLuhan M (1994) Understanding media: the extensions of man. The MIT Press, Cambridge, MA. (The original work was published in 1964)

Mosca I (2013) From fiction to reality and back: ontology of ludic simulations. Int J Gaming Comp Mediat Simul 5(1):13–31

Musil R (1996) The man without qualities, vol I. Vintage International, New York. (The original work was published in 1930)

Postman N (2005) Amusing ourselves to death: public discourse in the age of show business. Penguin Books Ltd., London. (The original work was published in 1986)

Rayner T (2007) Foucault's Heidegger: philosophy and transformative experience. Bloomsbury Academic, London

Salen K, Zimmermann E (2003) Rules of play: game design fundamentals. The MIT Press, Cambridge, MA

Sicart M (2011) Against procedurality. Game Stud Int J Game Stud 11(3). ISSN 1604–7982. Available online at: http://gamestudies.org/1103/articles/sicart_ap

Vattimo G (1991) The end of modernity. The John Hopkins University Press, Baltimore. (The original work was published in 1985)

Verbeek P (2011) Moralizing technology – understanding and designing the morality of things. The University of Chicago Press, Chicago

Yee N (2014) The proteus paradox – how online games and virtual worlds change us – and how they don't. Yale University Press, New Haven

Chapter 5
The Creative Manipulation of Time Through Digital Personal Narratives

María T. Soto-Sanfiel

5.1 Introduction

Digitalization increases people's possibilities for creating and publishing a variety of narratives about their own lives. Think of people uploading their childhood photos in Facebook or writing their opinions or stories on a blog as an example. These digital narratives reflect the narrators' notions about their identities and circumstances in different timeframes (present, past and future). They can also come to influence others and make them alter their own perceptions. We believe that these narrators also more or less deliberately wish to use their narration to modify the times of the actual experience (those of what is narrated and those of what is lived). We consider that people who narrate about their own lives more or less consciously see themselves as creative products, for whom it is a challenge to innovate regarding notions established in times gone by, in the present and in the processing of narratives in the future. All of this, as the reader might imagine, involves innumerable creative and persuasive possibilities. In fact, digitalization, which allows for the creative manipulation, storage and dissemination of individual narratives, is a powerful tool for the creation of discourses about the future, the present and, most of all, the past.

Before continuing, we shall further exemplify the above through three typical situations in which indications can already be found of how modern-day narrators, more than ever, try to alter the perception that they, and others, have of their identity through the manipulation of their represented past and in order to achieve an imagined projection of their future. Modern-day narrators, much more than in other times, have access to tools that give them enormous capacities to modify the time-frame of the narration and the experience of receiving their narratives. These

M.T. Soto-Sanfiel (✉)
Department of Audiovisual Communication and Advertising,
Universitat Autònoma de Barcelona, Barcelona, Spain
e-mail: MariaTeresa.Soto@uab.cat

© Springer-Verlag London 2015   75
N. Zagalo, P. Branco (eds.), *Creativity in the Digital Age*,
Springer Series on Cultural Computing, DOI 10.1007/978-1-4471-6681-8_5

circumstances lead us to speculate about the socially and culturally magnified impact of the times of their audiences. Let us see why.

An active Facebook user seeks to project a certain image of themselves in order to cause a specific impression of their life, identity or personality, through the careful selection (and manipulation) of the photographs that they post in their profile, the comments they add or the products that they say they like. This social network also provides other web applications that can help to magnify or expand this virtual identity, one which is created *ad hoc* and may have anything from a very close relation with the person's true reality to no relation whatsoever. This manipulation of identity is done in the present and involves altering the past (choosing which events to show and even changing or ignoring others). Nevertheless, when manipulating the reactions of their audiences through altered representations of themselves, they want to shape their own future. When individuals do this, they reveal their particular and social values, as well as helping to strengthen said values among certain groups. The information provided on the web may also, and likewise, be available in a more distant future. People of that time, the distant future, might perhaps evaluate our own time on the basis of this preconfigured information extracted from our present, which will be their past.

Let us consider another example of the idea expressed in the first paragraph. Day after day, we are witnessing an increase in the ability to record, store, edit and reveal the testimonies of the people of the present for the people of the future. Although in bygone days it was possible to conserve the autobiographies of human beings, digitalization has expanded and generalised that capacity: many more people of the world can transmit their opinions, their histories, their stories and their impressions on the web, because the instruments are increasingly more user-friendly, and the cloud is so much larger and more widespread. In doing so, they can also surround these testimonies with audiovisual resources to expressively emphasise sensations or emotions (such as the use of certain music, the inclusion of sound effects or the adding of animations or infographics). The emotional intensity of everyday experiences is thus made more powerful – it is 'spectacularised'. If they prefer, narrators can start creating their own versions of the past (enriching it, mixing it with images, selecting the details that matter or explaining one version of the reality, while ignoring another). In consequence, modern-day narrators can leave, as their legacy for the future, their own creative version of the present and also their creative version of the past. Given that there are fewer sources about the past, it is not outlandish to believe that there is an increasing possibility for present versions of the past to gain in relevance and have an impact on future explanations. Before moving on to a third and final example, readers should be reminded that the modification of history, of the past, is a recurring aspiration of certain governmental regimes and states, which means that reflections like these are more necessary than ever.

As a final example, let us imagine that somebody creates a narrative about a past circumstance (either their own or not) that includes distant people or places. Thanks to the use of immersive display techniques, such as 3D, augmented reality or metaverses, creators pursue high narrative engagement experiences for their audiences and achieve them. Due to the verisimilitude that narrators are able to imprint on their work, receptors identify with and feel empathy towards the people appearing in it and are transported into the represented world to the extent that they feel they are in it and are willing to consider it real, while they are consuming it. The emotional and cognitive impression that such living the narrative adds to the receptors' experience is so intense that it is automatically incorporated in their knowledge of the narrated facts, places or characters, whether real or fictional. This occurs to the extent that the receptor subconsciously believes that they have lived what happened way beyond the moment of reception and at every moment of their future, not only when they evoke the experience but also when they find themselves experiencing similar situations. The highly immersive experience of narrative, albeit fictitious, not only has effects on the receptor's cognition or emotions but also, at times, on their behaviour.

Having reached this point, and before continuing, we should make it clear that the need for transcendence, or to manipulate one's own image through the creation of narratives, is not exclusive to the human beings of our era. It is not that other people in the past were not aware of this capacity to leave their mark. But unlike what happened in other eras, the modern-day media sphere, to a large extent a product of digitalization, is public, personal, self-centred, rapidly accessible and expansible, as well as being rich in details. The more or less generalised access to these new forms of 'writings' or textures gives voice, in turn, to a greater number of individuals and their individualities. In the past, very few people understood the languages and mechanisms of expression; there are many more of us today. So, the volume of information associated to events increases, as do the points of view of how they are told.

Also, before continuing, we need to explain that personal narratives are a phenomenon that was already generating much interest among philosophers late in the last century. In fact, they led to the production of major theoretical diversity. Although they were still living in an entirely analogue world, the thinkers of the late twentieth century left us interesting, and still valid, reflections. The prominence of the concept, to begin with, led them to agree that knowledge, comprehension and notions of ourselves, beyond consciousness as an organic or somatic product, were produced through our own narratives (Fireman et al. 2003). They agreed that we are impelled to give sense to our lives in narrative format (McAdams 1993, p. 134). The mechanism they identified for this is very obvious: the organisation of and search for continuity or coherence between the experiences that lead us to associate our memories from the past to situations that we live in the present and to those that we expect in the future. We determine the meaning and sense of the experience on the basis of the product of the relation that we establish between the experience that inspires us to create a personal history and the personal history that structures our experience (Fireman et al. 2003, p. 4). Thinkers on the phenomenon, meanwhile, also came to the agreement that because narration is the medium through which we learn about the social world, our community and ourselves (Bruner 1986, 1990), it is present in practically all human activities and products (Gardner 1991). So, our narratives, according to these thinkers, not only describe, communicate and examine our own self but also construct it (Fireman et al. 2003, p. 5). In this text, we shall be sharing these thoughts.

On another point, we were also saying earlier that digitalization implies that the subject that narrates about themselves turns that self into a creative product. Before looking in greater depth at the knowledge that supports this consideration, we should make it clear that by 'creative product' we mean, as Cropley et al. (2008) said, the result of a process that is not only new (in relation to what preceded it) but also relevant and effective. A creative product surprises and gets noticed, but most of all it seeks to satisfy a need. In fact, if there was no need, the act of creation would merely be aesthetic. It is an original approach to the subject (Solomon et al. 1999), to oneself, that leads to a specific manifestation (Andreasen 1987). Creativity, one of the greatest forms for the expression of individuality (Bandura 1997, p. 239), makes our creation diverse, subtle even. As well as being creative in the manifestation of our persona, of the processes in which we are immersed and in the products into which we are converted, the result of our creativity, our individual expression, will have a social dimension: our public face (Runco 2007).

The aim of this chapter is to sustain these ideas through the presentation and discussion of the evidence provided by previous interdisciplinary research and the authors that support it. As the reader will find in the text, there is a large body of knowledge that has come from different academic disciplines. As a whole, this literature suggests that the increase in narrations in computer networks, in times of the 'spectacularisation' of reality, is something that should not be ignored but should instead be carefully observed due to its possible individual and cultural effects. In this chapter, the data that has led to the construction of such a view will be gradually and inductively presented.

5.2 Narrating One's Life

What do we understand narrative to mean in terms of this reflection? We should deal with this definition immediately. To do this, we shall fundamentally recur to narratology and, within it, to structuralism. As we shall see, the definition of the concept implies dealing with the inseparable relation between the creation of narratives, the identity of the narrators and the conceptions that these have of times lived and narrated. As already made clear, we believe that the act of creating and publishing one's own narrative is not banal, but rather is full of meaning. In fact, as shall be driven home throughout this epigraph, narrations are a reflection of a form of individual and collective consciousness of existence.

When defining narrative, it is useful to remember that the etymological origin of the world is associated to the idea of knowing, of conveying information and its function as an instrument for learning or showing the world to others (Tomascikova 2009). The word 'narrative' comes from the Latin narrat (related, told) and from its verbal form narrare, which is derived from gnarus (knowing). It is generally accepted that a narrative is any account of connected events presented to the audience in a sequence.

When we, like Rankin (2002), speak of narratives, we are referring to a story that can be factual, fictitious or somewhere between the two. In this reflection, narrative is therefore not only fiction, as one may think *a priori*. We also consider that, although their oral or written expressions may be the most frequent types, narratives can also be transmitted by other systems of symbolic languages, maybe for communicative or artistic purposes. However, regardless of the forms they adopt, like Rankin, we feel that narratives are a *cultural artefact* whose ultimate, those perhaps not deliberate, purpose is to tell a story. When somebody tells, speaks, talks, explains or describes themselves or others, they create a narrative. This is regardless of its realism or form. So, in order for there to be a narrative, it is not indispensable for there to be fiction, but rather the desire to express, communicate or transmit information. And this, in turn, is the expression and vehicle of culture.

The above leads to the requirement, in any narrative, for it to be possible to structurally distinguish between the story (the *content* or the chain of events and the beings or the characters and settings) and the discourse (the way in which the content is expressed) (Chatman 1978). Propp, when studying the morphologies of stories, speaks of the 'story' (fable), which is what happens in life in chronological order, and the 'plot', which is how the creator presents the story to his or her audience; how it is read, seen or heard (Propp 1968). This means that narrators can explain a series of facts by modelling them into the typical structures of different genres or packaging formats. We can explain the same thing using a format taken from the journalistic genre (e.g. a news story) or from entertainment (e.g. a piece of fiction). We could, to end the clarification, say how we want others to perceive us and create an identity for ourselves, on the basis of a written text, of photos posted in a social network or of an audiovisual production. In fact, any manifestation that someone uses to express themselves contains a story (certain facts or thoughts that are referred to) and a discourse (a way of telling, which can be verbal, nonverbal, textual, audiovisual, etc.). In short, practically everything a person does says something, regardless of the explicit relevance that the narrator seems to give to his or her work or of the relevance that the receptor admits that it contains.

The aforesaid also leads us to clarify that when we speak of narratives, we should distinguish not only how these are constructed or produced but also the role that they play in certain contexts (their function; Threadgold 2005). In reality, narratives are, apart from a product, the fundamental mode of human consciousness and self-consciousness (Rankin 2002). Narratives forcibly require the development of a product constructed in a version of time, and out of which emerges other more or less intentional processes of dialogue and consciousness with our past, present and future worlds. We represent today what might have happened in the past, and, when we do so, the current representation reveals notions of the passage of time. From these concepts of time expressed through narrative, a version of personal identity eventually emerges. Identity, therefore, is similar to the narrative of the times we live in. In fact, identity is an expression of the narrative of time itself.

We also consider that the forms acquired by dialogues among fragments, the relation between the events in a narrative, are an expression of consciousness, of creativity and, particularly, of temporal creativity. We shall now be discussing these last ideas, one's narrative as an application representation of consciousness of the world (and of its times) and, in consequence, of identity. But first, we should remember that the purpose of all this discourse is to show that people's narratives possess a powerful symbolic load, which even transcends their own consciousness and that of its effects.

5.3   Narrative and Consciousness

The idea that narrative is a form of consciousness and comprehension of the world, developed on the basis of each individual's concept of time, is not new. Beyond the perspectives of strictly literary theories, thinkers associated to different disciplines, in particular philosophers, as stated in the introduction, have dealt with the subject. We shall now offer some related academic contributions. We will start at the beginning.

Some suggest that life is nothing more than a biological phenomenon until it is interpreted (Ricoeur 1991). Narratives are born because in order to understand the world, humans have to configure it symbolically. To do so, we articulate our perceptions into signs, rules and standards (Bell 1990). This means that, as we order the world from its very reception, human experience is already semantically and linguistically preconfigured at birth. In any case, narrative is produced when, in order to write life, construct it, invent it or describe it, we have no option but to design a plot: to consider the structural relations among the elements.

So, the concept of the plot, as Carr (1991) points out, forcibly implies developing a temporal consciousness of the objects that form part of this narrative. And this is only possible because of our memory and our experience of time. In reality, consciousness of a happening, of an action or of an experience is its process. Its consciousness is, in short, its course, change or permanence. We experience objects retained in subjective conceptions of the past and their projection into the future. So this would constitute, in itself, a conception in the present. Narrative form, or a story, is therefore a representation of our real perception (Rankin 2002), and consciousness, in turn, is narrative in essence, i.e. the signs, rules and standards that form part of a narrative being told are always those of consciousness: those of retention and anticipation, of before and after and of the preceding and posterior states. And this is so even though said facts are reproduced and refigured in different forms of narrative communication. Narrative, in short, is consciousness and, particularly, consciousness of time.[1]

The idea of narrative communication challenges any attempt to believe that narrative, our narrative, as a product derived from our consciousness, is an egoistic, individual and personal product. Actually, to a large extent, it is quite the opposite. To begin with, the projection of our identity, our narrative as a product, is a form of

---

[1]The psychological relation between time and consciousness is discussed by Bergson in his seminal contribution (Bergson 1960).

communication based on the handling of shared languages. So, from its very conception, expressed individual identity, together with its consciousness, is the result of the influence of other people and of our connection with them. These individuals that influence us, and connections with them, in turn, do not necessarily have to form part of the present of the narrative. In fact, they can be from the past or the future. Therefore, reflections regarding our identity can only be produced through our comparisons with other people at specific times. The reflections are only produced when we see ourselves in others that are, were or will be (Rankin 2002). All of this leads us to explore the forms in which we reflect our conception of time in narratives. We shall now deal with this topic.

5.4 Narrative Time

As we have said, the ordering of the fragments of narratives implies making decisions about the temporal organisation of the story one wishes to tell. It implies considering that the arrangement of the fragments will affect their perception and effects. For example, from the plot point of view, going into the past of a story that is represented in the present implies placing ourselves in the past from our memory of the past. Considering the discourse, the pace at which changes in the fragments occur, their succession, we can provoke different emotional relations depending on whether it is fast or slow. In whatever case, due to the mental projection of time, whether a subjective view of the past, through memory, or the subjective ideation of the future, through imagination, these are processes guided by the ego (Tulving 2002) and not so different, as we shall shortly be seeing. To imagine the future, we travel with our notion of time, with our subjective time, determined by memory. Projecting ourselves into the future, therefore, implies going back over our autobiography. This approach has led to a large number of empirical studies, particularly associated to cognitive sciences, which we will be looking at in more detail later.

5.5 The Accepted Notions of Time

The immediately preceding reflections are based on one of the most popular and interdisciplinary conceptions of time: time's arrow (Coveney and Hughfield 1990; Davies 1995; Gould 1987). Based on Heraclitus' ever-flowing river, and in whose water is impossible to bathe twice, time is considered to be something irreversible that goes from the past to present. In this conception, change is more important than stability, events are more important than laws, contexts are more important than universals and possibilities are more salient than predictions (Mainemelis 2002; Maturana 1995; Maturana and Varela 1992; Prigogine 1990). Considering time from this lineal perspective leads us to believe that the personal experience of life is an irreversible process, which goes from birth to death, and whose most important moments are certain happenings (Mainemelis 2002).

In opposition to the linearity of time, we frequently find the notion of cyclic time. This conception is inspired by the observation of periodical repetitive movements, such as the seasons or phases (Mainemelis 2002) and is based on ideas of renewal, replication, recurrence, repetition and prediction. Although this position is epistemologically the complete opposite to that of time's arrow, they both coexist in real life as complementary modes of temporal experience. Actually, both notions can overlap in everyday life, are socially constructed and determine the way in which we as individuals perceive ourselves. In fact, as Freud, James and Bergson have (essentially) suggested, self-consciousness and time consciousness are two interdependent and inseparable processes that are delineated in the psyche.

However, there is another conception of time, a merely psychological one that our previous research has referred to and that is relevant to our discussion. The two previous notions of time are more ideological or philosophical, close to experience in the interpretative macroscopic sense; they are perhaps more cognitive or intellectual. The following, however, is individual, intimate and profoundly existential. We are referring to 'timelessness', a psychological experience.

Before examining this consideration of time as a psychological experience, we should remember that the notions of cyclic and lineal time have been widely explored by written or audiovisual narratives, whether as the object of the story (Chatman 1978; Propp 1968), or as variations in the discourse, in the ways that the former are articulated. Since they have been technologically possible, audiovisual montage and post-production techniques have, moreover, fostered the alteration of the times of representation of the sequence of events in any narration in the present. We can go back to what belongs in the story's past (flashback) or go into its future (flashforward) to project/imagine what will happen after. We can do this, and we do this, with our own narratives, regardless of the language of expression. In fact, not only have numerous audiovisual works widely reflected on the indefectible passage of time, but these reflections are part of our everyday lives, especially during adulthood. Meanwhile, the audiovisual industry has also created narratives whose fragments are organised as periods or whose plots are based on the idea of the eternal beginning. We, likewise, can explain our experiences on the basis of seasons or on the idea of starting over again. Both the idea of lineal time and the cyclic idea, therefore, are not only part of our cultural heritage, but are indefectibly reflected in our explaining, telling or narrating.

In the creation and reception of narratives, the three aforementioned views of time may coexist. A narrator of one's own life can experience the living of timelessness at the very moment of creation or can reflect on aspects associated to the notions of lineal or cyclic time. A receptor of that narrative, in turn, can experience the notion of timelessness when they receive a message that reflects, or invites them to think, about the conventional conceptions of time. However, in the following paragraphs, we will explain that the identification of the experience of timelessness involves distinguishing, when we speak of time in narratives, between what we live and what we know. Narrating is what we live, or make live, in the time we know.

5.6 Timelessness

We often get the feeling that time is going by slowly or passing very quickly. This is because our conception of time depends on our emotional state and our attention (Mitchon 1990; Ornstein 1970). When we are bored, time passes slowly; when we are anxious, it goes fast (Csikszentmihalyi 1990). However, when we are able to disregard the demands and expectations of the ego, the experience of time ceases, at least for short whiles. It is then that the notion of timelessness appears (Hartocollis 1983), the experience of transcending oneself and the socio-temporal reality, because one is captivated by the activity being done in the present. If cyclic and lineal time is a succession of instants, timelessness occurs when attention is removed from oneself and invested in the profundity of the experience of here and now (Mainemelis 2002).

The state of timelessness can be induced in different ways, e.g. by highly motivated activities, intense concentration when doing certain tasks, or through mystic experiences, drugs and epipahines (Arlow 1996; Csikszentmihalyi 1990; Hartocollis 1983; Mainemelis 2002; Ornstein 1986). Temporal experience, therefore, is merely subjective sensitive.

Researchers of cognitive sciences have traditionally defended the existence of two subjective temporalities. We consider them both indispensable for the fundamentation of our thesis. Klein et al. (2002) coin two forms of temporal experience: lived and known. The former, time lived, enables somebody to experience time as a present in motion. Known time, in contrast, consists of the chronological knowledge that enables someone to know about the events and their fixed temporal relations (before and after). It is this type of temporality, anchored in semantic memory, that makes it possible to anticipate and plan future contingencies and learn about the relations between cause and effect.

The idea of time lived is significant. The abandonment of the notion of the static present to submerge oneself in the narrative experience and become captivated by it, offers, thanks to digitalization, significant creative and existential possibilities. Some of these possibilities have already been exploited in the form of artificial virtual worlds, for example. In fact, nowadays there are scenarios for interaction, fundamentally for purposes of education and/or entertainment, such as metaverses, that through the use of synthetic images and interactivity invite us to live experiences in real time (on this issue, we recommend Jansson's (2013) exploration of the notion of transmedia textures). We gave an example of this at the start of the text. However, what we consider especially relevant, having reached this point of the discussion, is not so much the possibility of living in present-time experiences that are constructed in the same present. What we find striking is the increased possibility of living in present time narrations produced in the past, in what was then the present, or in more distant pasts, with the total appearance of immediacy and the sensation of immersion. The increasing capacity to create representations, or spaces for consumption, based on real, and not necessarily fictitious, people or facts, with much verisimilitude, invites us to experience the time lived of the past narration in the present, with improved aesthetic qualities and hyperrealism. The notion of timeless-ness, together with these representations, can have cognitive and emotional effects. In this regard, we can observe how recordings of people from the immediate past have already been used to interact with people of the present, for example. By superimposing their images and voices, show business has been able to get Natalie Cole to sing with her late father Nat King Cole at a live gala.[2] What we are alluding to here in particular, however, is the exacerbation of these capacities, made possible by technological development. This increased capacity will even lead to the genera-tion of new representations of people and facts from the past for immersive con-sumption in the present and future that will, moreover, be available to everybody. We are not far from being able to recover/simulate the image of dead human beings, whether affectively close or not, and make them part of our real present (and future) narrative with a high degree of accuracy, verisimilitude and realism. These experi-ences, to continue with the example, could even shift from being one-off into con-stant experiences. Our perspective system, which is able to become engaged in the audiovisual contract and accept simulations as real, can integrate them in our con-ception of the present (and future) reality. And all of this leads us to ask: what will the characteristics be of a future imagined on the basis of narratives taken from the past and modified by the creative use of digital instruments? How will the future be affected by our increased narrative modification of the past?

5.7   Projecting Ourselves Into the Future: Memory and the Future

A large body of researchers in the field of cognitive sciences sustains that all organisms capable of having a long-term memory are necessarily future orientated (Klein 2013a). The greater the capacity of our memory, the more capacity we have to imagine the future. So, if we have a better memory of the past, we could have more variability in the future. Research sustains that the capacity to imagine and plan one's personal future (especially those plans that are not associated to current urges and needs) is essentially based on the memory of past circumstances and contingencies, which produces enor-mous selective advantages for those who have such an ability (Klein 2013b).

   The above means that we are future to a great extent through the past. This is because humans typically have complex memories and a broad temporal range on which we orientate ourselves and produce our imaginations. Thanks to this sophis-tication, we protect ourselves from future contingencies, from those that transcend our needs and emotional states (Bischof-Koehler 1985; Klein et al. 2010; Suddendorf and Corballis 1997). Remembering, therefore, is evolutional because it serves to anticipate. In an adaptive sense, it is believed that as flexibility, complexity and the temporal extension of imaginations about the future increase, the capacity to have proactive and goal-orientated responses to one's environment increases (Klein 2013b). We therefore need to remember.

---

[2] See an example of this at http://www.youtube.com/watch?v=MKCyUe4syc4

Some studies have shown that not only neural mechanisms but also the cognitive processes on which both imagining the past and looking into the future rely are similar; both processes are strongly correlated (Addis et al. 2007; Schacter et al. 2012; Spreng and Grady 2010). This suggests that, existentially, outside of the present moment of what is lived resides what is known. However, despite this, research has shown that the phenomenological quality of the description of past happenings is superior to that of the future. We are much richer when providing sensorial details and localising events from the past (Bernsten and Boh 2010; D'Argembeau and Van der Linden 2004; Gamboz et al. 2010; Grysman et al. 2013). It is perhaps because of this that we possess more literary or audiovisual narratives about the past than about the future. It is perhaps also because of this that we more frequently recur to our past and its experience for inspiration when we represent our identity. Simulation of the future, in fact, is a much harder task than remembering because, although both activities are related, imagining the future is not a simple replica of past memories placed in new situations. Imagining what is not known requires construction (we add that this is an expression of personal creativity), rather than recuperation. Moreover, it may require the creation of unfamiliar environments (Arnold et al. 2011).

In terms of the creation of one's own narratives, research in cognitive sciences provides us with data for understanding why, and for what, we can create our own versions of stories. For example, evidence sustains that we tend to consider future events more positively than those of the past (Grysman et al. 2013): imagining the future is guided by personal goals and expectations (D'Argembeau and Mathy 2011; Shao et al. 2010). The self, in consequence, has an organisational role. In fact, both memories of the past and imagination of the future are guided by identity statements arranged in temporal clusters that, in turn, reflect how these characteristics of identity were modelled in the past and expect to be modelled in the future (Rathbone et al. 2011). Imagination of the future, in turn, is to a greater extent affect by self-enhancement biases. We need to believe that our lives constantly evolve (Sedikides and Gregg 2008). So, a large number of the narrations that project our identity towards the future have at their core the idea that we have improved our circumstances and will improve them even more. Likewise, and coherent with temporal self-appraisal theory (Wilson and Ross 2001), human beings feel the need to see ourselves constantly evolving towards the point where we are capable of denigrating the past in order to exalt the present. For example, the presentation of narrations of our past lives on Facebook may contain the idea not just that we have progressed, but that our past was, at least, improvable. Finally, the process of remembering the past and imagining the future supposes the application of knowledge of memory to new and future situations, although this involves a bias that leads us to construct our life histories around the idea of the perpetually improving self (D'Argembeau and Van der Linden 2004), which achieves the desired goals (D'Argembeau and Mathy 2011; Shao et al. 2010). In line with theories that defend our tendency to exaggerate optimism with regard to the future (Markus and Nurius 1986), our narrations regarding the past will contain the idea that our past has been improved, our present is being modified and our future will be better for us all.

5.8 Narratives in Cultural Evolution

Having reached this point, we might assume that digitalization could enable us to possess more, and more varied, narratives of ourselves and of others, which could question our experiences or knowledge of time and which could modify narratives of the past (a past whose story could be considered improvable). We might also consider that digitalization could offer us a greater number of narratives that modify the present, fundamentally our experiences, in which we are immersed (be that by manipulation of the formal times of narrated stories, by reflection on the time in plots or by absolutely timeless immersion in the consumption experience). Finally, we might consider that digitalization when applied creatively to narratives could present us with a greater number of narratives whose core leads to the idea of obtaining something different in the future that is changeable and always more positive.

However, what collective effects could all the above have? Honestly, the future cannot be known; we can only speculate on the basis of the tracks available to us. But if we insist on hypothesising with certain rigour, we come to the theory of accumulative cultural evolution, which sustains that each generation benefits from the progress made by previous generations, producing cultural artefacts of increasing complexity and sophistication. Following the principles of this theory, the narratives that people might produce about their lives in the future, not only due to technological but also cultural evolution, should be more sophisticated and complex than in the past (in fact, they already are with respect to just a few years ago). But there is another element worth considering.

The processes of cumulative cultural evolution, in addition to the above, involve social learning that guarantees the storage of successive modifications over time (Cadwell and Millen 2008). Cultural evolution is not just about showing creative invention, but also, just as or more importantly, is about social transmission ensuring that recently invented artefacts or practices are maintained until they are modified or improved in the process (Tomasello 1999). We believe that computer networks, with their unlimited capacity to store information, are magnificent, unique, in this regard. Never in human history have we possessed such efficient repositories for cultural knowledge or for the establishment of social relations. In fact, until now, these functions, as a whole, were especially complied with by cities (Mumford 1961). Because of computer networks, access to information, to our digital narratives, is transformed into knowledge in a context in which modern-day people (and we assume that this will increase for the people of the future) use past experiences or narratives, those of our present, in a way that is orientated at transformation and, therefore, at the future. Cultural evolution, which depends on innovation, is heading towards an increasingly greater bed (a richer and more varied memory of the past) on which the imagination of the future may rest. Previous narratives, and their experience, can provide the lessons that need to be overcome, in accordance with our current knowledge. The evolution of knowledge, cultural evolution, the changing of stories, of human beings' narratives, seems like it will never cease.

5.9   Conclusions

Throughout this text, we have defended the idea that as the people of the world become more able to use computer networks to create and disseminate their own narratives about their pasts and their presents, whether with more or less deliberate intention of transcending or influencing their futures, knowledge will also increase of beliefs about the past and the effect that human consumers or narratives have of experiences of times lived and known. We have sustained that digitalization applied to narrative creativity makes it possible to suppose that we are heading towards the construction of more sophisticated, lived and different narrative experiences in the present, while we configure the future in a new way and on the basis of an exponentially recreated and reinterpreted past. But, moreover, we have defended the idea that the richness of individual expressions in narration could make it possible to document the present and past using vivid details to the extent that, in the experience of these narratives, after the synthesis of the interpersonal variabilities in the description of the events, versions of both will be produced that are indistinctive, that contain a high level of verisimilitude, and with the appearance of reality (it goes without saying that the idea is not for the experience to be real, but for it to appear to be real). Finally, we have defended the idea that experiences of narratives from the past in the present, through the verisimilar simulation of disappeared people and realities, and their incorporation in our experiences of current life by a greater number of citizens of the world, could be added to the ways of narrating and recognising the world, with cognitive, affective and behavioural effects of increased magnitudes.

Despite the above, we believe that when someone creates their own narrative, they are transformed by the process, and some of the changes to that person depend on the process that they themselves believe to design. The tools they use, the representations that inspire them and the cultural environments in which they live are also influential. In fact, the narrator may be very aware that he or she has control over said factors. However, there is a limit to the amount of control one has of the narrative. It is impossible for the narrator to be sure about the effect that the narrative might have on others. Paradoxically, knowledge of the effects of narrations on individuals is currently very fast in comparison with earlier periods and will become even faster. However, narrations will gradually penetrate more, through moments of fleeting influence, and will only produce visible changes through convergent strategies that are maintained in time and creatively persistent. The narrator, however, changes himself or herself during the process of creating and disseminating the narration, even through the very sphere of the effects of their manipulations. The narrator that narrates himself or herself changes in his or her own times.

To conclude, we should make it clear that we believe that the person that constructs themselves through their digital narrations more or less consciously displays contradictory attitudes. On the one hand, they seem to want to liberate themselves from some of the identity labels imposed by their social environments in the present (many of which stem from their past) and impose their own creative criteria (their perceptions of time, of their identity and of the quality of their narration) in the present and in different (immediate or distant) futures. On the other hand, they imagine themselves to be the protagonist of the narration that builds towards the future, from their limited perception of the present, and partially sustained in the past. In other words, they label themselves now and seek to manipulate what is to come. They do not know, however, what the future will bring.

All narrators live inserted in natural and social narrations, in their times and circumstances. It is not possible, however, to avoid this. Fortunately?

References

Addis DR, Wrong AT, Schacter DL (2007) Remembering the past and imagining the future: common and distinct neural substrates during event construction and elaboration. Neuropyschologia 47(11):1363–1377

Andreasen NC (1987) Creativity and mental illness: prevalence rates in writers and their first-degree relatives. Am J Psychiatr 144:1288–1292

Arlow JA (1996) The concept of psychic reality. How useful? Int J Psychoanal 77(4):659–666

Arnold KM, McDermott KB, Szpunar KK (2011) Imagining the near and far future: the role of location familiarity. Mem Cognit 39(6):954–967

Bandura A (1997) Self-efficacy: the exercise of control. Freeman, New York

Bell M (1990) How primordial is narrative? In: Nash C (ed) Narrative in culture: the use of storytelling in the sciences, philosophy, and literature. Routledge, London

Bergson H (1960) Time and free will: an essay on the immediate data of consciousness. Harper & Row, New York. (Original work published in 1910)

Bernsten D, Boh A (2010) Remembering and forecasting: the relationship between autobiographical memory and episodic future thinking. Mem Cognit 38(3):265–278

Bischof-Koehler D (1985) On the phylogeny of human motivation. In: Eckensberger LH, Lnatermann ED (eds) Emotion and Reflexivitaet. Urban & Schwarzenberg, Vienna, pp 3–47

Bruner J (1986) Actual minds, possible worlds. Harvard University Press, Cambridge, MA

Bruner J (1990) Acts of meaning. Harvard University, Cambridge, MA

Cadwell CA, Millen AE (2008) Studying cumulative cultural evolution in the laboratory. Philos Trans R Soc B 363:3529–3539

Carr D (1991) Time, narrative and history. Indiana University Press, Indianapolis

Chatman S (1978) Story and discourse: narrative structure in fiction and film. Cornell University Press, New York

Coveney P, Hughfield R (1990) The arrow of time. Fawcett Columbine, New York

Cropley DH, Kaufman JC, Cropley AJ (2008) Malevolent creativity: a functional model of creativity in terrorism and crime. Creat Res J 20(2):105–118

Csikszentmihalyi M (1990) Flow: the psychology of optimal experience. Harper & Row, New York

Davies P (1995) About time: Einstein's unfinished revolution. Simon & Schuster, New York

D'Argembeau A, Van der Linden M (2004) Phenomenal characteristics associated with projecting oneself back into the past and forward into the future: influence of valence and temporal distance. Conscious Cogn 13(4):813–823

D'Argembeau A, Mathy A (2011) Tracking the construction of episodic future thoughts. J Exp Psychol Gen 140(2):258–271

Fireman GD, McVay TE Jr, Flanagan OW (2003) Narrative and consciousness: literature, psychology and the brain. Oxford University Press, New York

Gamboz N, Brandimonte MA, De Vito S (2010) The role of past in the simulation of autobiographical future episodes. Exp Psychol 57(6):419–428

Gardner H (1991) The unschooled mind. Basic Books, New York

Grysman A, Prabhakar J, Anglin SM, Hudson JA (2013) The time travelling self: comparing self and other in narratives of past and future events. Conscious Cogn 22:742–755

Gould SJ (1987) Time's arrow, time's cycle. Harvard University Press, Cambridge, MA

Hartocollis P (1983) Time and timelessness: a psychoanalytic inquiry into the varieties of temporal experience. International University Press, Madison

Jansson A (2013) Mediatization and social space: reconstructing mediatization for the transmedia age. Commun Theory 23(3):279–296

Klein SB (2013a) The complex act of projecting oneself into the future. WIREs Cogn Sci 4:63–79

Klein SB (2013b) Future mental time travel: types of memory, types of selves and types of temporality. Soc Cogn 31(3):417–426

Klein SB, Loftus J, Kihlstrom JF (2002) Memory and temporal experience: the effects of episodic memory loss on an amnesic patient's ability to remember the past and imagine the future. Soc Cogn 20:353–370

Klein SB, Robertson TE, Delton AW (2010) Facing the future: memory as an evolved system for planning future acts. Mem Cogn 38:13–22

Mainemelis C (2002) Time and timelessness: creativity in (and out of) the temporal dimension. Creat Res J 14(2):227–238

Markus H, Nurius P (1986) Possible selves. Am Psychol 41(9):954–969

Maturana HR (1995) On the nature of time. Instituto de Terapia Cognitiva, Santiago de Chile

Maturana HR, Varela FJ (1992) The tree of knowledge: the biological roots of human understanding. Shambhala, Boston

McAdams DP (1993) The stories we live by: personal myths and the making of the self. Guilford, New York

Mitchon JA (1990) Implicit and explicit representations of time. In: Block RA (ed) Cognitive models of psychological time. Lawrence Erlbaum, Hillsdale, pp 37–58

Mumford L (1961) The city in history: its origins, its transformations and its prospects. Secker & Arburg, London

Ornstein RE (1970) On the experience of time. Penguin, New York

Ornstein R (1986) Multimind. Doubleday, New York

Prigogine I (1990) Foreword. In: Coveney P, Highfield R (eds) The arrow of time. Fawcett Columbine, New York, pp 15–17

Propp V (1968) Morphology of the folktale. University of Texas Press, Austin

Rankin J (2002) What is a narrative? Ricoeur, Bakhtin, and process approaches. Concr Australas J Process Thought 3:1–12

Rathbone CJ, Conwoy MA, Moulin CJA (2011) Remembering and imagining: the role of the self. Conscious Cogn 20(4):1175–1182

Ricoeur P (1991) Life in quest of narrative. In: Wood D (ed) On Paul Ricoeur: narrative and interpretation. Routledge, London, pp 20–33

Runco MA (2007) Creativity: theories and themes: research, development and practice. Elsevier Academic Press, San Diego

Schacter DL, Addis DR, Hassabis D, Martin VC, Spreng RN, Spuzner KK (2012) The future of memory: remembering, imagining, and the brain. Neuron 76(4):677–694

Sedikides C, Gregg AP (2008) Self-enhancement: food for thought. Perspect Psychol Sci 3(2):102–116

Solomon B, Powell K, Gardner H (1999) Multiple intelligences. In: Runco MA, Pritzker S (eds) Encyclopedia of creativity. Academic, San Diego, pp 259–273

Spreng RN, Grady CL (2010) Patterns of brain activity supporting autobiographical memory, prospection and theory of mind and their relationship to the default mode network. J Cogn Neurosci 22(6):1112–1123

Shao Y, Yao X, Ceci SJ, Wag Q (2010) Does the self drive mental time travel? Memory 18(8):855–862

Suddendorf T, Corballis MC (1997) Mental time travel and the evolution of the human mind. Genet Soc Gen Psychol Monogr 123(2):133–167

Threadgold T (2005) Performing theories of narrative: theorising narrative performance. In: Thornborrow J, Coates J (eds) The sociolinguistics of narrative. John Benjamins, Amsterdam, pp 261–278

Tomascikova S (2009) Narrative theories and narrative discourse. Bull Transilv Univ Brasov 2(51):281–290

Tomasello M (1999) The cultural origins of human cognition. Harvard University Press, Cambridge, MA

Tulving E (2002) Episodic memory: from mind to brain. Annu Rev Psychol 53:1–25

Wilson AE, Ross M (2001) From chump to champ: people's appraisals of their earlier and present selves. J Pers Soc Psychol 80(4):572–584

Chapter 6
Interaction Aesthetics and Ubiquitous Music

Damián Keller, Nuno Otero, Victor Lazzarini, Marcelo Soares Pimenta, Maria Helena de Lima, Marcelo Johann, and Leandro Costalonga

6.1 Introduction

Two recent approaches to interaction design have good potential to address creative practice in everyday settings: interaction aesthetics and ubiquitous music. We discuss the theoretical and methodological issues raised by both perspectives and highlight the similarities and differences among the two approaches. Through the analysis of a series of experiments, a common theme emerges: relational properties may provide a useful target for creativity-oriented experimental work.

The first section presents the conceptual and methodological issues raised by interaction aesthetics research. Engagement, temporal patterns of behavior, alternative forms of design with innovative material combinations, and user identities inserted in cultural contexts are approached through methods based on situated experience, consensual rationale, and reflective practice. A recent definition of ubiquitous music encompasses the issues dealt within interaction aesthetics and highlights the need to account for everyday creative phenomena. Creative potentials, everyday creativity, and distributed creativity emerge as targets for the

D. Keller (✉)
NAP, Federal University of Acre, Rio Branco, Acre, Brazil
e-mail: dkeller@ccrma.stanford.edu

N. Otero
Linnaeus University, Kalmar, Sweden
e-mail: nuno.otero@lnu.se

V. Lazzarini
National University of Ireland, Maynooth, Ireland

M.S. Pimenta • M.H. de Lima • M. Johann
Federal University of Rio Grande do Sul, Porto Alegre, Brazil

L. Costalonga
Federal University of Espirito Santo, Vitória, Brazil

© Springer-Verlag London 2015
N. Zagalo, P. Branco (eds.), *Creativity in the Digital Age*,
Springer Series on Cultural Computing, DOI 10.1007/978-1-4471-6681-8_6

experimental research carried out in ubiquitous music. The implications of adopting material relational properties and social relational properties as targets for experimental work are discussed within the context of a series of ubimus design studies. The last section of the chapter points to the methodological challenges faced by creativity-aware interaction aesthetics, including factors related to the profile of the participants, the profile of the by-products, and the observation of situated behaviors.

6.1.1 Interaction Aesthetics

A promising approach for supporting the design of everyday creative activities.

Advances in interaction design have highlighted the need for a wider view on technological developments and their applicability in everyday activities (Löwgren 2009). The utilitarian focus of previous human-computer interaction research is being questioned by researchers interested in the creative enhancement of technology usage (Mitchell et al. 2003; Shneiderman 2007) and by investigators dealing with the aesthetics of interaction design (Redström 2007; Wright et al. 2008). In 2005, Udsen and Jørgensen stated: "at present, the aesthetic turn is not a full-fledged shift in paradigm. However, it is undoubtedly an indication of a new awareness of the wide-ranging dimensions of interaction between humans and computers." We have reasons to believe this situation has changed, particularly within the practices of interaction design.

Interaction aesthetics is surfacing as a strong alternative to mainstream human-computer interaction theories and methods (Hallnäs and Redström 2002; Löwgren 2009; Redström 2007; Stolterman 2008; Udsen and Jørgensen 2005). Löwgren (2009) and Stolterman (2008) propose a shift in focus from task-oriented, utilitarian approaches to human-centered and experience-centered methods, described as a "rational, disciplined, designerly way" (Stolterman 2008). Redström (2007) suggests that a central idea is the need to create a richer relation to computational things, through the exploration of:

- Engagement rather than efficiency
- Temporal patterns of behavior
- Alternative forms of design that challenge expectations
- User identities, cultural contexts, and traditions, within specific design domains
- Innovative material combinations

Despite the significant theoretical advances in interaction aesthetics, how to approach the variety of methodological issues raised by this perspective on technology is still an open question. In one of the initial studies in this area, Redström (2007) endorsed a radical change of focus, i.e., how to design for living with, rather than just using, computational technology. To design for everyday life involves more than supporting people to accomplish certain tasks effectively. Designs for usability and functionality are not sufficient. This broader view of interaction explores aspects for which the traditional usability assessment methods are incapable of providing useful information. New techniques are necessary.

As a general trend, situated experience, consensual rationale, and reflective practice are surfacing as key aspects of interaction aesthetics. From an aesthetically aware perspective, Stolterman (2008) proposes the following methods: "(i) precise and simple tools or techniques, (ii) frameworks that do not prescribe but that support reflection and decision-making, (iii) individual concepts that are intriguing and open for interpretation and reflection on how they can be used, (iv) high-level theoretical and/or philosophical ideas and approaches that expand design thinking but do not prescribe design action." Sketching and prototyping (Buxton 2007) are examples of item (i). Instead of prescribing solutions for well-defined problems, interaction aesthetics techniques employ design patterns, design actions, and interaction metaphors to handle open-ended research problems. Given that these techniques reduce the development cycle ensuing multiple iterations through the design process, they may eventually serve to fill the gap indicated in item (ii). Specific examples are personas, scenarios, probes, and affordance-based methods. These tools provide inspiration to deal with situated issues, fostering reflection and understanding of the implications of each design decision (iii). Despite their misleading name, design actions (De Bruijn and Spence 2008) are high-level applications of cognitive theories that can be used to guide aesthetically informed design decisions. When similar technological solutions are observed in various contexts, interaction patterns may provide a useful generalization. Interaction patterns can be applied to the task of finding suitable techniques to deal with recurring implementation issues. We can think of interaction metaphors and patterns as results of opposite design trends. While metaphors provide instantiations of general interaction mechanisms, patterns are generalizations of specific solutions. This means that solutions encountered by inductive or bottom-up processes (patterns) could eventually match solutions reached top-down – through deduction of general principles (metaphors). These specific cases are the strongest candidates for useful applications in multiple design contexts. Design actions, design patterns, and interaction metaphors provide non-prescriptive frameworks for design thinking (iv).

6.2 Goals of Ubimus Design

Ubiquitous music (ubimus) research (Keller et al. 2011a) has also targeted aspects of interaction design that have not been dealt with within the mainstream human-computer interaction perspectives. *Ubiquitous music deals with systems of human agents and material resources that afford musical activities through sustainable creativity support tools.* Viewing Redström's (2007) interaction aesthetics proposal from a ubiquitous music perspective, we see a convergence of interests and methods, including engagement, temporal patterns of behavior, alternative forms of design with innovative material combinations, and user identities inserted in cultural contexts. Despite these common themes, there are three ubimus design concepts that have not been considered within aesthetically informed trends: creative potentials, distributed creativity, and everyday creativity. Let us review the convergent approaches first and we will tackle the differences afterwards.

Engagement has surfaced as one of the constructs that impact creativity outcomes (Bryan-Kinns 2011; Brown and Dillon 2007; Keller et al. 2011b). This factor is particularly relevant when the activities involve intense social interaction (Pimenta et al. 2012). Engagement may encompass multiple mechanisms related to personal (Keller and Capasso 2000) and social aspects of the creative activity (Lima et al. 2012).

The study of *temporal patterns of behavior* has gained increased relevance in the context of creative activity. Eaglestone et al. (2008) and Shneiderman (2007) have proposed longitudinal studies as the method of choice to capture design requirements that are not addressed in short, task-focused experimental studies. Activity-based computing (Bardram 2005; Bødker and Klokmose 2011) may provide conceptual tools to tackle aspects of the interaction support involved in creative activity. Characterizing creative activities has become one of the major goals of the experimental ubimus research program (Keller et al. 2010).

Alternative forms of design and innovative material combinations were already present in ecocompositional practices (Keller 2000) but have gained new strength with the introduction of the technique of repurposing within ubiquitous music systems design (Flores et al. 2010, 2014). Multimodality (Keller 2004) also seems to be an emerging common theme that may be further developed by the exploration of aesthetically informed design qualities. A quality that shows promise for creative musical applications is ambiguity (Gaver et al. 2003). The semantic content of musical products is usually open to multiple interpretations. These interpretations depend on the personal history of interactions with everyday sounds (Keller 2004; Keller and Capasso 2000). Therefore, the function and emergent properties of ubiquitous musical experiences open opportunities to explore ambiguous design. This goal may separate the ubimus research agenda from the utilitarian objectives laid out by sonic interaction design (Serafin et al. 2011). An aesthetic ubimus experience involves not only new materials or combinations of materials; it also provides new forms of engagement.

User identities, cultural contexts, and traditions have been partially explored within the domain of ubiquitous music design. Brazilian creativity traits were introduced in interaction design by Pimenta et al. (2012). This line of research may be expanded through cross-cultural and ethnographic studies, although the current emphasis seems to be on the impact of user identities on aspects of everyday creativity. In other words, rather than applying large-scale comparative studies indicating general cultural traits, everyday creativity may demand detailed micro-observations of creative activities in ecologically valid contexts.

Ubiquitous music research may provide a contribution to interaction aesthetics by expanding the design goals to account for creative potentials (DiLiello and Houghton 2008). While existing approaches – synthesized in Redström (2007) – propose alternative forms of design and innovative material combinations to obtain new artifacts, ubiquitous music techniques target the increase of creative potentials.

Thus, one objective is the empowerment of participants in creative actions rather than just the implementation of creative products. For example, sonic sketching involves various exploratory activities that increase the knowledge of potential sonic results (Lima et al. 2014). This experiential knowledge may materialize as creative products but it may also induce new paths for exploration. Methodologically, having alternative goals indicates the need for multiple forms of assessment, including products, processes, and potential resources.

Ubiquitous music design decisions are materialized as technological prototypes that afford but do not enforce creative behavior. This proposal is rooted in the Brazilian dialogical education movement (Freire 1999; Lima et al. 2012). As we will see in the next section, relational properties result both from agent-object interactions and agent-agent (or social) interactions. When the social dynamic is nonhierarchical, creative products and processes may not necessarily fit within the division of labor traditionally applied in the industry: users may become cocreators. In this sense, the dialogical approach has strongly influenced the participatory design movement (Ehn 1988).[1] A focus that is missing from current research efforts in interaction aesthetics is the socially distributed nature of creative activity. This aspect is featured in the application of communities of practice within ubiquitous music research (Pimenta et al. 2012). Musical prototyping (Miletto et al. 2011) – encompassing a process of negotiations among participants, working on a shared creative product – provides another example of non-prescriptive support for aesthetically grounded decision-making.

A new focus on activities carried in everyday settings has opened the door to the study of everyday musical creativity (Pinheiro da Silva et al. 2013). Because creative ubiquitous musical experiences occur in everyday contexts featuring ordinary people, experiments are done outside of the institutionalized spaces for music making. Hence, another objective of the ubiquitous music design process is the support of manifestations of everyday creativity (Richards et al. 1988), defined as the processes and products that are both innovative and socially relevant but that do not attain status of artworks. Site-specific creative experiences – rather than digital musical instruments, instrumental virtuosity, or isolated sound objects (Schaeffer 1977) – are the material for study of aesthetically informed ubimus design. Hummels and Overbeeke (2010) stated that "design is about being-in-the-world." Paraphrasing, we can say that ubiquitous music design is about being creative in the everyday world.

Summing up, although there are several parallels between the interaction aesthetics and the ubimus research agendas, targeting creativity implies dealing with phenomena that have not been considered within the aesthetics-oriented human-computer interaction perspectives. Engagement, temporal patterns of behavior, alternative forms of design with innovative material combinations, and user identities inserted in cultural contexts are common themes. Creative potentials, everyday

---

[1] Pele Ehn (1988: 9) stated: "The research approach I advocated was action research together with trade unions, and here I was strongly influenced by Paulo Freire and his 'pedagogy of the oppressed' as well as by Kristen Nygaard and the work he was doing together with the Norwegian Metal Workers' Union."

creativity, and distributed creativity are emerging phenomena highlighted through the experimental research carried out in ubiquitous music. The next two sections will discuss the implications of adopting material relational properties and social relational properties as targets for experimental work. This discussion will provide the necessary context to define a common ground for interaction aesthetics and ubimus research methods. The last section will point to the methodological challenges faced by creativity-aware interaction aesthetics.

6.3   Material Relational Properties and Creativity Support Metaphors: Implementation of the Metaphors and Testing the Solutions Through User Studies

Keller et al. (2010) have proposed anchoring as an affordance-formation process for supporting creative practice. Affordances are not properties of the environment or properties of the human agents. They are relational properties that arise while activities are been carried out. Activities involve cognitive and proprioceptive processes that engage both material resources and conceptual operations. By understanding affordances as dynamic properties emergent from agent-object (natural or material affordances) and agent-agent interactions (social affordances), a key aspect of the design process emerges: how affordances are shaped. Anchoring is one of the key mechanisms for cognition and proprioception integration (Hutchins 2005). It may also play an important role in affordance formation. Two examples of the application of anchoring within the context of design are the creativity support metaphors: time tagging (Keller et al. 2010) and spatial tagging (Keller et al. 2011a, b).

1. The *time-tagging metaphor* provides direct couplings between sonic cues and conceptual operations making it possible to define how a set of unordered virtual elements or processes is layered onto a tagged timeline.
2. The *spatial-tagging metaphor* makes use of virtual or material visual cues – anchors – to support creative musical activity.

Creativity support metaphors embody methodological solutions that are not bound to technical specificities. Time tagging defines a process by which a set of unordered virtual elements or processes is layered onto an abstract one-dimensional structure – a tagged timeline. The time-tagging interaction metaphor is applicable to mixing on stationary or on portable devices. It can be applied on sonic data or on control sequences. It could also be extended to video applications. As a creativity support metaphor, time tagging materializes relational properties that fulfill part of the human and the technological demands of the mixing activity.

This metaphor was used to implement a series of prototypes grouped under the label mixDroid first generation (mixDroid1G). MixDroid1G is a compositional tool that allows the user to record sonic performances which can be merged into complete artworks. Usage consists of selecting and triggering multiple sound resources, doing the mix while sounds are being played. Several experiments encompassing domestic and public settings have shown that time tagging provides effective support for creative musical activities in everyday settings (Keller et al. 2010, 2013; Pinheiro da Silva et al. 2013, 2014; Radanovitsck et al. 2011).

As previously stated, spatial tagging is defined as an interaction metaphor that makes use of virtual or material visual cues – anchors – to support creative activity. The spatial-tagging metaphor was encapsulated in the Harpix prototypes. In Harpix 1.0, the visual elements of the interface can be manipulated directly, establishing a straightforward relationship between user actions and sound events. Keller et al. (2011b) tested the application of spatial tagging in musical epistemic activities. Three subjects realized 37 interaction essays, comprising exploratory, imitative, and product-oriented activities. Six creativity support factors were assessed: productivity, expressiveness, explorability, concentration, enjoyment, and collaboration. Enjoyment and expressiveness were highly rated during product-oriented activities, while exploratory activities yielded high enjoyment scores. Contrastingly, collaboration was poorly judged in all conditions.

The results of this experiment – encompassing three types of musical activities by three subjects – indicated good support for creative and exploratory activities, with particular emphasis on two factors: enjoyment and expressiveness. However, the collaboration and explorability factors were not evaluated positively, and imitative activities did not yield high scores.

Recapitulating, anchoring serves as a mechanism for linking constraints of the external structure of the environment to constraints on cognitive operations. This view implies that both memory and processing loads can be reduced if the constraints of the activity can be built into the physical structure of the material resources. The problem faced by system designers is thus reduced to finding consistent relationships between the abstract concepts and the local resources available during the activity. In other words, appropriate metaphors for creative activity may handle material relational properties through direct couplings between material and conceptual operations. This hypothesis was tested through the implementation of two interaction metaphors: time tagging and spatial tagging. Time tagging used local sound cues to support creative decisions. Spatial tagging employed visual cues to enable exploratory creative actions. Both metaphors showed good support for creative musical activities but did not fare well when collaboration was involved.

6.4 Social Relational Properties: Distributed Creativity

Converging trends in creative practice research (Keller and Capasso 2006; Truax 2002), educational research (Loi and Dillon 2006), and music education (Burnard 2007) point to the local context as a key factor in shaping creative experiences. These approaches propose creativity as a research focus within socially informed paradigms, gathering support from ecological methodologies (Keller 2000; Loi and Dillon 2006) and activity theory research (Burnard 2007; Keller et al. 2010; Leont'ev

1978). Loi and Dillon (2006) propose adaptive educational environments that can be designed as creative spaces to foster interaction through situational and social dynamics. Technological infrastructure is a key resource in this type of educational environments. Burnard (2007) places creativity and technology as the two central forces enabling innovative educational practices. She cites the use of online and collaborative technology, proposing practice, participation, and collaborative networking as objectives of music education research. These situated, socially informed approaches provide a stark contrast to the standard educational views on musical creativity (see Keller et al. 2011b for a review). While standard models are concerned with activities that (in theory) can be carried out without the need for social interaction or place-specific experience, such as "problem solving" and abstract "thinking," situated approaches bring socially acquired musical experience to the forefront of the research agenda. Thus, they highlight two aspects that need to be considered in aesthetically informed approaches to design: the local resources for creative action and the mutual processes of adaptation that emerge through social interactions.

The dialogical conception challenges the view of creativity as a purely mental, individual process (Freire 1999; Lima et al. 2012). Through hands-on activity and social interaction among peers, students are stimulated to evaluate their work. Given the relevance of the local referents, participants are encouraged to reflect about their own processes and products during musical activities. While keeping tabs on the local reality, they develop a critical view on their products and creative processes. Through iterative cycles of exchanges, dialogical methods foster individual and collective reflections. In line with other socially oriented perspectives, the dialogical view is based on the premise that knowledge is constructed. This knowledge is considered the basis for reflective actions. Freire's educational philosophy encourages pupils to assume an active role in the educational process, reflecting and justifying their creative choices and independently seeking resources within a context of open proposals. This consensus-building process opens a space for coexistence of diverse and sometimes opposing views. Thus, Freire's proposal emphasizes exchanges without confrontations, providing a foundation for the emergence of communities.

Liikkanen et al. (2011) argue for the adoption of practice-based design methods focused on creativity. Their proposal is situated within the participatory design initiative, integrating users as co-designers (Ehn 1988). On a similar vein, Botero et al. (2010) propose the exploration of a continuum from use to creation involving strategies such as repurposing of existing technology for rapid prototyping. A central aspect of this emerging trend is the focus on creativity and sustainability allied to the adoption of participatory techniques. Two recent studies carried out by our group applied this design approach within the context of ubiquitous music practice (Lima et al. 2012).

Lima et al. (2012) developed and applied a set of design techniques – the ubimus planning and the ubimus design protocols – to assess relevant aspects of social and procedural creativity dimensions that have been usually excluded from musical creativity field studies. Two workshops were conducted to assess both technological and domain-specific requirements for support of creative musical activities. The first workshop was conducted with music teachers and schoolteachers that had no formal musical training. The objective of this workshop was to assess domain-specific requirements for musical activities by educational staff. The second workshop focused on technological support for tool development by nonmusicians. This workshop yielded two software projects which involved user evaluations of creative musical processes. Participants in the user studies included both musicians and nonmusicians.

The ubimus planning protocol served to raise important questions regarding technological usage by musicians and naive subjects in educational contexts. Nontechnical approaches, such as those proposed by traditional soundscape activities (Schafer 1977), may not be suited for introducing nonmusicians to sonic composition. Naive subjects may respond better to technologically based approaches which emphasize aspects of the relationship between the personal experience and the environment. The ubimus design approach was effective to assess the usability of musical tools at early stages of development. Prototypes were implemented and usability studies were carried out by undergraduate information technology students within a 3-week time-slot. Sharp differences were observed in the type of requirements expressed by musicians and nonmusicians regarding creativity support tools. Despite these differences, both groups of subjects regarded the use of software prototypes within exploratory musical activities as being fun and expressive.

The ubimus planning and ubimus design protocols highlighted the existing limitations in the evaluation of creative activities in real-world settings. Although the protocols included careful consideration of the role of the participants within the design cycle, the data obtained did not provide enough information on the dynamics of the creative processes. Place and product creativity factors were considered both as individual and group manifestations of creative behavior. But the assessment of procedures was limited to the analysis of the participants' self reports. The study helped to identify a methodological gap in the development of procedural support for creativity, namely, the lack of time-based methods to study long-term creative musical practice.

This section explored the implications of adopting social relational properties within the context of aesthetically oriented ubiquitous music design. Experimental results indicated that nonmusicians responded better to technologically based support for creative activities when compared to musically trained subjects. A procedural limitation of the studies was the lack of time-based methods to deal with the assessment of local resource usage in creative activities. Support for distributed creativity poses at least two challenges: (1) the availability of local resources for creative action and (2) the emergence of consensus through shared social resources.

6.5 Relational Properties in Ubimus Design: Methodological Implications

Given the radical shift set forth by the interaction aesthetics and the ubiquitous music research programs, existing approaches to interaction design are being reformulated bringing new issues to the foreground. Relational properties – such as pliability (Löwgren 2009) and anchoring (Keller et al. 2010) – capture the tight agent-object interaction dynamic that has been at the center of the embedded-embodied approaches to cognition (Gibson 1979). In line with the enactive perspective (Di Paolo et al. 2010), these design qualities emerge as a result of mutual adaptations between agents and objects. Because they demand the active engagement of an agent, relational properties cannot be "attached" to objects. They can only be experienced "in the act." There are several methodological implications of adopting relational properties as theoretical constructs.

Firstly, design experiments must take into account both subjective and material constraints and opportunities. Experiments that adopt closed epistemic fields – where subjects are given a task to complete in laboratory settings and the results measure their efficiency in completing the task – do not provide information on the ecosystem's support for the emergence of relational properties. In this case, the material resources are chosen by the experimenter and may not fulfill the creative needs of the subject. This is an example of the problem that ubiquitous music research has labeled as the "auto-referentiality of the theoretical-experimental construct" (Keller et al. 2011b): the experimental situation does not take into account the conditions of real-world settings. Relational properties may be absent from a laboratory task but may be accessible when participants are interacting on site.

Second, the adoption of a tool at the initial stages of the design process may forgo the emergence of relational properties. Sometimes, the agent-object ecosystem's potentials to support relational properties are not enough to ensure creative outcomes. These potentials have to be materialized in products and behaviors. Given that behaviors are constrained by personal factors (including both cognitive and social resources), understanding the creative profiles of the subjects is an integral part of the design process. From a ubiquitous music perspective, this procedural limitation is defined as "early domain restriction" (Keller et al. 2011b).

Third, assessments purely based on products may not provide a complete picture of the creative factors at play. There is a rich literature of product evaluation methods in creativity studies (Baer and McKool 2009; Mumford et al. 2011). Creative products give reliable information on creative outcomes. This information can be enhanced by the analysis of domain-specific products. Nevertheless, despite its untapped potential, this retrospective approach has an epistemological limitation: products and procedures are usually not equivalent. Whether considering synchronous or asynchronous creative activities, if a relational property emerges as a by-product, it may not be discernible through the analysis of the finished product but it may be observable while the product is being made or used. Asynchronous creative activities furnish procedural data that needs to be collected during the creative activity (Coughlan and Johnson 2006). This data is not easily recoverable from the finished products. Contrastingly, synchronous creative proposals (such as improvisatory musical practices) fuse products and processes into a unified entity. In this case, the assessment of the product imposes the same requirements as the assessment of the creative performance: time-based methods.

Furthermore, while creative products are not enough to enhance the knowledge of aesthetically aware designs, creative processes may be insufficient to assess the level of support for creative behavior. Creative potentials are externalized as creative actions, which may yield creative by-products (Runco 2007). The creative magnitude of these by-products can only be assessed in relation to a specific social context (or social niche – Keller 2012). This context is shaped by the life histories of the participants of the creative experiences. Therefore, evaluations of technological support for creative behavior demand: (1) assessments of by-products, (2) observations of situated behaviors, and (3) analysis of the profiles of the participants. As Mumford et al. (2011) suggest, creativity evaluation methods are necessarily multidimensional. Ubiquitous music research is no exception.

This section discussed the adoption of relational properties in ubiquitous music experimental research, highlighting the methodological implications of creativity-aware interaction aesthetics. The requirements for multidimensional assessment encompass the evaluation of by-products, the observation of situated behaviors and the analysis of the personal factors.

6.6 Conclusions and Future Work

Generally speaking, since the late 1990s, musical practices have incorporated resources that were absent from purely instrumental music performance and from studio-centered creative practice. Ubiquitous music making has expanded this trend by embracing personal experiences that lead to creative musical phenomena that were excluded from professional musical practices. Creative music making has incorporated the creative experience as a target of compositional practice. Furthermore, music making through technological means has become the rule, rather than the exception.

We believe that considering the conceptual framing provided by relational properties is useful to help researchers and practitioners find common ground concerning the understanding of everyday creative activities and foster the emergence of design solutions for supportive digital artifacts. The time- and spatial-tagging metaphors can, in fact, be applied to other domains than the creation of sonic products. For example, tools to support digital storytelling are, in some cases, already using time- and spatial-tagging metaphors to facilitate the organization of collected content and enable the emergence of contextualized narratives based on people in situ experiences (see, e.g., Nordmark and Milrad 2012).

To overcome the limitations of previous methodological approaches, three strategies were identified: (1) usage of real-world resources and conditions, (2) furnishing potential material resources that match the profiles of the participants, and (3) adopting time-based multidimensional evaluation methods targeting by-products' profiles, situated behaviors, and subjective evaluations. Given the complementary goals of interaction aesthetics and ubiquitous music research and the methodological implications of adopting relational properties as experimental variables, what are the consequences of the application of the ubimus agenda in interaction aesthetics? Would ubimus concepts provide a sharper focus to aesthetically aware design? We believe that the methodologies presented in this chapter point to an affirmative response to these questions.

In the previous section, we mentioned three important aspects connected to the third strategy just mentioned above: (1) acknowledging the significance of by-products of the overall creative process instead of just focusing on end products, (2) considering strategies that enable the observation of situated creative behaviors, and (3) taking into serious consideration an analysis of participants' profiles. Let us try to reflect further on these and foresee possible implications for the creative technologies community and society in general.

In relation to the first aspect, the immediate question is: what are by-products good for? Recent developments of digital tools are widening the ability of people to create their own digital art forms, disseminate them, and store them. We believe that by-products cannot only be a useful learning resource allowing creators to go back, check, and reflect upon past learning trajectories and creative processes, but they can also provide a repository of past collaborative experiences, probably strengthening the group members' feelings of shared and common ground. Furthermore, such repositories of by-products can become invaluable resources for music historians in their quest to understand the creative product and process.

The second aspect emphasizes the need to understand people's in situ dealings with creative tools. The observation of situated behaviors, from a research point of view, seems crucial if we want to design better tools to support people's opportunistic adoptions and use of digital tools. Furthermore, we also envision the possibility of providing appropriate scaffolding to the creative processes themselves, and such scaffolding needs to be grounded in authentic and meaningful situations; otherwise, people might miss the relevance of the scaffolding cues and suggestions.

The third aspect emphasizes the potential of facilitating people's choices of digital tools based on their own strengths, weaknesses, likes, and dislikes. This is a major issue for at least two reasons. Firstly, it provides opportunities for creative action to a potential community of users that has been excluded by the expert-oriented approaches. Second, it empowers nonspecialists to shape design decisions by tinkering with digital tools, yielding precious information on the relationships among design choices, local resources, and personal profiles.

Concluding, we also hope that these aspects can function as triggers to the widening of informed discussions about the nature of the creative act, its function in society, and its associated costs.

References

Baer J, McKool SS (2009) Assessing creativity using the consensual assessment technique. In: Schreiner C (ed) Handbook of research on assessment technologies, methods, and applications in higher education. Information Science Reference, Hershey, pp 65–77

Bardram E (2005) Activity-based computing: support for mobility and collaboration in ubiquitous computing. Pers Ubiquit Comput 9(5):312–322. doi:10.1007/s00779-004-0335-2

Bødker S, Klokmose CN (2011) The human-artifact model: an activity theoretical approach to artifact ecologies. Hum Comput Interact 26(4):315–371. doi:10.1080/07370024.2011.626709

Botero A, Kommonen K-H, Marttila S (2010) Expanding design space: design-in-use activities and strategies. In: Durling D, Bousbaci R, Chen L-L, Gautier P, Poldma T, Roworth-Stokes S, Stolterman E (eds) Proceedings of the DRS 2010 conference: design and complexity. DRS, Montreal

Brown AR, Dillon SC (2007) Networked improvisational musical environments: learning through online collaborative music making. In: Finney J, Burnard P (eds) Teaching music in the digital age. Continuum International Publishing Group, London, pp 96–106

Bryan-Kinns N (2011) Annotating distributed scores for mutual engagement in daisyphone and beyond. Leon Music J 21:51–55

Burnard P (2007) Reframing creativity and technology: promoting pedagogic change in music education. J Music Technol Educ 1(1):37–55. doi:10.1386/jmte.1.1.37/1

Buxton W (2007) Sketching user experiences: getting the design right and the right design. Elsevier/Morgan Kaufmann, New York. ISBN 9780123740373

Coughlan T, Johnson P (2006) Interaction in creative tasks. In: Proceedings of the SIGCHI conference on human factors in computing systems. ACM, New York, pp 531–540. ISBN: 1-59593-372-7

De Bruijn O, Spence R (2008) A new framework for theory-based interaction design, applied to serendipitous information retrieval. ACM Trans Comput Hum Interact 15(1):5:1–5:38. doi:10.1145/1352782.1352787

DiLiello TC, Houghton JD (2008) Creative potential and practised creativity: identifying untapped creativity in organizations. Creat Innov Manag 17:37–46. doi:10.1111/j.1467-8691.2007.00464.x

Di Paolo EA, Rohde M, Jaegher HD (2010) Horizons for the enactive mind: values, social interaction, and play. In: Stewart JR, Gapenne O, Paolo EAD (eds) Enaction: toward a new paradigm for cognitive science. MIT Press, Cambridge, MA, pp 33–88

Eaglestone B, Ford N, Holdridge P, Carter J, Upton C (2008) Cognitive styles and computer-based creativity support systems: two linked studies of electro-acoustic music composers. In: Kronland-Martinet R, Ystad S, Jensen K (eds) Computer music modeling and retrieval: sense of sounds. Springer, Berlin/Heidelberg, pp 74–97. ISBN 978-3-540-85034-2

Ehn P (1988) Work-oriented design of computer artifacts. Arbetslivscentrum, Stockholm. ISBN 9789186158453

Flores L, Miletto E, Pimenta M, Miranda E, Keller D (2010) Musical interaction patterns: communicating computer music knowledge in a multidisciplinary project. In: Proceedings of the 28th ACM international conference on design of communication. ACM, New York, pp 199–206. ISBN 978-1-4503-0403-0

Flores LV, Pimenta MS, Keller D (2014) Patterns of musical interaction with computing devices. Cadernos de Informática 8(2):68–81

Freire P (1999) Pedagogy of Hope/Pedagogia da Esperança: Um Reencontro com a Pedagogia do Oprimido. Paz e Terra, Rio de Janeiro

Gaver WW, Beaver J, Benford S (2003) Ambiguity as a resource for design. In: Proceedings of the SIGCHI conference on human factors in computing systems (CHI 2003). ACM, New York, pp 233–240. ISBN 1-58113-630-7

Gibson JJ (1979) The ecological approach to visual perception. Houghton Mifflin, Boston. ISBN 0898599598

Hallnäs L, Redström J (2002) From use to presence: on the expressions and aesthetics of everyday computational things. ACM Trans Comput Hum Interact 9(2):106–124. doi:10.1145/ 513665.513668

Hummels C, Overbeeke K (2010) Special issue editorial: aesthetics of interaction. Int J Des 4(2):1–2

Hutchins E (2005) Material anchors for conceptual blends. J Pragmat 37:1555–1577

Keller D (2000) Compositional processes from an ecological perspective. Leonardo Music J 10:55–60. doi:10.1162/096112100570459

Keller D (2004) Paititi: a multimodal journey to El Dorado. Doctor in Musical Arts thesis. Stanford University, Stanford, CA, USA

Keller D (2012) Sonic ecologies. In: Brown AR (ed) Sound musicianship: understanding the crafts of music. Cambridge Scholars Publishing, Newcastle upon Tyne, pp 213–227. ISBN 978-1-4438-3912-9

Keller D, Capasso A (2000) Social and perceptual processes in the installation the trade. Organ Sound 5(2):85–94. doi:10.1017/S1355771800002053

Keller D, Capasso A (2006) New concepts and techniques in eco-composition. Organ Sound 11(1):55–62. doi:10.1017/S1355771806000082

Keller D, Barreiro DL, Queiroz M, Pimenta MS (2010) Anchoring in ubiquitous musical activities. In: Proceedings of the international computer music conference. MPublishing, University of Michigan Library, Ann Arbor, pp 319–326

Keller D, Flores LV, Pimenta MS, Capasso A, Tinajero P (2011a) Convergent trends toward ubiquitous music. J N Music R 40(3):265–276. doi:10.1080/09298215.2011.594514

Keller D, Lima MH, Pimenta MS, Queiroz M (2011b) Assessing musical creativity: material, procedural and contextual dimensions. In: Proceedings of the National Association of Music Research and Post-Graduation Congress – ANPPOM. ANPPOM, Uberlândia, pp 708–714

Keller D, Ferreira da Silva E, Pinheiro da Silva F, Lima MH, Pimenta MS, Lazzarini V (2013) Everyday musical creativity: an exploratory study with vocal percussion (Criatividade musical cotidiana: Um estudo exploratório com sons vocais percussivos). In: Proceedings of the National Association of Music Research and Post-Graduation Congress – ANPPOM. ANPPOM, Natal

Leont'ev AN (1978) Activity, consciousness and personality. Prentice Hall, Englewood Cliffs. ISBN 0130035335

Liikkanen LA, Laakso M, Björklund T (2011) Foundations for studying creative design practices. In: Proceedings of the second conference on creativity and innovation in design (DESIRE '11). ACM, New York, pp 309–315. ISBN 978-1-4503-0754-3

Lima MH, Keller D, Pimenta MS, Lazzarini V, Miletto EM (2012) Creativity-centred design for ubiquitous musical activities: two case studies. J Music Technol Educ 5(2):195–222. doi:10.1386/jmte.5.2.195_1

Lima MH, Keller D, Otero N, Pimenta MS, Lazzarini V, Johann M, Costalonga L (2014) Ecocompositional techniques in ubiquitous music practices in educational settings: sonic sketching. In: Himonides E, King A (eds) Proceedings of the Sempre (MET2014). Researching music, education, technology: critical insights. University of London, London, pp 123–127

Loi D, Dillon P (2006) Adaptive educational environments as creative spaces. Camb J Educ 36(3):363–381. doi:10.1080/03057640600865959

Löwgren J (2009) Toward an articulation of interaction esthetics. N Rev Hypermed Multimed 15(2):129–146. doi:10.1080/13614560903117822

Miletto EM, Pimenta MS, Bouchet F, Sansonnet J-P, Keller D (2011) Principles for music creation by novices in networked music environments. J N Music Res 40(3):205–216. doi:10.1080/092 98215.2011.603832

Mitchell WJ, Inouye AS, Blumenthal MS (2003) Beyond productivity: information technology, innovation, and creativity. The National Academies Press, Washington, DC

Mumford MD, Hester K, Robledo I (2011) Methods in creativity research: multiple approaches, multiple methods. In: Mumford MD (ed) Handbook of organizational creativity. Elsevier Science, Waltham, pp 39–64. ISBN 9780080879109

Nordmark S, Milrad M (2012) Mobile digital storytelling for promoting creative collaborative learning. In: Proceedings of the seventh IEEE international conference on Wireless, Mobile and Ubiquitous Technology in Education (WMUTE 2012). IEEE, Takamatsu, Japan, pp 9–16

Pimenta MS, Miletto EM, Keller D, Flores LV (2012) Technological support for online communities focusing on music creation: adopting collaboration, flexibility and multiculturality from Brazilian creativity styles. In: Azab NA (ed) Cases on Web 2.0 in developing countries: studies on implementation, application and use. IGI Global Press, Vancouver. ISBN 1466625155

Pinheiro da Silva F, Keller D, Ferreira da Silva E, Pimenta MS, Lazzarini V (2013) Everyday musical creativity: exploratory study of ubiquitous musical activities (Criatividade musical cotidiana: Estudo exploratório de atividades musicais ubíquas). Música Hodie 13:64–79

Pinheiro da Silva F, Pimenta MS, Lazzarini V, Keller D (2014) Time tagging in its niche: engagement, explorability and creative attention (A marcação temporal no seu nicho: Engajamento, explorabilidade e atenção criativa). Cadernos de Informática 8(2):45–56

Radanovitsck EAA, Keller D, Flores LV, Pimenta MS, Queiroz M (2011) mixDroid: time tagging for creative activities (mixDroid: Marcação temporal para atividades criativas). In: Proceedings of the XIII Brazilian symposium on computer music (SBCM). SBC, Vitória

Redström J (2007) Aesthetic concerns. In: Giaglis G, Kourouthanassis P (eds) Pervasive information systems. M.E. Sharpe Inc., Armonk, pp 197–209

Richards R, Kinney D, Benet M, Merzel A (1988) Assessing everyday creativity: characteristics of the lifetime creativity scales and validation with three large samples. J Pers Soc Psychol 54:476–485

Runco MA (2007) A hierarchical framework for the study of creativity. New Horiz Educ 55(3):1–9

Schaeffer P (1977) Traité des objets musicaux: Essai interdisciplines. Éditions du Seuil, Paris. ISBN 9782020026086

Schafer RM (1977) The tuning of the world. Knopf, New York

Serafin S, Franinović K, Hermann T, Lemaitre G, Rinott M, Rocchesso D (2011) Sonic interaction design. In: Hermann T, Hunt A, Neuhoff JG (eds) The sonification handbook. Logos Publishing House, Berlin, pp 87–110. ISBN 978-3-8325-2819-5

Shneiderman B (2007) Creativity support tools: accelerating discovery and innovation. Commun ACM 50(12):20–32. doi:10.1145/1323688.1323689

Stolterman E (2008) The nature of design practice and implications for interaction design research. Int J Des [Online] 2(1):55–65

Truax B (2002) Genres and techniques of soundscape composition as developed at Simon Fraser University. Organ Sound 7(1):5–14. doi:10.1017/S1355771802001024

Udsen LE, Jørgensen AH (2005) The aesthetic turn: unravelling recent aesthetic approaches to human-computer interaction. Digit Creat 16:205–216. doi:10.1080/14626260500476564

Wright P, Wallace J, McCarthy J (2008) Aesthetics and experience-centered design. ACM Trans Comput Hum Interact 15(4):1–21. doi:10.1145/1460355.1460360

Part III
Co-creation and Collaboration

Chapter 7
An Enactive Model of Creativity for Computational Collaboration and Co-creation

Nicholas Davis, Chih-Pin Hsiao, Yanna Popova, and Brian Magerko

7.1 Introduction

The modern landscape of computing has rapidly evolved with breakthroughs in new input modalities and interaction designs, but the fundamental model of humans giving commands to computers is still largely dominant. A small but growing number of projects in the computational creativity field are beginning to study and build creative computers that are able to collaborate with human users as partners by simulating, to various degrees, the collaboration that naturally occurs between humans in creative domains (Biles 2003; Lubart 2005; Hoffman and Weinberg 2010; Zook et al. 2011; Davis et al. 2014). If this endeavor proves successful, the implications for HCI and the field of computing in general could be significant. Creative computers could understand and work alongside humans in a new hybrid form of human-computer co-creativity that could inspire, motivate, and perhaps even teach creativity to human users through collaboration.

To reach this optimistic future, the field of computational creativity needs a conceptual framework and model of creativity that can account for the collaborative and improvisational nature of human creativity. Traditional cognitive science theories view cognition and creativity as an abstracted manipulation of symbols that happens solely in the brain (e.g., Newell et al. 1959). The new cognitive science

N. Davis (✉) • B. Magerko
School of Interactive Computing, Georgia Institute of Technology, Atlanta, GA, USA
e-mail: nicholas.davis@gmail.com; magerko@gatech.edu

C.-P. Hsiao
College of Architecture, Georgia Institute of Technology, Atlanta, GA, USA
e-mail: chsiao9@gatech.edu

Y. Popova
Department of Cognitive Science, Case Western Reserve University, Cleveland, OH, USA
e-mail: yanna.popova@case.edu

© Springer-Verlag London 2015
N. Zagalo, P. Branco (eds.), *Creativity in the Digital Age*,
Springer Series on Cultural Computing, DOI 10.1007/978-1-4471-6681-8_7

theory of enaction claims that cognition and creativity always emerge through a real-time and improvised interaction with the environment and other agents in that environment (Varela et al. 1991; Stewart et al. 2010). While traditional theories could work to incorporate this perception-action feedback loop to model continuous improvised interaction, the enaction theory begins with the assumption that all cognition is based on this principle of improvised interactions guided by feedback from the environment. Starting from this basic assumption makes developing an enactive model of collaborative creativity and co-creation much easier due to their improvisational nature.

The overall aim of this chapter is to show how an enactive approach to computational creativity can make it easier to think about, design, and build creative computers, especially those that are able to improvise in real-time collaboration with human users. To situate and motivate our contribution, we first describe the field of computational creativity. Next, we introduce the cognitive science theory of enaction and describe creativity through its theoretical lens. Then, we present our enactive model of creativity and explain how its principles helped design "enactive" creative systems in two different domains: visual art and design.

7.2 Computational Creativity

Computational creativity is an outgrowth of artificial intelligence, cognitive science, and creativity research. It studies and builds creative systems involving different combinations of creative humans and creative computers. Making creative computers is a kind of grand challenge for the modern era of computing, and the recent efforts in computational creativity show a promising path forward. The field of computational creativity can be segmented into three broad categories that each have different motivations and goals. *Creativity support tools* augment and enhance human creativity, such as Adobe's Photoshop or Computer Aided Design tools. *Generative systems* produce creative artifacts (semi-)autonomously, such as computers that paint pictures (see Fig. 7.1) (McCorduck 1991; Colton and Wiggins 2012) or generate poetry (Colton et al. 2012). *Computer colleagues* collaborate with human users on creative tasks much like another human would (see Fig. 7.2).

Once it was established that creativity could be trained, facilitated, and measured, researchers began to develop techniques to support creativity (Smith et al. 1995; Guilford 1970; Csikszentmihalyi 1997). Initially, these techniques were procedural activities one could engage in to stimulate creativity, such as brainstorming and lateral thinking exercises (Rawlinson 1981; Bono 1970). Researchers also began developing a new class of technology referred to as creativity support tools (CSTs) (Shneiderman 2002; Shneiderman et al. 2006; Hewett et al. 2005; Carroll et al. 2009). CSTs are designed to help users explore a creative domain, record decision histories, and scaffold skills to allow and encourage users to learn expertise (Candy 1997; Shneiderman 2007).

Fig. 7.1 Art-generating computational creativity systems. *Left*: Artwork by The Painting Fool (Colton and Wiggins 2012). *Right*: Artwork by Aaron (McCorduck 1991)

Creativity Support Tool
Track history, simulate and explore alternatives to support a creative person

Accelerate Creativity

Generative Systems
Programs that automatically generate novel, surprising, and valuable creative products

Generate Creative Products

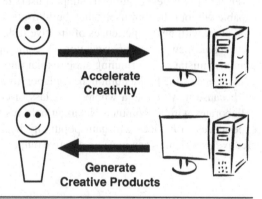

Computer Colleagues
Co-creative agents collaborate with humans in *continuous* real time improvisation to enrich the creative process

Collaborative Improvisation

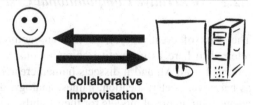

Fig. 7.2 Three approaches in the field of computational creativity

7.2.1 Creativity Support Tools

Shneiderman distinguishes creativity support tools (CSTs) from productivity support tools through three criteria: clarity of task domain and requirements, clarity of success measures, and nature of the user base (2007). Productivity support tools are designed around a clear task with known requirements, have well-defined success metrics, and are characterized by a known and relatively well-understood set of users. In contrast, CSTs often work in ill-defined domains that have unknown requirements, vague success measures, and an unpredictable user base. For example, consider productivity support tools for the well-defined goals of product supply scheduling, which include many clearly defined variables like cost metrics for shipping efficiency. Contrast this with a drawing support tool, like ShadowDraw (Lee et al. 2011) or iCanDraw (Dixon et al. 2010), that helps users learn drawing skills and inspires creativity.

Creativity support tools can take many forms. Nakakoji (2006) organizes the range of creativity support tools with three metaphors: running shoes, dumbbells, and skis (Nakakoji 2006). Running shoes improve the abilities of users to execute a creative task they are already capable of; they improve the results users get from a given set of abilities. Dumbbells support users learning about a domain to become capable without the tool itself; they build users' knowledge and abilities. Skis provide users with new experiences of creative tasks that were previously impossible; they enable new forms of execution. A contemporary text editor that highlights grammar mistakes is a running shoe; explaining why those wordings are ungrammatical makes the tool a dumbbell. Collaborative drawing tools would be a type of ski because they enable a whole new class of creative expression where the user collaborates with a computer. Nakakoji believes CSTs that introduce new creative experiences to novices will gain popularity because of the positive impact novel creative experiences can have on creative output (Nakakoji 2006).

7.2.2 Generative Computational Creativity

The class of creative systems that autonomously produce creative products is referred to here as generative computational creativity. This approach is largely inherited from AI, and it dissects human creativity into observable behaviors such as narrative, poetry, ideation, games, analogy, design, etc. These researchers then create computational models for their tightly delineated creativity module with the hope and effort to try to integrate those components with other embodied and situated aspects of creativity later.

The typical software architecture for generative computational creativity progresses as follows: The system first "reads" or interprets a large corpus of material into structured representations that it uses as its knowledge base. To make the systems more "creative," the corpus is carefully selected to lead to more interesting combinations, such as twitter posts and news articles (Veale and Hao 2008; Colton et al. 2012). These representations form the "conceptual space" the agent traverses to find interesting combinations to produce novel output (Boden 2004). For example, a poetry-generating system might parse a news article into structured representations that can then be spliced and recombined according to hard-coded rules of poetry (meter constraints, rhyming patterns, etc.). The conceptual space itself can be restructured to reveal additional mappings and traversals within it, which is called "transformational creativity" (Boden 2004). Finally, those spaces are systematically traversed to piece together a novel creative product, which is outputted to the user. These types of creative systems typically yield bounded and discrete creative artifacts as their output. The recent 2014 International Conference on Computational Creativity, for example, was largely dominated by this approach.

Based on this distinction, a system can be referred to as generative if it does not constantly interact with its environment through both perception and action to create an artifact. Instead, it relies on building a large knowledge base from a corpus and then manipulating elements of that corpus to develop new artifacts. The "creativity" that generative systems exhibit occurs in an abstracted manipulation of symbols without a perception-action feedback loop with the environment. While the end product may resemble something we might expect of a "creative" human, we argue these systems leave out one of the most fundamental ingredients to human cognition—the environmental feedback loop.

7.2.3 Computer Colleagues

Computer colleagues are the newest and perhaps most ambitious venture in the space of computational creativity because they require a method for controlling real-time improvisational interaction with a user in addition to some mechanism for generating original creative contributions to the shared artifact. There are several options for algorithms that generate creative contributions (as discussed previously), but understanding how to get the agent to improvise in real time is difficult. A good starting point is to understand collaboration and co-creativity in humans, which is classified as multiple parties contributing to the creative process in a blended manner (Mamykina et al. 2002). It arises through collaboration where each contributor plays an equal role. Contrast this blended model with cooperation, for example, which can be modeled as a distribution of labor where the result only represents the sum of each individual contribution (Mamykina et al. 2002).

Co-creativity allows participants to improvise based on decisions of their peers. Ideas can be fused and built upon in ways that stem from the unique mix of personalities and motivations of the team members (Mamykina et al. 2002). Here, the creative product emerges through interaction and negotiation between multiple parties, and the sum is greater than individual contribution. These interaction principles can be extended to include a sufficiently creative agent that can collaborate with human users in a new kind of human-computer creativity.

Some approaches that have yielded interesting examples of computer colleagues use mimicry, structured improvisation, and shared mental models. For example, the improvisational percussion robot Shimon mimics human musicians by analyzing the rhythm and pitch of musical performances and generating synchronized melodic improvisations (Hoffman and Weinberg 2010). In practice, the human and robot develop a call-and-response interaction where each party modifies and builds on the previous contribution. Some co-creative agents use sensory input to construct mental models of agents, actions, intentions, and objects in the environment (Hodhod et al. 2012). Mental models help agents effectively structure, organize, interpret, and act on sensory data in real time, which is critical for meaningful improvisation.

Although there are only a few examples of computer colleagues today, they raise interesting questions about what it means to collaborate with a computer. These projects also point to the need for a general cognitive theory of collaboration and improvisational creativity that can be used to guide their interaction design and software architectures. We contend that enaction can fulfill this need.

7.3   The Enactive Paradigm

In the following sections, we describe how the enactive approach reframes perception into an active and dynamic process critical for participatory sensemaking, i.e., negotiating emergent actions and meaning in concert with the environment and other agents. Next, we examine the role of goals and planning in the enactive perspective. Finally, we review some sketching and design research to show evidence that enaction plays a key role in the creative process when creative individuals "think by doing."

Enactive cognition is an outgrowth of the embodiment paradigm in cognitive science. Embodiment claims cognition is largely structured by the manner in which our bodies enable us to interact with the environment (Varela et al. 1991). This approach is contrasted with earlier cognitive theories that conceptualized the mind as a machine and cognition as a complex but disembodied manipulation of symbolic representations (Newell et al. 1959). In particular, enaction emphasizes the role that perception plays in guiding and facilitating emergent action (De Jaegher 2009). A short definition of enactivism by Havelange (2010) will help summarize this distinction.

Here, cognition is no longer considered as a linear input/output sequence (as was the case in classical cognitivism) but rather in terms of a dynamic sensorimotor loop by taking into account the fact that actions themselves produce feedback effects on subsequent sensations. Action is thus no longer a simple output; it becomes actually constitutive of perception. What is perceived and recognized in perception are the invariants of the sensorimotor loops, which are inseparable from the actions of the subject.

The enactive approach takes first person experience and awareness of the cognitive agent as the starting point. It advocates for an intelligent perception and action system that pairs interesting actions and related percepts as a coupling that are stored to guide future interactions. Enaction is rooted in the notion that cognitive agents always experience reality as a continuous interaction with the world and any investigation or model should have interaction as its fundamental constituent.

7.3.1   Enactive Perception

Perception is not a passive reception of sensory data but rather an active process of visually reaching out into the environment to understand how objects can be manipulated (Gibson 1979; Noë 2004). In the enactive view, cognition is seen as a process of anticipation, assimilation, and adaptation, all of which are embedded in and contributing to a continuous process of perception and action. This type of enactive perception minimally involves a negotiation among the following factors: (1) the subject's intentional state, (2) the skills and bodily capabilities of the individual, and (3) perceptually available features of the environment that afford different actions such as size, shape, and weight (e.g., is it graspable, liftable, draggable, etc., as elaborated in Norman (1999)). Sensory data enters the cognitive system and irrelevant data is suppressed and filtered (Gaspar and McDonald 2014). Objects and details of the environment that relate to the subject's intentional goals appear to conscious perception as affordances, which can grab, direct, and guide attention and action (Norman 1999). Each time the individual physically moves through or acts upon the environment, that action changes the perceptually available features of the environment, which can reveal new relationships and opportunities for interaction.

7.3.2   Participatory Sensemaking

The enactive view accentuates the participatory nature of meaning generation, often called participatory sensemaking. Each interaction with the environment can (and often does) reveal new goals, which leads to a circuitous, rather than a linear, creative process. Creative individuals engage in a dialogue with the materials in their environment (and other agents) to define and refine creative intentions (Schön 1992).

In human daily interactions, for example, there is evidence that some form of natural coordination takes place in the shape of movement anticipation and synchronization. A good example of participatory sensemaking would be the familiar situation where you encounter someone coming from the opposite direction in a narrow passageway (De Jaegher 2009). While trying to negotiate a safe and quick passage, both participants look toward their intended path (providing a social cue) while also trying to assess the projected path of other agents. Interaction then, in the form of coordination of movements, is the decisive factor in how quickly the individuals achieve their goal of passing each other. Rather than adopting a plan with a fixed and concrete goal to control locomotion, an enactive analysis would posit that individuals remain flexible throughout the situated action by dynamically accommodating the choice of the other agent.

7.3.3 Goals and Directives

In the traditional view of information processing, in order to accomplish goals, an agent would follow certain steps according to a preset plan for solving the particular problems defined by concrete goals. From an enactive perspective, intelligence and creativity involve knowing how to change the flow of sensory information in order to explore possibilities for action, i.e., leaning in closer to get a better look at something. It is often simply easier to act on the environment and experiment with how different interactions affect the system than representing it in its entirety and performing symbolic processing on those representations like the information processing perspective proposes (Noë 2004). Even at the level of social interaction with an intelligent agent, an enactive approach tries to avoid postulating high-level cognitive mechanisms at the core of our intersubjective skills. The coevolution of a communicative/creative process is seen here as a gradual unfolding in real time of a dynamic system spanning a human subject, the environment, and agents within it. In this view, intentions emerge but are also transformed in and through the interaction with other agents and the environment.

Thus, instead of describing creative behavior as goal-based planning and information processing, we have adopted the enactive terminology of directives (Engel 2010). A "directive" is a loose intention that directly influences what things appear interesting or salient in the environment and how specific types of interactions might provide more information about emerging hypotheses. A directive is similar to a goal in that it can be reflected on, elaborated, and specified in more detail, but it is critically different from the current notion of "goal" in planning-based AI because it does not constitute action in any way. A directive constrains and suggests potential actions that could yield productive changes in an emergent process of sensemaking. See Fig. 7.3 for an illustration of goals compared to directives.

To illustrate the distinction between directives and goals, let us consider an example in the creative domain, such as painting a picture. Yokochi and Okada (2005) analyzed the painting process of a famous Japanese painter. He found that the artist began with a vague "directive" (our term) that is then refined and explored through interacting with the painting. Each new line adds an additional constraint and affects all the existing constraints created by previous lines. Whenever the painter decides to alter some part of the image, the enactive perspective would claim he has defined a "task" for himself. This task is similar to a goal in goal-based AI; in Fig. 7.3, tasks correspond to the small actions that serve to explore the problem space of the directive. Accomplishing a task can be modeled in an enactive manner

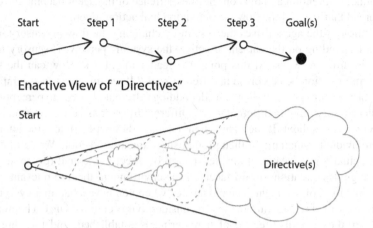

Fig. 7.3 Comparing goals and directives. Goals are linear with a series of steps whereas directives are vague and gradually refined through a process of interacting with the environment and defining tasks that explore the problem space outlined by the directive

(improvisation and affordance-based interactions) or using any number of search and planning procedures defined in goal-based AI.

Once the painter takes a step back to understand his last contribution in terms of the overall picture, however, he may find that his last contribution actually disrupted the overall balance of the piece. Although he doesn't have a specific end state for the painting in mind, one of the directives guiding his work may relate to achieving an overall balance in the composition. This directive does not tell him what contributions to make, but it helps point out inconsistencies and visual tensions that need to be addressed.

Let us suppose that the artist found five areas of the drawing that all violated his sense of balance due to his last contribution. He then selects one of those areas and defines a specific painting tasks that he predicts will help achieve balance. Once the first of those five areas is complete, the artist could take another step back and realize that his latest contribution makes the left side of the artwork look kind of like a face, which he likes. The artist might then update his overall directive to creating some kind of abstract face. Once this directive is adopted, the entire canvas is analyzed with respect to face-like features. Given this new constraint, he sees additional opportunities to change the drawing and would then select specific painting tasks that contribute toward the current directive. Here, the directive is dynamic and always evolving through interaction with the environment. The feedback offered by actually producing a change in the environment spurs new ideas and interpretations that can change the overall directive. The directive determines the constraints and affordances that are consciously available to the painter's perceptual processes.

Ultimately, it is the continuous perception-action feedback loop that actually determines actions. Instead of thinking of action as a series of behaviors executed like scripts or plans, we can think of action as a continuous improvisation with the environment. Attention and the conscious experience of the agent become the common thread that stitches the flow of each individual action together.

Attention of the agent drives the system by changing the flow of sensory information. Depending on the current directive, the system "perceives" sensory information in different ways. At this point, the reader might ask: How can the same sensory information be perceived in different ways? If we imagine sensory input as a flow through time, we can then consider adding different "lenses" to perception to filter that sensory input in different ways. Different filters make different features of the environment salient. If they are salient enough, they will demand the attention of the individual, which might then prompt subsequent interaction. We call this filter perceptual logic because it enables a form of direct perceptual reasoning. The directive guides attention toward facets of the environment that are relevant to the current intention of the agent. The old adage "when you have a hammer everything looks like a nail" is quite illuminating to consider in this context. Once a hammer is picked up, the general directive of hammering is established, and this directive guides attention and action, which results in things being perceived in terms of their "hammerability."

To summarize the idea of a directive, a directive does not dictate action; it selects a filter for perception that (we propose) enables a perception-based reasoning process we call perceptual logic. Actions are not discrete units but rather exist as an emergent flow of interactions with the environment. Some actions are executed in service of tasks, while other actions help gain different perspectives, including changing physical location as well as changing the directive with which a scene is analyzed. This process is guided by attention and the awareness of the agent and is inherently based on the temporal flow of experience and the dynamics of interaction with the environment.

7.3.4   Enactive Creativity Thesis

To account for the emergent nature of cognition and of creativity, we can make systems that are designed from the ground up as improvisational collaborative agents. Their "intelligence" and "creativity" would then emerge organically through interacting with intelligent and creative humans. Current AI systems are good at constrained and specialized tasks, but tasks that require common sense and creativity (like collaboration and improvisation) are notoriously difficult to model computationally. Humans use what is referred to as "commonsense knowledge" to adapt their actions and understand everyday situations. The so-called commonsense problem in AI refers to the huge knowledge databases required to achieve what humans normally take for granted as common sense. Building such a large database of knowledge is notoriously difficult and labor intensive, which is one reason why a general purpose AI does not exist today. Creativity goes a few steps beyond the commonsense problem because it introduces open-ended domains that do not necessarily have correct solutions. Collaboration further complicates this issue because it involves coordinating with other agents in a creative process. For these reasons, collaborative creativity is an extremely difficult target for traditional AI approaches.

This crack in the theoretical foundation of AI and computational creativity once seemed like a problem that would only take more computing power, larger knowledge bases, and more sophisticated machine-learning algorithms to solve. However, we think this problem reflects a larger systemic issue stemming from the basic assumptions about the nature of human cognition in AI and computational creativity. Once cognition and creativity are reframed in an enactive perspective, these hard problems become much more manageable.

Computationally creative systems employing the enactive perspective are based on a continually flowing and dynamic interaction with an environment rather than discrete actions and goal-oriented planning. An enactive investigation of creativity therefore begins at the level of perception, action, an environment, and the feedback loop that emerges during interaction. Enactive agents learn by experimentally interacting with their environment and perceiving the effects of those actions in a feedback loop, similar to a baby first learning to make sense of her senses. From this perspective, learning takes place when actions that produce a pleasing perceptual correlate (including a reaction from another agent, such as a mother cooing) are remembered as a percept-action pairing. These percept-action pairings are then repeated and built upon in an attempt to create shared meaning and experiences through participatory sensemaking, whereby agents coordinate their intentions through interaction and negotiation (Stewart et al. 2010).

The enaction theory describes creativity as a continual process whereby cognitive agents adaptively and experimentally interact with their environment through a continuous perception-action feedback loop to produce structured, organized, and meaningful interactions in an emergent process of sensemaking (or participatory sensemaking when multiple agents are collaborating). The emergent sensemaking process that results in creativity is fundamentally based on (and therefore inextricably bound to) continuous real-time interaction between an agent and its environment. During this type of emergent creativity, loose "directives" that guide actions are negotiated and fluidly defined, refined, or discarded altogether depending on how other collaborating agents and the environment respond to the agent's actions. While an enactive agent still defines directives that serve to guide actions, these directives merely constrain (rather than constitute) possible opportunities to explore in the environment.

In this process, experience, practice, and concentration help develop more nuanced and detailed percept-action couplings that afford a greater depth of interaction with the world. This means we cannot explain expertise relying exclusively on huge databases of representations manipulated in a rule-based manner (like case-based reasoning, analogical reasoning, blending, evolutionary algorithms, etc.). Experts know exactly where to look, what to look at, and when to look at it to figure out how to effectively navigate their domain of expertise. If the right information is not available, then experts know how to either restructure their sensory information (change viewpoints) or restructure the environment (take action) in order to explore further possibilities for interaction that will in turn help evaluate emerging theories and also reveal additional actions. It is the dynamics of this feedback loop that need to be understood and modeled in order to understand the improvisation that inherently undergirds creativity.

7.3.5 Enactive Creativity Examples

The literature on creativity provides evidence supporting the enactive perspective with research on "thinking by doing." There is a multitude of evidence demonstrating how both representational and nonrepresentational artists plan their artworks using sketches, studies, and other ways to simulate artistic alternatives (Mace and Ward 2002). Sketching reduces cognitive load and facilitates perceptually based reasoning (Schön 1992). In many creative domains, individuals generate vague ideas and then use some form of sketch or prototyping activities to creatively explore, evaluate, and refine artistic intentions (Davis et al. 2011). Sketching allows creative individuals to think by doing. When an action or idea is materialized in some way, the perceptual system is rewarded with richer data than pure mental simulations and abstract reasoning. Additionally, cognitive resources that would have been used to simulate the action (i.e., consciously visualizing the situation) are now freed for other tasks such as interpretation and analysis (Shneiderman 2007).

7.3.5.1 Architectural Design

One obvious example of using sketch to "think by doing" can be found in the task of planning the spatial configurations in the architectural design process. As addressed above, generating an entire artifact with all of its details directly from the mind is virtually impossible for a designer (Schön 1992). Instead, designers experience these improvised real-time adjustments in the design procedures with the tools and materials they are using. When starting the design process, designers choose different materials, tools, and media to present the initial ideas from their minds to explore the constraints of their problem (Schön 1992). When they interact with these tools, they might need to adjust their actions in order to achieve their needs. For instance, when drawing a sketch to study the forms, they may need to constantly adjust the "next steps" in order to solve the design constraints, such as not enough space, too long, too much curvature, etc.

Figure 7.4 illustrates a typical spatial plan of a student center in a bubble diagram. Since the plan entails many spaces, the designers would have to write down all the space names so that related spaces are located next to each other. They would also use arrows to represent the main circulation paths between two spaces. Each time a new space is added or an arrow is inserted, the designer's flow of sensory information changes and they might discover new problems or opportunities that were not apparent before (Suwa and Tversky 1997). Sketching facilitates their

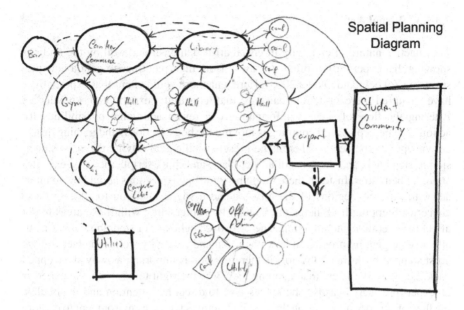

Fig. 7.4 Spatial layout of a school student center design (Courtesy of Kyle Doggett)

creativity and reasoning process through a dynamic perception-action feedback loop whereby new meanings are gradually constructed through a negotiation with the design materials (i.e., sketch, physical models, computational models, etc.).

Experienced designers also change the granularity of their perception to reason about sketches at different levels. When focusing on individual details, an architect might imagine how a particular corridor might feel to walk through. Then, they could shift to a global perspective that considers the overall theme and consistency of the whole building design (Suwa and Tversky 1997; Goldschmidt 1991).

7.3.5.2 Musical Performance

The enactive nature of creativity can also be seen in live musical performance. A classical musician, for example, a trumpet player, will need to feel the acoustic effects in a concert hall before his performances. For instance, he may extend the ending of a sound in a concert hall that has a "dry" acoustic effect. We propose the expert trumpet player has a well-established set of percept-action pairings (creating his expert perceptual logic) that have to be tuned to the particular performance space because the actions he will take in the performance will result in a slightly different perceptual feedback process than his normal practice space. Thus, he has to actively feel and explore the sounds of the space to align his perceptual logic with the specifics of the exact situation. Furthermore, during performance, he will also listen to the mixture of his trumpet sound with other sounds to make real-time adjustments to achieve the desired general effective (i.e., the directive, such as playing a "sad" tune).

7.3.5.3 Visual Art

The enactive nature of creativity in visual art is demonstrated well by the findings showing that expert artists often step away from their paintings to gain a new perspective (Yokochi and Okada 2005). Here, enaction would claim that expert artists have acquired percept-action pairings that constitute experiential knowledge: Altering the flow of sensory information can reveal additional possibilities for action. The percept-action coupling is moving the body (actions) and gaining different viewpoints (percepts). There is no preset specific goal driving the artist's decision to step back, and there is not a "step-back-and-think script" the artist executes at predefined times. Instead, there might be some open questions about how to interact with different regions of the artwork and a vague intention to address those concerns. Stepping back helps think about how interacting with those areas might affect the overall vague intention. The "creative" behavior of stepping back is actually an emergent by-product of how cognition and creativity work. The fact that the artist stepped back (her behavior) is therefore not as important as why she stepped back, i.e., how she knew that stepping back was the right thing to do. An expert is an expert precisely because she knows how to direct her attention and manipulate the flow of sensory information through interactions with the environment to explore and evaluate possibilities for further action.

The domain-independent examples above provide evidence that creativity does not only come from executing planned steps and actions but emerges through improvisational micro interactions between the human and the surrounding environments, including other humans, tools, and, most importantly, the continuous results generated during the percept-action feedback loop. We consider these interaction processes as an improvised interaction processes. Humans often experience the results from unplanned micro interactions that match or mismatch their expectations, which will then become perceptual logic for future interactions. We argue that this enactive feature of cognition is fundamental to understanding how to understand human creativity and also build computer colleagues.

7.3.6 Enactive Model of Creativity

The argument here is that the traditional cognitive science theories used by AI are inadequate to explain the entirety of human creativity (and cognition more broadly) and should thus be supplemented, augmented, or potentially replaced entirely with an enactive conceptualization of cognition. In the enactive view, cognition (including creativity) is inherently composed of a continuous interaction with the environment and other agents in that environment to adapt and thrive (Stewart et al. 2010); it is improvisational and ever changing based on the demands and opportunities of the moment. The enactive view encapsulates the embodied, situated, distributed cognition perspectives that have recently gained popularity (Suchman 1986; Hutchins 1995). From this view, cognition is not inherently goal-based planning procedures, as the search and planning-centric approaches in AI suggest. Although we certainly construct plans to try to organize our interactions with the environment, they are never constitutive of the actual creative process, which is enacted in concert with feedback from the environment. We cannot cut off this real-time interaction feedback loop with the environment in any way if we hope to create a realistic model of creativity and cognition.

7.3.6.1   Model Description

We first explain the visual conventions of the enactive model of creativity and describe how it can be applied to model creative cognition through time. Then, we describe in detail a new concept derived from our model called perceptual logic, which is a perceptual filter that highlights relevant affordances in the environment while suppressing irrelevant affordances. Next, we explain how modulating perceptual logic leads to different ways of seeing and interacting with the world in a way that can account for the diverse array of human creative behavior.

In the enactive model of creativity (see Fig. 7.5), the awareness of the agent is represented by the vertical rectangle situated on a spectrum of cognition, which essentially means that the agent is "aware" of what is perceived and its current intention. Perception is constituted partly by the mental model the agent has constructed for the current situation (top-down cognition) as well as the sensory input coming from the environment (bottom-up cognition) (Gibson 1979; Glenberg 1997; Varela et al. 1991; Stewart et al. 2010; Gabora 2010).

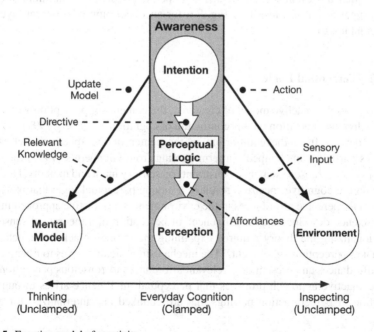

Fig. 7.5 Enactive model of creativity

To get a sense of the intended dynamism of this model, imagine the entire "awareness" rectangle as one unit that can shift to the left or right on the cognitive continuum as a function of the agent's concentration. Routine actions only require minimal thought and a limited amount of highly relevant sensory data. The enactive model of routine actions, such as driving, would be visually depicted by having the awareness rectangle resting at equilibrium in the center of the spectrum with small deviations to the left to update and revise strategy and deviations to the right to interactively evaluate those ideas.

To simulate bounds on working memory, the agent only has a limited amount of cognitive resources. These resources are used through a process of directed attention, i.e., concentration. During this simulated form of concentration, agents devote their attention to reflecting on the situation (building more detailed mental models, running complex mental simulations, etc.) or acting in a deliberate and interactive manner to inspect the world.

If the agent is performing an unfamiliar task, however, cognitive resources are recruited to actively build a mental model of the situation, which requires performing experimental interactions, closely examining the results in the environment, and then updating the mental model in a slower global model of perceptual logic. Initially, novices have to think a lot about what they are doing, which means they are using a lot of the previous attention resources to build up a cognitive model by performing micro experiments interacting with the world to hypothesize about this particular domain. As novices build up this model, they begin to interact without having to pay as much attention to what they are doing. The enactive model claims this happens because the experienced individual is able to use the new perceptual logic to filter irrelevant sensory details and operate effectively with minimum conscious supervision of a task (see Fig. 7.6 for an illustration of different layers of perceptual logic).

7.3.6.2 Perceptual Logic

According to the enactive model of creativity, the contents of perception vary based on an individual's position on this continuum of cognition (Glenberg 1997). As individuals deviate from the equilibrium in the center of the spectrum, perception becomes partially "unclamped" (a term coming from Glenberg's (1997) theory of memory) which loosens semantic constraints on sensory input and memory. Different points on the cognitive spectrum result in a unique perceptual logic that is used to intelligently perceive affordances in the environment. The enactive approach in cognitive science describes the "intelligence" of perception in a theoretical sense, but operationalizing the theory required explaining the implicit black box mechanism that makes perception "intelligent." The mechanism basically serves to filter all possible affordances and present only relevant affordances to conscious perception.

The enactive approach proposes that perceptual intelligence arises through the formation of percept-action pairings that are chunked and internalized for quick retrieval (Noë 2004). Perceptual logic is a proposed cognitive mechanism that filters sensory data, identifies relevant percept-action pairings, and presents these percept-action pairings as affordances to perception. Perceptual logic performs a similar role as the "simulator" in Perceptual Symbol Systems (Barsalou 1999). The simulator activates all the associated neural correlates related to a percept, including the various ways it can be interacted with based on experiential knowledge and physical characteristics.

7.3.6.3   Clamping Perception

Research indicates that perception filters irrelevant sensory input to reduce distractions and facilitate everyday cognition (Gaspar and McDonald 2014). When the agent is engaged in a routine task and following well-established affordances, sensory data is "clamped" to filter out unnecessary details and unconventional ways of seeing objects (Glenberg 1997). Everyday cognition is represented in EMC by situating the awareness rectangle in the center of the spectrum of cognition, creating a point of equilibrium. Shifting to either the left or right on this spectrum requires the agent to either concentrate on the details of her mental model or closely inspect details in the environment. At equilibrium, perception is clamped to a combination of sensory input and cognitive input that optimizes routine interactions (Glenberg 1997). When minor problems arise, such as small improvisational adjustments to the action based on environmental feedback, this equilibrium is slightly perturbed. The agent could generate various alternative actions by thinking (moving slightly left on the spectrum) and explore various ideas by interacting with the environment (moving slightly right on the spectrum).

7.3.6.4   Unclamping Perception

If there is a severe disruption to the current task (e.g., a great new idea, distraction, or some kind of failure), it might become necessary to disengage from the current task to reevaluate the situation. When an individual "disengages" from a task, perception becomes "unclamped" and attention shifts to thinking and simulating solutions (moving far left on spectrum) and closely examining the detail of the environment to discover new affordances (moving far right on the spectrum). The degree of concentration devoted to thinking about or acting on the environment determines how far, in either direction, awareness is situated on the spectrum of cognition. At the extreme left of the continuum (thinking) would be closing one's eyes to try to think deeply about a topic, which removes most sensory input from perception altogether. At the extreme right of the continuum (inspecting) would be an individual fully concentrated on acting skillfully, carefully, and deliberately on the environment.

7.3.6.5 Modulating Semantic Constraints

During these periods of disengaged evaluation, EMC proposes that the semantic constraints for recalling associated ideas from memory and interpreting elements in the environment become "unclamped" to enable reconceptualization. Unclamping semantic constraints helps overcome functional fixedness, which is a phenomenon where individuals have trouble dissociating objects from their entrenched meaning during insight problem-solving (Adamson 1952).

In the cognitive science literature, the abovementioned type of meaning reassignment is referred to as a *conceptual shift* (Nersessian 2008). Colloquially termed the Eureka! or Aha! moment, conceptual shifts occur when two separate knowledge domains are connected in the mind (Boden 2004; Nersessian 2008). It is often partially or wholly responsible for insights that lead to creative discoveries and solutions. The enactive model suggests that conceptual shifts and creative reconceptualizations are made possible by unclamping perception, thereby allowing new meanings to be associated with objects and concepts.

Interestingly, this model identifies an important role for distraction in the creative process. Distraction is one way to prompt an individual to disengage from everyday cognition. In abstract art, for example, unfinished segments of the artwork (or unexpected contributions from a collaborator) may distract the artist while they are drawing. These newly discovered areas might not align with the artist's current intention. As a result, the artist might want to resolve that tension by drawing additional lines, which can catalyze the creative process. However, too many distractions might frustrate the artist.

Now that we have introduced enaction and presented the enactive model of creativity, we will describe how this model was helpful in designing two computer colleagues in the domains of visual art and design.

7.4 Building Co-creative Agents with the Enactive Model

The enactive model of creativity served as a productive framework to design co-creative agents because it enables agents to interactively adapt their perceptual reasoning strategies and creative behavior to that of the user, which increases the probability the user will find the contributions of the system meaningful and creatively engaging.

7.4.1 Layers of Perceptual Logic

There are three layers of perceptual logic in the enactive model of creativity (local, regional, and global) that are determined by the position of awareness on the spectrum of cognition (see Fig. 7.6). Each successive layer of perceptual logic considers a larger portion of the creative artifact (i.e., more sensory data) at a higher level of

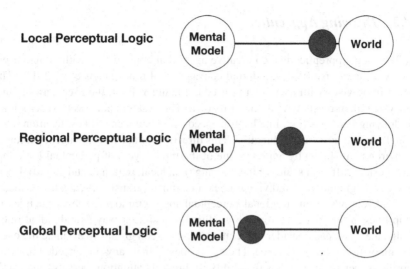

Fig. 7.6 The layers of perceptual logic: The position of awareness (*gray ball*) on the spectrum of cognition corresponds to the layer of perceptual logic the system uses

conceptual abstraction (global being the most complex). Since each layer is more complex than the next, we found the most effective implementation strategy to be implementing them progressively in stages starting with the most basic local layer of perceptual logic.

Local perceptual logic considers granular details of the user's contributions, such as individual lines added to a drawing. Regional perceptual logic, on the other hand, groups the user's inputs into regions and containers based on principles of gestalt grouping, such as proximity, similarity, common fate, and continuity (Arnheim 1954). The principles of gestalt grouping were encoded into this layer of perceptual logic to provide a means for the system to begin to make sense of creative contributions in a similar way as humans.

Global perceptual logic considers the creative artifact as a whole, like when an artist takes a step back from their painting. This form of perceptual logic considers the relationship between the different regions of the drawing to analyze the overall composition. When this perceptual logic is applied, the system may decide to completely decouple its contribution from the human's recent input, i.e., it can select non-active regions of the artifact on which to operate if those regions present significant creative opportunities. For example, a drawing system might examine the overall composition and determine that the left side of the drawing is imbalanced because it has significantly less lines overall than the right side of the drawing. The system employs global perceptual logic to reason about the drawing as a whole and set a directive of "do work on the left-hand side of the drawing." After this directive is determined, the system would then employ either regional or local perceptual logic to determine the exact lines to draw on the left-hand side of the page. The directive therefore constrains the possible actions the system could potentially take and guides interaction going forward, but it does not determine actions in any way, which is the critical difference between directives and goals.

7.4.2 Drawing Apprentice

The Drawing Apprentice is a co-creative agent that collaborates with human users to draw abstract artworks on a digital canvas in real time (Davis et al. 2014). The system improvises with users in a turn-taking manner. First, the user draws a line. The system then reacts with a line of its own. The system analyzes the user's lines and drawing behavior (i.e., line length, speed, time between strokes, location, etc.) through time to construct a directive. This directive guides how the agent perceives its environment (lines) by applying one of the three layers of perceptual logic that each consider different scales of the drawing (i.e., local, regional, and global). Local perceptual logic modifies individual lines (i.e., mirror, translate, scale, trace, shade, etc.) and redraws them. Regional perceptual logic employs gestalt principles to group lines into regions that can be modified in a similar way as individual lines. Finally, the agent can consider the relationship between groups to evaluate the overall composition, such as balance. The agent doesn't have any pre-encoded drawing algorithms, per se. It only has the ability to direct its attention, perceive the user's lines, and manipulate and interact with those lines according to its perceptual logic. The program will be provided with some perceptual rules of gestalt grouping to inform perception how to group sensory input into larger gestalt wholes (i.e., principles of perceptual grouping: good continuity, closure, proximity, flow, etc.) that allow the system to build its own knowledge base through its experience collaborating with artists (Fig. 7.7).

7.4.3 Multiple Sets of Perceptual Logic

The argument we have built in this chapter contends that experts gradually develop perceptual logic that enables them to intelligently perceive their environment to navigate specific situations. When a creative expert attempts to accomplish their creation process on a creativity support tool, like a designer using a traditional CAD tool, they have to acquire a completely different set of perceptual logic relating to how to navigate the interface and accomplish tasks. Users have to alternate between these sets of perceptual logic when they interact with creativity support tools, which can take users out of the immersive and interactive flow that the enactive model of creativity proposes is critical for facilitating creativity. As a result, people often use CAD tools at late stages in the design process to finalize their design, instead of using them to facilitate creative thinking and exploration early in the design process. One overarching design principle of an enactive approach is to design interactions as conversations, where each party tries to understand and build meaning through negotiation and feedback over time. In a conversation, each person actively works to understand what was said and respond appropriately. This suggests that creativity support tools might develop a dynamic model of the user over time based on their interactions and behaviors such that we might understand what type of perceptual

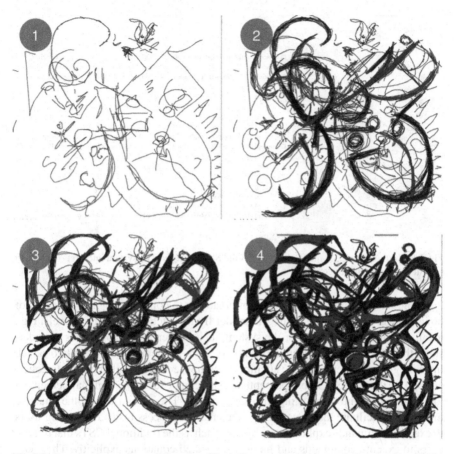

Fig. 7.7 Drawing Apprentice collaboration. User's lines are *black*; AI agent's lines are *blue* (Color figure online)

logic and creative strategy the user is currently employing and offer the right tools at the right time.

7.4.4 Solid Sketch

Solid Sketch is an example of a CST that utilizes the concepts we describe in the previous section. It is a sketch program for 3D model creation that constantly observes the user's sketch inputs and reacts in real time based on the context determined by the previous and surrounding sketches. The enactive model of creativity serves two roles in this prototype. One is to help the system understand the perceptual logic the user employs throughout their creative process. The other use is to facilitate natural interactions when designing the prototype. For the first purpose,

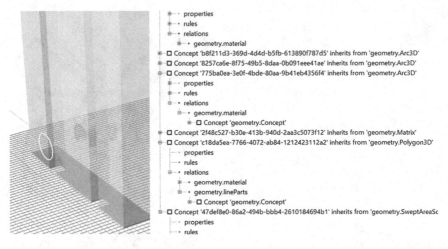

⊕—• properties
⊕—• rules
⊕—• relations
  ⊕—• geometry.material
⊕—☐ Concept 'b8f211d3-369d-4d4d-b5fb-613890f787d5' inherits from 'geometry.Arc3D'
⊕—☐ Concept '8257ca6e-8f75-49b5-8daa-0b091eee41ae' inherits from 'geometry.Arc3D'
⊖—☐ Concept '775ba0ea-3e0f-4bde-80aa-9b41eb4356f4' inherits from 'geometry.Arc3D'
  ⊕—• properties
  ⊕—• rules
  ⊖—• relations
    ⊖—• geometry.material
      ⊕—☐ Concept 'geometry.Concept'
⊕—☐ Concept '2f48c527-b30e-413b-940d-2aa3c5073f12' inherits from 'geometry.Matrix'
⊖—☐ Concept 'c18da5ea-7766-4072-ab84-1212423112a2' inherits from 'geometry.Polygon3D'
  ⌐—• properties
  ⌐—• rules
  ⊖—• relations
    ⊕—• geometry.material
    ⊖—• geometry.lineParts
      ⊕—☐ Concept 'geometry.Concept'
⊖—☐ Concept '47def8e0-86a2-494b-bbb4-2610184694b1' inherits from 'geometry.SweptAreaSc
  ⌐—• properties
  ⌐—• rules

Fig. 7.8 *Left*: A simple 3D model done with Solid Sketch. *Right*: The system interprets the human natural sketch into parametric information

the program uses the enactive model of creativity to construct cognitive models of how humans construct the entire 3D model from sketches at different levels, e.g., local, regional, and global. For the system, its local perceptual logic tries to understand the relationship between the geometry, such as the angle between two sketch lines. Regional perceptual logic attempts to compose nearby sketch lines into coherent part of the model. Global perceptual logic composes those regional perceptual logic groupings into a meaningful overall model. The second use of the enactive model is to facilitate the conversation like creation process instead of having users to execute commands explicitly one by one, such as the traditional CSTs that require users to execute commands and input complicated equations explicitly. The enactive agent in Solid Sketch sits in the background, perceives the user's actions, interprets his intentions, and leverages its understanding of the user's intention to help the user achieve their current goal. The final products after interacting with the system will include not only a 3D model but also a set of parametric rules that describe how the user created the model (Fig. 7.8).

7.5 Conclusions

Computational creativity has the potential to radically change what it means to interact with computers. However, in order to reach its full potential, the field needs a cognitive theory of creativity that accounts for the enactive nature of creativity, including improvisation, collaboration, and a tight feedback loop with the environment. In this chapter, we provided a brief summary of the current state of computational creativity and pointed out the shortcomings of the traditional information processing view of cognition. We argued that the new cognitive science paradigm of enaction provides a helpful way to reframe creativity and potentially solve some of the long-standing hard problems that both artificial intelligence and computational creativity face. The theory of enaction was used to describe creativity in design, music, and visual art to show its potential for generalizability and descriptive power. We also presented the enactive model of creativity that formalized the enaction theory in a computational model. Finally, we describe how the enactive model of creativity was helpful in designing two computer colleagues, one in the domain of visual art and the other in the domain of design. The primary design principle of the enactive model of creativity is to design interactions like a conversation where each party tries to make sense of contributions and respond appropriately given the history of interaction.

References

Adamson RE (1952) Functional fixedness as related to problem solving: a repetition of three experiments. J Exp Psychol 44(4):288–291

Arnheim R (1954) Art and visual perception. University of California Press, Oakland

Barsalou LW (1999) Perceptual symbol systems. Behav Brain Sci 22(04):637–660

Biles JA (2003) GenJam in perspective: a tentative taxonomy for GA music and art systems. Leonardo 36(1):43–45

Boden MA (2004) The creative mind: myths and mechanisms. Psychology Press, New York

Bono ED (1970) Lateral thinking: a textbook of creativity. Ward Lock Educational/El pensamiento lateral: manual de creatividad, Londres/Versión española

Candy L (1997) Computers and creativity support: knowledge, visualisation and collaboration. Knowl-Based Syst 10(1):3–13

Carroll EA, Latulipe C, Fung R, Terry M (2009) Creativity factor evaluation: towards a standardized survey metric for creativity support. In: Proceedings of the seventh ACM conference on creativity and cognition. ACM, New York, pp 127–136

Colton S, Wiggins GA (2012) Computational creativity: the final frontier? In: Proceedings of European conference on artificial intelligence, pp 21–26

Colton S, Goodwin J, Veale T (2012) Full face poetry generation. In: Proceedings of the third international conference on computational creativity. International Conference on Computational Creativity, pp 95–102

Csikszentmihalyi M (1997) Flow and the psychology of discovery and invention. HarperPerennial, New York

Davis N, Li B, O'Neill B, Riedl M, Nitsche M (2011) Distributed creative cognition in digital filmmaking. In: Proceedings of the 8th ACM conference on creativity and cognition. ACM, New York, pp 207–216

Davis N, Popova Y, Sysoev I, Hsiao CP, Zhang D, Magerko B (2014) Building artistic computer colleagues with an enactive model of creativity. In: Proceedings of the fifth international conference on computational creativity. The International Association for Computational Creativity, pp 38–45

De Jaegher H (2009) Social understanding through direct perception? Yes, by interacting. Conscious Cogn 18(2):535–542

Dixon D, Prasad M, Hammond T (2010) iCanDraw: using sketch recognition and corrective feedback to assist a user in drawing human faces. In: Proceedings of the SIGCHI conference on human factors in computing systems. ACM, New York, pp 897–906

Engel AK (2010) Directive minds: how dynamics shapes cognition. In: Enaction: towards a new paradigm for cognitive science. MIT Press, Cambridge, MA, pp 219–243

Gabora L (2010) Revenge of the "neurds": characterizing creative thought in terms of the structure and dynamics of memory. Creat Res J 22(1):1–13

Gaspar JM, McDonald JJ (2014) Suppression of salient objects prevents distraction in visual search. J Neurosci 34(16):5658–5666

Gibson JJ (1979) The ecological approach to visual perception. Lawrence Erlbaum Associates, Hillsdale

Glenberg AM (1997) What memory is for: creating meaning in the service of action. Behav Brain Sci 20(01):41–50

Goldschmidt G (1991) The dialectics of sketching. Creat Res J 4(2):123–143

Guilford JP (1970) Creativity: retrospect and prospect*. J Creat Behav 4(3):149–168

Havelange V (2010) The ontological constitution of cognition and the epistemological constitution of cognitive science: phenomenology, enaction and technology. In: Enaction: towards a new paradigm for cognitive science. MIT Press, Cambridge, MA, pp 335–360

Hewett T, Czerwinski M, Terry M, Nunamaker J, Candy L, Kules B, Sylvan E (2005) Creativity support tool evaluation methods and metrics. Creativity Support Tools, 10–24

Hodhod R, Piplica A, Magerko B (2012) A formal architecture of shared mental models for computational improvisational agents. In: Intelligent virtual agents. Springer, Berlin/Heidelberg, pp 440–446

Hoffman G, Weinberg G (2010) Shimon: an interactive improvisational robotic marimba player. In: CHI'10 extended abstracts on human factors in computing systems. ACM, New York, pp 3097–3102

Hutchins E (1995) Cognition in the wild. The MIT Press, Cambridge, MA

Lee YJ, Zitnick CL, Cohen MF (2011) ShadowDraw: real-time user guidance for freehand drawing. ACM Trans Graph 30(4):27:1–27:10. doi:10.1145/2010324.1964922

Lubart T (2005) How can computers be partners in the creative process: classification and commentary on the special issue. Int J Hum Comput Stud 63(4):365–369

Mace MA, Ward T (2002) Modeling the creative process: a grounded theory analysis of creativity in the domain of art making. Creat Res J 14(2):179–192

Mamykina L, Candy L, Edmonds E (2002) Collaborative creativity. Commun ACM 45(10):96–99

McCorduck P (1991) Aaron's code. WH Freeman & Co., New York

Nakakoji K (2006) Meanings of tools, support, and uses for creative design processes. In: International design research symposium '06, Seoul

Nersessian N (2008) Creating scientific concepts. MIT Press, Cambridge, MA

Newell A, Shaw JC, Simon HA (1959) The processes of creative thinking. Rand Corporation, Santa Monica

Noë A (2004) Action in perception. MIT Press, Cambridge, MA

Norman DA (1999) Affordance, conventions, and design. Interactions 6(3):38–43

Rawlinson JG (1981) Creative thinking and brainstorming. Gower, Farnborough

Schön DA (1992) Designing as reflective conversation with the materials of a design situation. Knowl-Based Syst 5(1):3–14

Shneiderman B (2002) Creativity support tools. Commun ACM 45(10):116–120

Shneiderman B (2007) Creativity support tools: accelerating discovery and innovation. Commun ACM 50(12):20–32. doi:10.1145/1323688.1323689

Shneiderman B, Fischer G, Czerwinski M, Resnick M, Myers B, Candy L, Terry M (2006) Creativity support tools: report from a US National Science Foundation sponsored workshop. Int J Hum Comput Interact 20(2):61–77

Smith SM, Ward TB, Finke RA (eds) (1995) The creative cognition approach. MIT Press, Cambridge, MA

Stewart JR, Gapenne O, Di Paolo EA (eds) (2010) Enaction: toward a new paradigm for cognitive science. MIT Press, Cambridge, MA

Suchman L (1986) Plans and situated actions. Cambridge University, New York

Suwa M, Tversky B (1997) What do architects and students perceive in their design sketches? A protocol analysis. Des Stud 18(4):385–403

Varela FJ, Rosch E, Thompson E (1991) The embodied mind: cognitive science and human experience. MIT Press, Cambridge, MA
Veale T, Hao Y (2008) A fluid knowledge representation for understanding and generating creative metaphors. In: Proceedings of the 22nd international conference on computational linguistics, vol 1. Association for Computational Linguistics, Stroudsburg, PA, pp 945–952
Yokochi S, Okada T (2005) Creative cognitive process of art making: a field study of a traditional Chinese ink painter. Creat Res J 17(2–3):241–255
Zook A, Magerko B, Riedl M (2011) Formally modeling pretend object play. In: Proceedings of the 8th ACM conference on creativity and cognition. ACM, New York, pp 147–156

Chapter 8
Creative Collaboration in Young Digital Communities

Pilar Lacasa, María Ruth García-Pernía, and Sara Cortés

8.1 Introduction

We recently attended several video game fairs in different European cities. Some researchers, such as Wortley (2013), refer to these contexts as a starting point for exploring creativity and innovation. These fairs are quite similar to film festivals, even if there are no real actors or celebrities there. Instead, we find large screens, consoles, new forms of entertainment, and the players (the visitors to the fair) take precedence. While walking around the different stands, they don't just observe; they play and discover the novelties created by the industry of these cultural objects. Wandering around people of all ages, families, and groups of friends (more boys than girls), the thought came to us that we are *witnessing the result of innovation, the ability to create in contemporary society.*

One cannot help but get the impression that we are experiencing something new, a different type of culture where a new form of entertainment is shared. While we were looking at the large posters advertising games and observing people while they played, we thought that creation has now become a collective activity. The great creators of classical art we learned about at school were individuals. They were individually named together with their masterpieces, for example, Michelangelo's David or Picasso's Guernica. *Video games are quite different.* In the case of video games, the environment from which specific distributors and freelance designers have emerged or the saga they have participated in is of greater importance. When people mention *The Sims,* fans are well aware, for instance, that the distributor is Electronic Arts and that its designer came from Will Wright's team. We are therefore faced with a different form of creation here.

P. Lacasa (✉) • M.R. García-Pernía • S. Cortés
Department of Philology, Communication and Information,
University of Alcalá, Madrid, Spain
e-mail: p.lacasa@uah.es; mruth.garcia@uah.es; sara.cortesg@uah.es

© Springer-Verlag London 2015   135
N. Zagalo, P. Branco (eds.), *Creativity in the Digital Age,*
Springer Series on Cultural Computing, DOI 10.1007/978-1-4471-6681-8_8

We could reflect on who created the products which have made these new popular cultural expressions possible, but there is no one answer or single factor involved. One should mention the technology behind them, the interdisciplinary team sometimes working for years toward the launch of a new game, the financing involved in presenting the product to the player, and, undoubtedly, the people who actively play and respond to it. Creative processes are embodied within video games, just like cinema, novels, or architecture. They are the result of their creator's application, but, as educators, we are convinced that interacting with them could foster the development of such creativity.

Summing up, *old and new media require collective creation processes* according to different contexts and work processes. In this research, creation is inseparable from a teenage community while creating video games as part of an after-school program. The goal of this chapter is to analyze the creative processes present in a community of teenagers when they design games and participate in a collective blog at school and several interviews in which they express their reflections during the process.

The specific objectives are the following:

1. To analyze the game creation processes taking place in the classroom and to define dialogical contexts favoring intersubjectivity and the creative process
2. To explore the creative process from the creators' perspective in a system defined by the roles assumed by the participants in the game creation process
3. To propose *educational strategies supporting the acquisition of creative ways of thinking and acting* when video games are considered as cultural tools present in the classroom

8.2 Theoretical Framework

This chapter focuses on the cultural practices of video game creation as involving new media, explored from the general frame of convergent culture. Creation is understood as *a cultural, collective, and historically situated process in which relationships are established between different conceptual elements that become meaningful in the social practices of the community* (John-Steiner 1985/1997, 2000). Sociocultural psychology, classic or contemporary, serves as a starting point. Figure 8.1 includes a synthesis of these theoretical models and their main concepts, as well as some possible relationships between them.

We understand creativity from the models provided by two classical authors (Bakhtin and Vygotsky) and others who more recently worked on their legacy. For Bakhtin, culture is immersed in intersubjective and discursive processes. Vygotsky, however, approaches creativity from emotions and thinks of community settings interpreted from the concept of ZPD (zone of proximal development). In the following pages we will delve into these models.

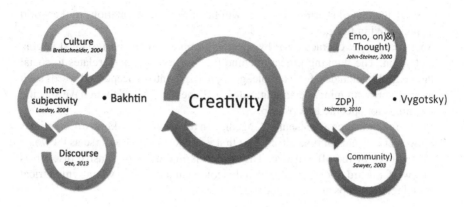

Fig. 8.1 Theoretical models

8.2.1   Dialogue, Creation, and Intersubjectivity

Bakhtin's words help us to understand how the creative dialogue takes place in the classroom (Brettschneider 2004). In a very general sense, creative comprehension does not become exhausted into itself:

> Creative understanding does not renounce itself, its own place in time, its own culture; and it forgets nothing. In order to understand, it is immensely important for the person who understands to be **located outside** the object of his or her creative understanding – in time, in space, in culture. (Bakhtin et al. 1986, p. 7)

In order to understand the integrity of a cultural production, rather than merely focusing on it as the author himself understood it, we should go further. True understanding is active and creative by nature. In that sense, a process of co-creativity of those who understand is being generated, and this is true whatever is the basis of our "outsideness," be it personal, spatial, temporal, national, or otherwise.

It is in this framework where we can place the notion of intersubjectivity, supporting creative processes. It is merged into cooperation considering that it is necessary to share goals and values. This collaboration needs to be understood as a process interwoven in history and culture where creative individuals develop.

According to this model, Landay (2004) identifies four principles of Bakhtinian theory which are a starting point to create educational environments favoring creativity. They are the following:

- Heteroglossia. The meaning of any utterance is never fixed; it differs in rich and complex ways according to the context and conditions in which it is used. The same words can have different meanings and create difficulties that must be overcome when designing a game collectively.
- Dialogue, which merges into the social world. Dialogism is embedded in speaking subjects. Meanings need to be shared, and when they are they create intersubjective communication contexts. Considering dialogues when the game is

created, the fact of sharing meanings will favor new representations of the world as presented in the game.

- Social language, characterized by specific group activities, professional jargon, and so on. The thinking process behind the creation of games relates to social language that includes, for example, going in depth into concepts and words such as story, programming, designing, rules, and enemies. All of them have specific meanings for specific groups of people.
- Power relationships as present in language. In that context, Bakhtin differentiates between two kinds of discourses. The first is authoritative discourse as the voice of tradition, of the official line. The second is internally persuasive discourses that work toward a concrete verbal and ideological unification when symmetrical social relationships are preponderant.

Through discourse analysis, we will examine how language contributes to favor certain processes of creativity.

8.2.2   Emotion, Thinking, and Creative Collaboration

Vygotsky's work on creativity complements this perspective and helps to clarify how the subject must go out of himself to create. Let's see how creators should do this in the real world to go beyond pure formal abstraction:

> From our point of view, imagination is a transforming, creative activity directed from the
> * concrete toward a new concrete. The movement itself from a given concrete toward a created concrete, the feasibility of creative construction is possible only with the help of abstraction. Thus, the abstract enters as a requisite constituent into the activity of imagination, but is not the center of this activity. The movement from the concrete through the abstract to the construction of a new concrete image is the path that imagination describes during the transitional age. (Vygotsky 1998, p. 162)

From that theoretical framework, creativity is understood as *a process in which the abstract and the concrete merge*. Also, emotion and cognition merge and need to be considered as involved in specific processes:

> Specifically the secrecy of the fantasy indicates that it is closely connected with internal desires, inventiveness, drives, and emotions of the personality and begins to serve this whole aspect of the adolescent's life. In this respect, the connection between fantasy and emotion is extremely significant. (Vygotsky 1998, p. 164)

From this point of view, Vygotsky proposes the idea of *zone of proximal development (ZPD)* to explain the relationships between development and learning:

> What we call the Zone of Proximal Development (…) is the distance between the actual developmental level as determined by independent problem solving, and the level of potential development as determined through problem solving under guidance or in collaboration with more capable peers. (Vygotsky 1978/1986, p. 86)

Following these Vygotskian ideas, Holzman (2010) relates ZPD and creativity. He refers not to an attribute of individuals but to social units that are present in everyday life creative processes. From this perspective, *development is the practice of becoming, where people shape and reshape* their relationships with themselves, with each other, and with the material and psychological tools and objects of their world.

By approaching social relationships as a nuclear process of creativity, John-Steiner (2000) faces the topic treating "self" and "community" as two poles in a form of dialectical interaction, even bearing in mind that a perfect synthesis between both poles is not always possible. Her approach is concerned with *creative collaboration* and with the principle that *humans come into being and mature in relation to others*. Moreover, in those relationships the partners may develop previously unknown aspects of themselves through *joint participation*.

8.3 Methodology

In this chapter, an ethnographic perspective is assumed and understood as a situated activity that places the researcher in specific communities that will be understood by specific processes of building meaning (Denzin and Lincoln 2011; Gee 2014; Tsui 2014; Hamera 2011). The validity of this approach relies on detailed descriptions of cases to explain how people build the meaning of their activities in specific socio-cultural contexts. We observe people's practices in specific environments, in this case the classroom (Lacasa 2013; Lacasa et al. 2009, 2013). In this chapter, we focus on creativity as a social and cultural phenomenon.

8.3.1 The Project, Contexts, and Participants

The project was carried out at a secondary education school during the 2012–2013 school year. The context is a private school[1] next to the university, where the research team worked for 3 years introducing video games as educational tools in the classroom.

A group of 20 students, 14 girls and 6 boys aged 14–16, participated in a workshop during 14 sessions (each 1 h and a half long). They worked in a large group and five small ones. Each student played a different role in the smaller groups, all of them oriented to reach specific goals that focused on the game's main elements: team director, designer, art director, sound director, and programmer. To define their roles, we considered Mitchell's (2012) proposal when he describes the different functions associated with work situations in relation to the creation of video games. The teacher and the interdisciplinary research team (consisting of an educational psychologist and a specialist in communication and computing) also took part in the experience. All of them planned and monitored the workshop.

---

[1] In Spain, public schools are funded by the government and private schools are not.

In this chapter, we focus on one of the groups (made up by three girls and two boys) as a unit of analysis. Each of them played a different role in the creative process. From a theoretical and methodological approach, the reason for this decision is related to the ethnographic perspective guiding this research. Both the large group and each of the five small groups became independent units of analysis related to each other but maintained some degree of autonomy. In the small groups, which make sense in the overall context of a large group, activities are considered from a holistic point of view. Moreover, we must take into account that the practices and meaning change over time. However, while all groups participated in similar activities, only the selected group had the opportunity to attend an interview on a local radio station to present the experience. That happened a month after the workshop ended. This gave the students the opportunity to reflect and synthesize collectively the meaning attributed to its activity and faced them with questions coming from both the broadcaster and a professional video game critic who also participated in the interview.

8.3.2 The Data

The corpus of data consists of video- and audio-recorded sessions, the photographs taken during the most relevant moments of the workshop, and the video games created by the students; moreover, the researchers elaborated an interpretative summary of the sessions, and we carried out interviews to the groups. Four focus-group interviews were carried out (one per team) at the end of the workshop. A final interview, as previously mentioned, took place at the local radio station in which the participants were the students in the group that will be examined in this chapter. Moreover, the whole class participated in a Weblog, presenting personal collective and personal reflections. All this allowed for different interpretations of the same activities. The data collected appear in Table 8.1.

Table 8.1 allows us to see the data collected throughout the workshop and, more specifically, those corresponding to the group whose activities will be analyzed in this chapter (group 2). All data have been combined following an interpretative approach, which allows us to examine both practices and mental representations as present in conversations.

8.3.3 Data Analysis

We adopted Gumperz's (1981) concept of ethnography. This is defined as a "thick description," including participant observation, interviews, mapping and charting, interaction analysis, study of historical records, and current public documents. It is assumed that ethnography is much more than a set of methods or techniques; it is understood as a way of approaching culture to understand people's practices in

Table 8.1 Data collected across the session during the workshop

Tools for collecting data	Total	Group 2
Video recording (14 sessions)	39:39:52	08:39:25
Audio recording	33:17:45	09:03:27
Group interviews	05:26:33	01:25:44
Photographs	1,290	268
Radio interview[a]		00:32:14
Researchers' summaries	11	1
Student materials		
Written material (texts)	10	22
Blog	54	12
Power point	3	1
Drawings	125	31
Sound files	50	8
Video games (3 trailers)	00:03:35	00:01:26
Researchers' materials		
Videos	01:13:53	
Power point presentations	7	
Texts	25	6

[a]Radio https://www.facebook.com/JessWePlay/info
http://www.ivoox.com/podcast-podcast-jess-we-play_sq_f133474_1.html (oj no es la correcta)

specific communities. Moreover, other authors (Gee 2010; Green and Wallat 1981) provide the rationale for conducting discourse analysis combined with an ethnographic approach. We looked for the flow of the classroom conversations to identify thematic units of varying length, to produce structural maps, and to identify insights related to people's ideas, explanations, and beliefs.

The analysis is considered as a circular process beginning during fieldwork (Holstein and Gabrium 2011). In this chapter, we analyze the process followed in the workshop to understand the process itself and not only the final product of the video game design activity (Pulsipher 2012b). From a discourse analysis perspective (Gee 2010), the enquiry was carried out with Transana software (2.5.3) in order to understand the adolescents' experiences in the context in which they occurred. The recordings of each session were segmented and transcribed in order to analyze the conversations to understand the meaning that this experience had for teenagers and researchers.

8.4 The Creative Process in the Classroom

Results are presented through an analysis of the workshop sessions, analyzing the conversations in small and large groups. In addition to this, other materials were considered to have the general contexts of these conversations. Through this analysis, we can see how students become aware of their creative processes and how that awareness is generated progressively throughout the sessions we'll present.

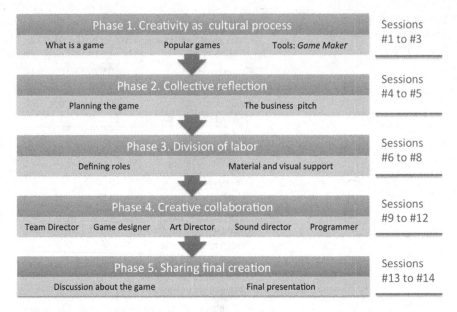

Fig. 8.2 Workshop context: phases and sessions

Figure 8.2 presents the main moments of the workshop; this is the result of the researchers' interpretation, and it serves as the general framework for the analysis of the creative process in one of the small groups participating there.

8.4.1 Phase 1. Creativity as a Cultural Process

This phase took place over three sessions, serving as an introduction and inviting the students to reflect on three main concepts. The brain storming generated awareness that video games are cultural tools, so it was uplifting to consider them as the starting point of the game creation. Also, to create a video game, some material elements support creative activity. At that moment Game Maker was considered as the software to develop the game.

8.4.1.1 Approaching the Game

A discussion on existing games in session 1 allowed to define the starting point. Guitar Hero, Space Invaders, Portal, SimCity, Pokemon, God of War, Final Fantasy VII, Prince of Persia, Dead Space, and Angry Birds were mentioned as those preferred by teenagers. All of them are popular and almost mythical games. Following Russ and Fiorelli (2010), it could be said that the creative process, contextualized in this scenario, implies that improvisation is complemented by a collective inspiration which focuses on certain cultural products. This is the theoretical framework to interpret the adolescents' conversations with the researcher.

Fragment 1. Analyzing commercial video games
Session 2. 2012 12 13
Researcher: Have you understood <u>why we are doing this exercise</u>? Student: Yes, to get an idea so that we can design our own, to get some inspiration. Researcher: To be inspired, that's the main idea. So today we will learn what games are (…). And I think we will learn to be critical, to look at games differently.

The researcher tried to promote the awareness that it is possible to create from something but, mainly, that creating may require a prior analysis of what others have created. Vera John-Steiner (2000) has referred to this process of inspiration that goes beyond the individual when it comes to artistic inspiration. The dialogue shows, moreover, that video games can be analyzed from different perspectives and the students express it clearly.

Fragment 2. Video games. Introduction to the workshop
Blog. 2012 12 19
We are Evany and Mar; we are in 9th grade in high school. We look forward to starting to develop our own game. <u>We have been exploring other games, and we have learned to look at them from new perspectives</u>. We hope to have more knowledge for the project in the coming sessions. Greetings!

8.4.1.2   What Is a Game for You?

After initial discussions, students reflect and write a text individually about the features that define games and video games. Let's consider, for example, the definition provided by the art director in the group being analyzed.

Fragment 3. What is a game?
Session 3. 2012 12 20
<u>What is a game?</u>
"A game <u>is an object or a set of conditions</u> defined in a given situation in order <u>to have fun and some time for entertainment</u>. Games can also be educational, that is, we can learn by playing." <u>What is a video game for you?</u> "To me, a game is <u>a kind of electronic game</u>. It is projected on a screen and you have a series of <u>commands or controls</u> that can be used to modify what appears on the screen. Video games, in my opinion, are the type of games to which teenagers dedicate most of the time."

Focusing on the representation that the student has about the game, we noticed that she refers to it as a *set of conditions*, which could be the rules or mechanics. In addition to this, she associated it with entertainment contexts. It is clear that, in her opinion, video games are not present in formal learning environments; they are often missing in schools. From this perspective, Holzman (2010) refers to the fact that "in nearly all schools the elements of ZPD-creating, freedom from knowing, creative imitation, and completion are absent" (p. 36), hence the motivation surely felt by students entering the game in formal learning contexts.

8.4.1.3 Tools and Creative Processes: Specific Software for Game Design

The use of specific instruments to create is relevant in the context of sociocultural psychology. In this case, one of them was the software, Game Maker. From this perspective, for example, Connery (2010) states that knowledge and creation are not directly internalized processes but through the use of instruments, not just the language but also the physical tools and materials. Managing this tool required interdisciplinary work between the different members of each group, i. e., scheduling the game involves creating a scenario, integrating the characters, defining a pattern of sounds, developing game options, and so on. The teacher and the student programmer were aware of it, and that's how it was described in an interview on a local radio station maintained once we finished the workshop.

Fragment 4. The meaning of software
Radio interview. 2013 05 25

Programmer: In general, I think none of the programmers of the four groups had any idea of programming.

Radio broadcaster: No idea? Did you start from scratch?

Programmer: Well, I for one did not know that the program existed.

Radio broadcaster: What program did you use?

Programmer: Game Maker

Radio broadcaster: So is it a program designed [asking the teacher] to make video games?

Teacher: Yes, it is a program that gives you the basics and, because it is otherwise (…) clear, it gives you ideas on how to establish forces, vectors, and so on. It is quite complicated. But through the program they can see what happens when a force is applied, something that they already know from their physics and chemistry lessons. That is, something like Newton's apple falling down [laughing]. They see it in their language, that is, the language of video games."

We will emphasize the importance given to the software by the students, which will allow them to build the game. The software presents another kind of language that the students must learn to communicate in a digital society. The teacher is concerned about how to apply school knowledge to everyday life.

8.4.2   Phase 2. Collective Reflection: Anticipating the Final Product

The dialogue among team members while planning the game helps to achieve awareness of the game's elements, anticipating the final product. This activity can be interpreted from the reflections of Moran and John-Steiner (2003) when they consider that creative thought starts as an imaginary sense of how things must be, which is expressed in an ongoing dialectic between the general categories of the culture and the specific materials and emotional experiences which with the individual works. These authors mention how Vygotsky (1986) emphasizes verbalization processes in creative thinking: *"There is a continuing interaction between generative thought, which is often condensed, fluctuating, and unstable and communicated thought, which is expanded and organized for maximum impact"* (Moran and John-Steiner 2003, p. 75).

The results of the reflections, focusing on the product planning that they would create, were expressed in a collective text, including the fundamentals of the game. The text was written in a session dedicated to planning a "business pitch" oriented to present the game model in which they were interested.

Fragment 5, session 4. Planning the pitch. Designer's text
Session 4. 2013 01 10
Synthesis
The game presents a parent who realizes his family has been infected by a virus passed on by his zombie mother-in-law.
Each floor is a level, and he will find specific challenges in every room and will have to face his infected family.
If he manages to get through all floors, he will reach the attic, where he will have to fight his mother-in-law, who will throw croquettes at him. If he beats her, he will win the game. If not, he must start all over.
Goal
The goal is to beat the mother-in-law, which cannot be done without killing the rest of the family so as not to be infected by the virus.
Apart from escaping death, he needs to be careful not to come in contact with bacteria in the house, because if he did, he would be infected and die a slow death unless he finds a new life in one of the bonus boxes.
Some mechanics
Five limited lives and limited time. Bacteria that will be eating you alive if infected unless an antidote is found in a bonus box. If this is not the case, the game will come to an end.

In this game's description, the narrative dimension and the rules orienting the player's activity are differentiated from player activity (Juul 2005). Both dimensions are intertwined. Looking at the story, the physical context is observed; it is defined by a multistory house around which the characters wander. They may be infected with the virus created by the mother-in-law, on the top floor. The goal, achieved by following the rules, is clear: to kill the mother-in-law without coming in contact with the rest of the characters. The mechanics of the game are also presented by proposing a limit on the characters' lives and the antidotes to prevent infection. Fantasy and imagination are present in the creative process (Vygotsky 1998, p. 164).

8.4.3   Phase 3. Specific Roles in the Creative Process

As indicated, this phase of the workshops focuses on the organization of work and the distribution of the roles that each of the members of the group will play in creating the game. Among them there will be collaborative processes. In these activities, students are guided by the research team, more specifically by the computer specialists. They provide two clear strategies. The first one relates to the distribution of roles. The second will provide techniques for work organization.

8.4.3.1   Division of Labor

Looking at Fig. 8.3, we can see that there is a very clear division of labor. If we apply Vera John-Steiner's (2000) contributions, it could be defined as complementary collaboration. In this case, it is not necessary for all people to be involved in the

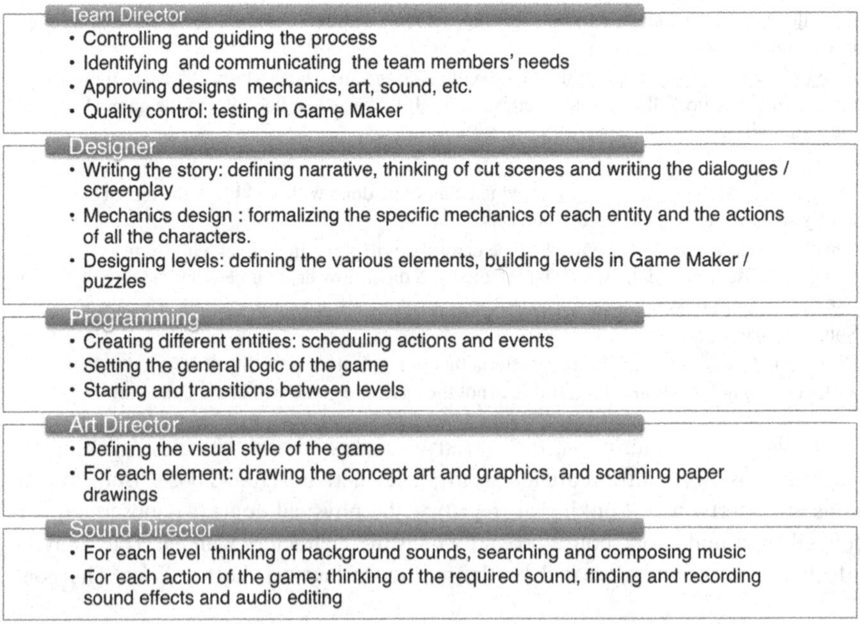

Team Director
- Controlling and guiding the process
- Identifying and communicating the team members' needs
- Approving designs mechanics, art, sound, etc.
- Quality control: testing in Game Maker

Designer
- Writing the story: defining narrative, thinking of cut scenes and writing the dialogues / screenplay
- Mechanics design : formalizing the specific mechanics of each entity and the actions of all the characters.
- Designing levels: defining the various elements, building levels in Game Maker / puzzles

Programming
- Creating different entities: scheduling actions and events
- Setting the general logic of the game
- Starting and transitions between levels

Art Director
- Defining the visual style of the game
- For each element: drawing the concept art and graphics, and scanning paper drawings

Sound Director
- For each level thinking of background sounds, searching and composing music
- For each action of the game: thinking of the required sound, finding and recording sound effects and audio editing

Fig. 8.3 The division of labor. Tasks assigned to each of the team members

creative process of the final production. Tasks can be segmented, and each sub-task must be done at the right time. Delays will cause a problem to the rest of the group. According to John-Steiner, there is another way of working, where each member of the group is present in all tasks. This way of acting leads to a transformation of the participants' global vision of the creative process. The latter is defined as "integrative collaboration." They are not mutually exclusive but complementary; this is the main reason why we mentioned both of them.

8.4.3.2 Material and Visual Support

Having described and distributed all roles, it was necessary to manage the setup. The students had not suggested any planning process over time. Therefore, the researchers proposed a dynamic strategy based on a division of tasks supported by the generation of different game elements. The strategy will allow them to go forward together and organize visually several tasks, displayed using Post-its and cards. Let's see how the researchers present their proposal for work organization.

Fragment 6. Work organization: The researchers' proposal
Session 6. 2013 01 24
Researcher:
We were thinking about <u>the process you can follow to organize all the work</u> you need to do…
The process we are proposing is quite visual; it employs cards and Post-its, okay?
Then, to organize the group, we will take a giant card and place stickers and move from side to side…
Now I'll tell you roughly, and then I will present an example of what I'm saying.
So the first thing for what it is used is to <u>identify all the elements</u> that you will see in the game.
I think we are being quite insistent on this idea all the time…
Later on this will be useful for planning, because each of these elements will require some work; you will need some graphics, sound, programming, planning…
And then <u>each of those elements, which requires work, will have to be passed from hand to hand.</u>
The first step might be to design, then draw graphs, and then look at the sound and audio, and finally the developer will have to gather everything in the process…
You have to distribute the elements of the game between you.
So <u>how do we identify the elements of the game?</u>
Well, with stickers, with Post-its. What we do when we start organizing the team…
What you will do at first is ask: What are the game's entities? And you will do one Post-it for each of them.

Reading the text in detail, we notice that the researcher has structured his speech stopping at the steps students must follow in their activity. Figure 8.4 shows the implementation of the strategy by the students in one of the sessions during the workshop.

In this context, the role of the team director is especially relevant, as she realized herself in the final interview on the local radio station.

Fig. 8.4 Planning tools in session 8. 2013 02 14

Fragment 7. Task coordination
Radio interview. 2013 05 25
Radio broadcaster: Are you the boss?
Team Manager: Yeah, well, <u>we are a good group</u>, but when there are many people, <u>it is more difficult to pay attention</u> and a firm hand is needed.
Radio broadcaster: But basically you function well as a group, right?
Team Manager: Yes, more or less. At first we used a system we were taught to organize the work consisting in a large card. I put the names of all the tasks for each of them, for example, the design of the main character, on the one hand, and then placed it in a column to organize everything and put it all together…

Students need to coordinate their work. Their ideas intersect, and the decision-making process is collective, although each of them performs their own work. According to John-Steiner (2000), collaboration involves a process of appropriation, in the sense of taking something that belongs to others to rebuild it together.

8.4.4 Phase 4. Creative Collaboration

The differences in the working mode do not impede shared creativity. Several authors reported distributions of collaborative work in creating video games when exploring specific contexts in companies, semiprofessional, or amateur teams (Mitchell 2012; Pulsipher 2012b; 2013, July). Over four workshop sessions, the team members performed their task relatively independently and integrated it all in a game programmed with Game Maker. The students explained it later on, during the interview, and this allowed us to understand what their roles were and how each

Fig. 8.5 Student interpretations of their own creative roles when designing the game

of them interpreted his/her work. A synthesis of the content of this conversation appears in Fig. 8.5.

The previous fragment presented the team director's explanations about her own role. Her main ideas, when she answered the questions of the radio broadcaster, are included in the conversation map: first, her role as group coordinator; second, how she distributed the tasks in order to create the final product; third, adopting the practices of brands and companies where she helped the team to organize a business pitch to present the project in session 5 and the final product on session 14. We will now focus on how they approached and interpreted the work of the rest of the team. To understand their roles, the following paragraphs will include both the video game elements as proposed by each of the team members and the student's explanation when replying to the radio broadcaster in the final interview. The process of creating the game would not have been possible without the cooperation that took place between them, always acting in a complementary way.

8.4.4.1   The Game Designer's Role

The designer had two tasks. She had to write the script for the game and also to integrate its rules into the story in order to guide the player's activities. Figure 8.6 is a summary of the chapter prepared for delivery to the programmer as an example of the game mechanics.

It's very clear how important game mechanics are for her. They focus on the confrontation between enemies. To achieve this, the hero must find the antidote in the bonus boxes. How the students interpreted her work is presented in the following fragment.

GAMEPLAY (MECHANICS 1)

In each room there are two enemies protecting the antidote. If a bullet or something launched by the enemy, reaches the protagonist he will become slowly infected, so he will have to be quick to get the antidote, which will be in a bonus box.

Once he has the antidote he will heal.

BONUS BOX DETAILS. They are protected by the corresponding enemy.

IMPORTANT! If there is more than one box (which would be normal) in the room ANTIDOTE WILL ONLY BE IN ONE OF THEM. In the other, there may be:

- Nothing
- A request for help to the grandparents
- A life
- Death (Game Over.)
- An extra enemy

As ihe walks, the protagonist will be able to collect coins (Like Mario Bros)

Fig. 8.6 Creating the game mechanics

Fragment 8. The designer's role
Local radio interview. 2013 05 25

Radio broadcaster: You're the designer, right? Why did you choose this plot?

Designer: Let's see. First, we wanted something different because I think there are many video games about families infected by zombies, and here we have a murderous mother-in-law infecting the whole family.

Radio broadcaster: Is there something like that in the market?

Designer: Yes, we were also watching different games, and the one we liked the most has action and zombies and such. Then I wanted to create an environment slightly recreating daily life. The mother-in-law idea infecting the whole family was oriented to having a more attractive game.

Radio broadcaster: That's fine, fine, and also the difference in your game (…). But you do something more constructive than to cure the zombies, which I think is the goal, right?

Designer: Yes, because killing the entire family was going to be a little (…) then (…) they have to find the antidote in the house and avoid those already infected.

Here, we can see that the game designer has two messages. First, the team wanted to be present in game markets, so they looked for something new that didn't exist and considered ordinary people. Anticipating the final product plays an important role from the beginning (Sawyer 2003). Second, she focuses on the game mechanics considering antidotes that will save those who have been infected. As she wrote in her proposal for the programmer, she was inspired by other games, for example, Mario Bros. Again, the presence of culture is undeniable; the designer not only integrates the work of their peers to be compatible with her own but also a cultural product on the market (Connery 2010).

8.4.4.2   The Art Director

Let's now consider the contributions of the art director, as she explained in the radio interview.

Fragment 9. Collective art: art uninspired and freehand
Local radio interview. 2013 05 25
Radio broadcaster: (…) what about the art director? Because I think it's you who were in charge of how the game looks like.
Art director: Yeah, more or less.
Art director: Well, all together, a little bit.
Radio broadcaster: Why did you choose this look for the game? It reminded me a little of some Japanese drawings.
(…)
Art director: No, the truth is that I started at home picking up a piece of paper and starting to draw with a set square, compass…. I didn't look at any other drawings for inspiration.

This student brings us two messages showing the potential importance in the game production process of both individual and collective creation (John-Steiner 1985/1997). First, the student recognizes that there is some collective work involved; perhaps, she refers to the ideas that helped her to generate her drawings from the group dialogues with peers or to the story they had previously built together. On the other hand, she refers to the result of her own creation, the product to be integrated into the whole game. Interestingly, according to her words, she was not inspired by other artworks; she just mentions the tools she was using. Figure 8.7 includes a sample of her characters as they were integrated in the overall context of the game.

8.4.4.3   The Sound Director

We will now see the sound director's interpretation. He also refers to creative activity in an individual and collective context (Sawyer 2010).

Fragment 10. Downloading and editing sound
Local radio interview. 2013 05 25
Audio manager: Well, I had the task of adding music in the background….
Radio broadcaster: Yes, did you add music?
Audio manager: I had to get into a Web page, obviously, to download sounds without copyright.
Radio broadcaster: Very good.

Audio manager: Editing them was the most difficult task, and after editing I added it to the game.
(…)
Radio broadcaster: Which style did you finally choose? Terror or tension? Or you added something different to have an intense break?
Audio manager: I used mainly two sounds, I added one of tension, and… I don't know how to say that… a sound that rises to create a special environment.

His task was to accompany the player with a music background when playing. He feels limited by copyright. He didn't compose the music. He downloaded and edited it. He chose the sound style according to the game, what he felt most appropriate, and then he combined sounds and controlled their intensity.

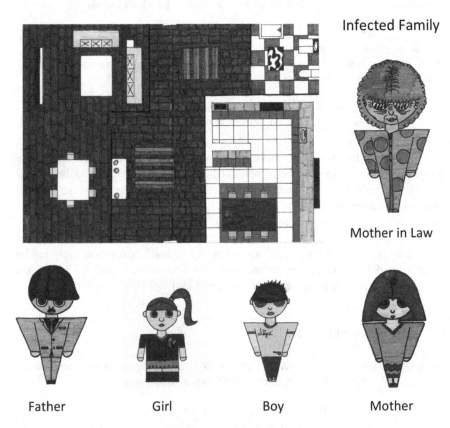

Fig. 8.7 Graphical representation and the game environment

8.4.4.4 The Programmer

Finally, the role of programmer is related to the integration of the previous creations in the game system. Although supported by the Game Maker software, he tells us that sometimes his work was not easy. The program imposes its limits, even if not all team members are fully aware of this fact.

Fragment 11. The programmer's perspective
Local radio interview. 2013 05 25
Programmer: It is a program that gives you the option of including codes, as you said, but if you don't know about programming, it gives you the main parts. For example, you can include a picture and it makes a graphic, as you said before, and you can create an object all together with that picture.   (…)   Game reviewer: So let's say you are going to have meetings with the members of your team, right? A meeting with the sound person, another meeting with the art director?   Programmer: Right, because, for example, Verónica (game designer) kept coming over, and she was always telling me, "take that" and "do that"! And it was difficult…   Radio broadcaster: Writers! (…) They give a lot of problems!   Programmer: Because you can't tell the game that the character must do that! No! You need to write some variables, things like that. And it is not as easy as it seems!

For this programmer, the specific software was helpful even though it was not necessary to program the code, but sometimes difficulties arise because peers are not aware of its limitations.

8.4.5 Phase 5. Sharing Final Creation: Awareness of Difficulties

Difficulties were present in the final phase of the workshop. They can be noticed through the conversations (intersubjective processes) that students had with the research team. Those allowed for progress in overcoming some problematic questions related, for example, to the game mechanics, specially its levels.

Fragment 12. Final presentation: difficulties appear
Session 14. 2013 04 11
Researcher   Well, I have noted that you have done very well; the narrative is well told and the game dynamic is well integrated. I also like how you developed the characters.   They've insisted that the first level is pretty hard. What you did is okay but move it to level 10! [laughs]   (…)

This game can be seen from above, many times. This is called aerial view. The overhead shot is not very realistic, of course, because you start to see angles and dimensions; you are somewhat aware of this problem.

What has been missing is explaining a little or telling a little bit about the other levels. Because level one was in the house, the rest consisting that in each level one character was saved and (...).

Director
Levels were defined in relation to the floors, adapted to the house, and then the house was to have five floors.

And then there would be several family members on each floor, and the upstairs floor would be entirely for the mother-in-law that was who was infecting everybody and who you must fight in the end.

The conversation between the researcher, in this case a computer person, and the team director shows that the students are aware of the game's elements. She tried to overcome the problems posed by the research. Verbalization processes, the use of language, are what helps to transcend and expand the students' awareness of the game elements. Reading the previous fragment carefully, we observe that the researcher, acting as a jury to choose the best game in the final presentation, values the narrative and the character design but also points out some problems with the mechanics that define the levels of the game. Sharing his doubts with the students helps them focus on the issues that remain to be defined. Responding to these issues, the team director expresses verbally how each level relates to a different scenario and how certain characters are associated with them. Once again, she is aware that some elements which were previously presented had not been integrated into the game.

It is relevant to show what this experience means for each of the participants. The radio broadcaster asked all the students to summarize the project and their personal experience while creating the game in one sentence. These were the responses of the team members.

Fragment 13. Final synthesis
Local radio interview. 2013 05 25

Programmer: Well, I don't know. This was a unique experience. As you mentioned, not everyone has this opportunity (...) to learn programming, and also (...) people buy and play games, but they are unaware of all the work behind them, no?

Audio manager: I think the best thing about this project was teamwork or the ability to work with others; usually in other subjects you have to do a project by yourself....

Art director: That is what is amazing; you create a video game, and like my colleagues said, it is very complicated, but later, knowing that you are playing your own game is incredible.

Designer: To me, what I find amazing is seeing that what you had in mind is working. There has been a whole process, sometime later, and working hard you see it on a screen. You are watching something that didn't exist before that you imagined, and that works!

Team director: Well, I think it would be a little mix of the four ideas. It gives you another perspective, another view on video games. Next time you grab a video game, you'll play but you'll also look at more things. Teamwork is also very important, and it is something you'll always need in your everyday life. And then there is the satisfaction of knowing that at the beginning we had nothing but now we have created something that is just ours.

In short, creating a game turns out to be a unique experience, emerging as a collective enterprise. It allows us to look at games from a different perspective. Moreover, that has contributed to the realization of a project, which was only a set of mental representations at the beginning of sessions but has become a reality, a video game that works.

8.5 Conclusions

Society demands that people face new challenges, implementing skills often lacking in formal educational environments. Among those skills is the ability to create something new and meaningful in specific social and cultural contexts (Connery et al. 2010; John-Steiner 1985/1997, 2000). In this chapter, we show how a formal educational setting can become an environment that encourages creativity. In any case, both the stage, organized around the game design activities in a school setting, and the process of collaboration among students must be taken into account. The innovative scenario was built on the following foundations.

First, the creative process was organized around a cultural product, the game relevant for the actors in entertainment environments (Gardner 2011; Gee 2013). The students, who at first understand games as an object designed for leisure, discover new ways to look at them, once it is they who have created them.

Second, people have created the video game using two instruments (Cole 1996): materials embedded in physical reality, which include not only software but also any type of technology, analogical or digital, which supports the activities during the workshop, and tools linked to the participants' mental representations and the collective ideas which have served as inspiration (Sawyer 2010, 2012).

Creativity is inseparable from the social context where it appears, and that can happen from a double perspective. First, when people dialogue in small or large groups, they are aware of their ideas, and they are forced to rebuild them, according to other perspectives, in an environment in which the subject interacts with others, which results in intersubjective processes. Moreover, we find collaborative creativity. Second, people act in small groups, taking on different roles with positions, goals, and functions (Moran 2010) associated to these roles.

At the end of the day, it's the role one plays in the creation of the game which allows him/her to integrate as an individual. Creation as a cultural becomes intertwined with individual activity (Sawyer 2010). The construction of meaning is not independent of the played role, which helps to bring different perspectives and to mix them.

Summing up, this research sets up particular creative universes that educators, parents, and researchers often forget. By being there and participating with the students, we understand the world without sacrificing fantasy, which is so often abandoned in schools. Playing, imagining, and creating are indispensable activities that humans, young or old, have to learn in the twenty-first century.

References

Bakhtin MM, Holquist M, Emerson C (1986) Speech genres and other late essays, 1st edn. University of Texas Press, Austin

Brettschneider AW (2004) Voices in dialogue – dialoguing about dialogism: form and content in Bakhtinian dialogue. In: Ball AF, Freedman SW (eds) Bakhtinian perspectives on language, literacy, and learning. Cambridge University Press, Cambridge, pp 99–106

Cole M (1996) Cultural psychology: a once and future discipline. Harvard University Press, Cambridge, MA

Connery MC (2010) The social construction of a visual language: on becoming a painter. In: Connery MC, John-Steiner V, Marjanovic-Shane A (eds) Vygotsky and creativity: a cultural-historical approach to play, meaning making, and the arts. Peter Lang, New York, pp 83–106

Connery MC, John-Steiner V, Marjanovic-Shane A (2010) Vygotsky and creativity: a cultural-historical approach to play, meaning making, and the arts. Peter Lang, New York

Denzin NK, Lincoln YS (2011) Introduction: the discipline and practice of qualitative research. In: Denzin NK, Lincoln YS (eds) The SAGE handbook of qualitative research, 4th edn. Sage Publications, Thousand Oaks/London, pp 1–21

Gardner H (2011) Creating minds: an anatomy of creativity seen through the lives of Freud, Einstein, Picasso, Stravinsky, Eliot, Graham, and Gandhi. Basic Books, New York

Gee JP (2010) How to do discourse analysis: a toolkit. Routledge, New York

Gee JP (2013) The anti-education era: creating smarter students through digital learning. Palgrave MacMillan, New York

Gee JP (2014) Discourse and the new literacy studies. In: Gee JP (ed) An introduction to discourse analysis: theory and method, 4th edn. Routledge, New York, pp 371–382

Green JL, Wallat C (1981) Mapping instructional conversations – a sociolinguistic ethnography. In: Green JL, Wallat C (eds) Ethnography and language. Ablex Publishing Corporation, Norwood, pp 161–205

Gumperz JJ (1981) Conversational inference and classroom learning. In: Green JL, Wallat C (eds) Ethnography and language. Ablex Publishing Corporation, Norwood, pp 3–24

Hamera J (2011) Performance ethnography. In: Denzin NK, Lincoln YS (eds) The SAGE handbook of qualitative research, 4th edn. Sage Publications, Thousand Oaks/London, pp 317–330

Holstein JA, Gabrium JF (2011) The constructionist analysis of interpretive practice. In: Denzin NK, Lincoln YS (eds) The SAGE handbook of qualitative research, 4th edn. Sage Publications, Thousand Oaks/London, pp 341–358

Holzman L (2010) Without creating ZPDs there is no creativity. In: Connery MC, John-Steiner V, Marjanovic-Shane A (eds) Vygotsky and creativity: a cultural-historical approach to play, meaning making, and the arts. Peter Lang, New York, pp 27–40

John-Steiner V (1985/1997) Notebooks of the mind: explorations of thinking, revised. Oxford University Press, New York/Oxford

John-Steiner V (2000) Creative collaboration. Oxford University Press, Oxford/New York

Juul J (2005) Half-real. Videogames between real rules and fictional worlds. The MIT Press, Cambridge

Lacasa P (2013) Learning in real and virtual worlds: commercial video games as educational tools. Palgrave MacMillan, New York

Lacasa P, Méndez L, Martínez R (2009) Using video games as educational tools: building bridges between commercial and serious games. In: Kankaanranta M, Neittaanmäki P (eds) Design and use of serious games. Springer, Milton Keynes, pp 107–126

Lacasa P, Martínez-Borda R, Méndez L (2013) Media as practice: narrative and conceptual approach for qualitative data analysis. Stud Media Commun 1(1): 132–149. http://redfame.com/journal/index.php/smc

Landay E (2004) Performance as the foundation for a secondary school literacy program. In: Ball AF, Freedman SW (eds) Bakhtinian perspectives on language, literacy, and learning. Cambridge University Press, Cambridge, pp 107–128

Mitchell BL (2012) Game design essentials. John Wiley & Sons, Indianapolis

Moran S (2010) The roles of creativity in society. In: Kaufman JC, Sternberg RJ (eds) The Cambridge handbook of creativity. Cambridge University Press, New York, pp 74–92

Moran S, John-Steiner V (2003) Creativity in the making: Vygotsky's contemporary contribution to the dialectic of development and creativity. In: Keith R, John-Steiner V, Sternberg R (eds) Creativity and development. Oxford University Press, New York, pp 61–90

Pulsipher L (2012a) Game design: how to create video and tabletop games, start to finish. McFarland & Company, Inc., Publishers, Jefferson

Pulsipher L (2012b) Opinion: don't train students on game design – educate them. Gamasutra. http://www.gamasutra.com/view/news/174068/Opinion_Dont_train_students_on_game_design__educate_them.php

Russ SW, Fiorelli JA (2010) Developmental approaches to creativity. In: Kaufman JC, Sternberg RJ (eds) The Cambridge handbook of creativity. Cambridge University Press, New York, pp 233–249

Sawyer RK (2003) Group creativity: music, theater. L. Erlbaum Associates, Mahwah

Sawyer RK (2010) Individual and group creativity. In: Kaufman JC, Sternberg RJ (eds) The Cambridge handbook of creativity. Cambridge University Press, New York, pp 366–380

Sawyer RK (2012) Explaining creativity: the science of human innovation, 2nd edn. Oxford University Press, New York

Tsui ABM (2014) Ethnography and classroom discourse. In: Gee JP (ed) An introduction to discourse analysis: theory and method, 4th edn. Routledge, New York, pp 383–394

Vygotsky LS (1978/1986) Mind in society: the development of higher psychological processes. Cole M, John-Steiner V, Scribner S, Souberman E (ed). Harvard University Press, Harvard

Vygotsky LS (1986) Thought and language: newly revised and edited by Alex Kozulin. The MIT Press, Cambridge, MA

Vygotsky LS (1998) In: Rieber RW (ed) The collected works of L.S. Vygotsky. Volume 5. Child psychology. Kluwer Academic & Plenum Publishers, New York

Wortley D (2013) Immersive technology strategies. Simul Gaming 44(2–3):452–465. doi:10.1177/1046878113488850

Chapter 9
When Ideas Generate Value: How LEGO Profitably Democratized Its Relationship with Fans

Vlada Botoric

9.1 Introduction

In a basement filled with buildings made of LEGO bricks, a young boy creates his own models. Adventures are being played out by his own imagination but on his father's LEGO setting. When that came into his father's eyes, he immediately starts to chastise his son for ruining the setting by creating hodgepodges of different models and playing themes. The story that a young boy created was actually the plot of The Lego Movie (2014) where an ordinary construction worker Emmet had been prophesied to save the LEGO universe from the tyrannical Lord Business. Later in the basement, the boy's father looked at his son's creations again and got impressed. Having realized that his son based the evil Lord Business on him, the father changes opinion and allows his son to play with his bricks however he sees them fit. The LEGO Movie, a computer-animated adventure comedy film, successfully managed to be a powerful story about the drawbacks of conformity while celebrating individuality and the creative potential of imagination. "Creative individuals are no longer viewed as iconoclasts; they are new mainstream" (Florida 2012) in the emergence of "a new economic democracy in which we all have a lead role" (Tapscott and Anthony 2007). According to Florida, that creative ethos that molds the core of our identities is critical for generating creativity and commercial innovations in a "produsage-based democratic model" (Bruns 2008); the real driving force is the rise of human creativity as the key factor in our economy and society. Both at work and in other spheres of our lives, we value creativity more highly and cultivate it more intensely than we ever before (Florida 2012).

To cope successfully with technological progress, competitive change, and the evolution of consumer behavior, companies continuously develop, adapt, or

V. Botoric (✉)
Department of Aesthetics and Communication, Aarhus University, Aarhus, Denmark
e-mail: vbotoric@dac.au.dk

© Springer-Verlag London 2015
N. Zagalo, P. Branco (eds.), *Creativity in the Digital Age*,
Springer Series on Cultural Computing, DOI 10.1007/978-1-4471-6681-8_9

reinvent their business models. "Opening up a business model to external ideas can capture greater value using key assets or resources, not only in the company's own business but also in relation to other partners such as customers (Djelassi and Decoopman 2013)." It is evident that new business models emerge and gain control over ideas and creative potential outside the company, while developing new ways of earning revenues. "Bringing the two together – ideas and companies – and getting them to cooperate could seriously foster innovation and offer many more people the chance to benefit from their ideas (Weiers 2014)." Given this trajectory, using the LEGO Group and its fans, as an example of one of the most active fan communities in the world (Antorini 2007), will provide an important key for understanding many forms of fans empowerment (Baym and Burnett 2009) and corporate strategies for value co-creation (Zwick et al. 2008) in order to shed light on the broader ontological and epistemological changes that occurred within fan/corporate practices (Lanier and Fowler 2013). Theoretical links between fan culture and a set of corporate practices that seek to capture and exploit participatory culture (Jenkins et al. 2013, p. 48), such a complex discourse in the sense of innovation and user appropriation, are central to this chapter.

9.2   The Infusion of New Interactions

In the year 2000, the LEGO Group had a loss of DKK 831 million (LEGO Annual Report 2000). That year was a very difficult year for the entire toy industry, but despite many strengths and high points, the LEGO Company was impacted because they had lost focus. Even though the year of 2002 may in the circumstances be regarded as a good year (LEGO Annual Report 2002), 2003 was a very disappointing year for LEGO Company, when the negative development reflected an unsuccessful growth strategy with a consequent loss of market shares. At the end of the year, it was decided to change the business strategy and set out a series of specific initiatives in order to ensure a stable platform for the company's development. The successful implementation of these initiatives was crucial for LEGO Company to ensure profitable growth and, at the same time, uphold its strong, global brand position among families with children. The following year, the LEGO Group took radical new steps in order to tackle its most serious financial crisis to date. The main objective was to restore competitiveness by focusing on customers. The Lego Group, therefore, and many firms and industries had to make fundamental changes to long-held business models in order to adapt (von Hippel 2005). The Lego Group realized the fundamental transformations of user-producer relations, where the infusion of new technologies in such interactions has redefined the roles in innovation and value creation processes (Thomke and von Hippel 2002).

9.3 Bringing Ideas and Companies Together

Over the past decade, research has viewed the customer as a component of the business model, but the business model literature has recently emphasized going further and considering the customer as a "content generator" (Plé et al. 2010). Companies need to both market to and collaborate with their customers. This is more important today, especially given generation Y's tendency to actively share, contribute, search, and work using social media and its expectation that it will participate in value co-creation (Bolton et al. 2013). "Considering the gradual shift towards co-creative media work and a corresponding industry-wide framing of the audience as collaborators or otherwise 'active' publics, the key issues moderating such corporate appropriation of participatory culture are notions of transparency (of all parties involved) and control (over all communications)," as Mark Deuze (2008) argued. From this, it becomes clear that the broad participatory culture is becoming more democratic, because users are enabled to produce culture themselves, and not just to listen or follow the prewritten rules, without an active engagement in such content creation. LEGO business could thus be built through the incorporation of customer interaction as a core value generation strategy.

According to the recent data from the LEGO Group, there are more than 200 LEGO User Groups with over 135.000 registered members; more than 400 events organized, with over six million visitors at these events in 2012; 1,170,000 LEGO movies on YouTube, where top five videos has over 100 million views combined; over 1.400.000 LEGO tagged images on Flickr; hundreds of LEGO related blogs; thousands of LEGO-related websites, etc. For example, a YouTube *Lego Star Wars – For the millionth time, I didn't make this video*, uploaded in 2005 has been viewed by 30,887,650 people since[1] [Accessed: July 27, 2014]; Henrik Ludvigsen, from Roskilde in Denmark, spent GBP 50,000 and 18 months planning creation of the world's largest LEGO railway[2]; Alice Finch built a massive LEGO Hogwarts from 400,000 bricks,[3] a mini-scale rendition of Hogwarts School of Witchcraft & Wizardry from J.K. Rowling's Harry Potter series of books and the corresponding movies; and inspired by fantasy buildings featured in sagas like Star Wars and The Lord of the Rings, LEGO fan Gerry Burrows built an impressive 250,000 LEGO-Brick Mega-Structure called the Garrison of Moriah.[4] Having realized the amazing number of diverse posts, images, and videos of LEGO creations on numerous online platforms, the LEGO Group celebrated those creations with the ReBrick,[5] a social bookmarking platform where adult users can share, organize, and discuss

---

[1] https://www.youtube.com/watch?v=O61Do03ZCjw

[2] http://www.dailymail.co.uk/news/article-2364154/Lego-fan-builds-worlds-longest-toy-train-circuit-93-000-bricks.html

[3] http://www.brothers-brick.com/2013/02/26/alice-finch-builds-massive-lego-hogwarts-from-400000-bricks/

[4] http://www.wired.com/2011/05/lego-garrison-of-moriah/

[5] LEGO Rebrick [online] Available at: http://rebrick.lego.com/. Accessed 15 July 2014

user-created LEGO content. The content on ReBrick is not what LEGO sets can be bought in a shop, but creations made by teenage and adult builders, who use their creativity to build their own models called MOCs (My Own Creation).

More than 400.000 h is being spent weekly on LEGO activities (LEGO Group 2014). Such an open innovation suggests that valuable ideas and creations come from both outside and inside the company. This approach placed external ideas and external path to market on the same level of importance as that reserved for internal ideas and path to markets in the earlier era (Chesbrough et al. 2006). "Open Innovation is a paradigm that assumed that LEGO should use external ideas as well as internal ideas, and internal and external path to market. New LEGO business model supported by the open innovation processes utilized both external and internal ideas to create value." The LEGO Group, therefore, had placed more emphasis on using leading-edge technologies in ways that support its brand values, such as extending the "intelligent brick" concept of LEGO MINDSTORMS to open up whole new ways of playing and learning, as well as initiatives such as LEGO Studios, putting the power of moviemaking in the hands of children (LEGO Annual Report 2000). Mindstorms consists of computational LEGO bricks that allow you to create your own robots. Mindstorms was developed in close contact with the MIT Epistemology and Learning Group founded by Seymour Papert. It is named after Papert's book Mindstorms: children, computers, and powerful ideas (1993). In 1985, the LEGO Company started working together with Papert "with an eye toward introducing a computer-driven LEGO product" (Wiencek 1987, p. 102 in Lauwaert 2009). Papert is the founding father of the educational theory constructionism ("learning by making"), based on the work by Swiss philosopher and psychologist Jean Piaget (Papert 1991). In 1998, the LEGO Group launched the Mindstorms User Groups (MUGs) which allowed for social interaction, knowledge sharing, and which gave online and face-to-face access to inspiration and input from like-minded others. LEGO Mindstroms consumers did not accept the products as they were, but they constantly modified, improved, and created new products and service solutions that better fitted their needs and wants. "They did not wait for the firm to take action on things which concerned the products, nor did they contact the firm to learn more about the products, or to have answers and problems regarding the use of the products solved. Instead, they did it for themselves via the communities, the guidebooks, the online resources, and the many other things they created (Antorini 2007)." Zwick et al. (2008) argue in this context that the discourse of value co-creation stands for a notion of modern corporate power that is no longer aimed at disciplining consumers and shaping actions according to a given norm but at working with and through the freedom of the consumer. For Prahalad and Ramaswamy and others (c.f. Tapscott and Williams 2006), consumers have specialized competencies and skills that companies are unable to match or even understand. The most popular section of the LEGO Club was "Cool Creations." It was a place where members could show pictures of their own LEGO models and tell other members a little about themselves. LEGO Company's "What will you make?" road tour of North America and the LEGO World Event in the Netherlands, attended by more than 40,000 visitors, demonstrated the extent to which LEGO fans had become involved in the arrangement of events (LEGO Annual Report 2003). A collaboration of this nature benefits both fans and company. LEGO therefore started building solid foundations in order to fight two special challenges: first, attracting and retaining these consumers and, second, providing a creative and open communication environment (Zwick et al. 2008).

For example, the popularity of Mindstorms 2.0 prompted the LEGO Group to develop a second edition of the robotics construction toy. "One of the goals was to appeal not only to adults but to children as well. Mindstorms 2.0 is a toy with a specific (adult) user embedded in its design, use of technology and requirements on both the financial and computational level. Mindstorms NXT products, launched in 2006, has shown how the cooperation with fans changes over time, becomes more important and results in the adjustment of the LEGO Group to a totally new paradigm (Lauwaert 2009)." Through simplifying the programming language, the LEGO Company wanted to broaden the scope of possible NXT users (Koerner 2006). The new system is PC and Mac compatible, and the programming software has been redesigned and is now far more intuitive and easier to use. The American nonprofit organization FIRST (For Inspiration and Recognition of Science and Technology) aimed to stimulate interest among children and young people for science and technology subjects by organizing projects in which children themselves were the driving force. FIRST LEGO League was a robotics competition for teams of children and young people between the ages of 9 and 16 years, who competed in several disciplines. Teams were required to build and program a LEGO MINDSTORMS robot to perform certain tasks on a robot track, solve a research task, and demonstrate cooperation and innovation. In 2003, the theme was Mission Mars, and robots had to carry out assignments on Mars, for example, collect mineral samples, build houses, collect ice samples, and free a Mars Rover which had become stuck on a sand bank. In 2003, approx. 42,000 children participated in the competition representing 14 countries: USA, Canada, Brazil, South Korea, Germany, Britain, France, Netherlands, Norway, Sweden, Denmark, Austria, Singapore, and China (LEGO Annual Report 2003).

The market thus becomes a platform for participation in a culture of exchange, where companies offer consumers resources to create, and where consumers offer to companies "a contact with the fast-moving world of knowledge in general" (Terranova 2000, p. 37). The market, in the view of the co-creationists, has been transformed into a channel through which "human intelligence" renews its capacity to produce (Terranova, ibid). For example, these dedicated Mindstorms users are considered as "lead users," a term introduced by innovation expert Eric von Hippel (2005, p. 22). Lead users are not only quick in adopting new products by making a purchase of them, but importantly, also in adapting these products so that they might better fit their personal needs. Hippel defines lead users as either persons or companies that are at the edge of market trends and therefore experience needs that others will soon experience as well. More so, lead users innovate products because they anticipate a relatively high benefit from doing so (ibid.).

"While user-generated websites present arguably some of the 'purest' examples of consumer government through co-creation, the same principle operates successfully in industries and businesses as diverse as John Deere's DeereTrax farm machinery management system, Sumerset Houseboats' dialogical method of bespoke houseboat production, LEGO Group's Mindstorms and LEGO Factory applications, and Build-a-Bear Workshop's consumer-operated production process (Zwick et al. 2008)." In November 2004, the LEGO Group launched a new website: www.LEGOfactory.com. Children and other building enthusiasts visiting the site were invited to design LEGO models and take part in competitions for LEGO prizes. The idea behind the website was to develop the Group's contacts with LEGO fans of all ages. If children were looking for advice or ideas, they could see inspirational material at the site posted by LEGO designers and adult LEGO fans. Visitors could build 3D LEGO models using a special software application, LEGO Digital Designer (LDD), and join the LEGO Factory competition. Every week, new winners were selected. On top of receiving LEGO products, they automatically competed for the certification of "professional LEGO Factory designer," which entitled them to have their model mass produced and sold on the official corporate website. Many of the better-designed products uploaded by consumers are in fact appropriated by LEGO for general production and sale, with design recognition (but no financial recognition) granted to the creator. In this way, LEGO taps into the mass intellectuality of a globally networked community of consumers to speed up innovation and market response rates. The first version of LDD appeared a year ago on www.LEGO.com. The program can be downloaded free of charge. The LEGO Factory is not only a creative tool, it also provides the LEGO Company with a digital database of user creations and thus with invaluable information about their most active fans (ibid, 2008).

9.4 Enthusiastic Labor

Organized cooperation in which users interact within communities is also common. Innovation communities are often stocked with useful tools and infrastructure that increase the speed and effectiveness with which users can develop and test and diffuse their innovations (von Hippel 2005, p. 93). Von Hippel defines innovation communities as "meaning nodes consisting of individuals or firms interconnected by information transfer links which may involve face-to-face, electronic, or other communication. Innovation communities can have users and/or manufacturers as members and contributors. They can flourish when at least some innovate and voluntarily reveal their innovations, and when others find the information revealed to be of interest (p. 96)." A growing number of adult LEGO enthusiasts begun setting up groups to discuss their LEGO hobby. They call themselves AFOLs: Adult Fans of LEGO. Over a period of years, the LEGO Group has actively developed relations with many AFOL groups, who have their own websites, organize public events, and take part in LEGO development projects. In January 2005, the LEGO Group announced its "LEGO Ambassador" program for AFOLs worldwide. The purpose of this program is to expand mutually useful relations between the LEGO Group and its loyal, talented, and committed consumers (LEGO Annual Report 2005). For example, loyal LEGO fans are serviced through a number of measures, such as LEGO Factory. It was the ambition that product development and process improvements should take place in close dialogue with LEGO fans, which should through different channels have the possibility of presenting ideas to the Group's designers. The many adult LEGO enthusiasts all over the world, comprising an increasingly active group of fans, were also involved. The Ambassador Program is an official program which invites adult LEGO fans to share their enthusiasm for the LEGO idea and LEGO products and encourages interaction in the global LEGO communities. Moreover, the LEGO Certified Professionals program caters for adult fans who, wholly or partly, live by their LEGO hobby and therefore wish to enter into cooperation with the LEGO Group. The idea of putting customers to work is not entirely new. Ritzer (2004) argued about the increasing rationalization processes of companies in a McDonaldizing world that have long relied on the appropriation of consumers' work. McDonald's restaurants turn customers into waiters and cleaning personnel, for example, while the automated teller machine (ATM) "allows everyone to work, for at least a few moments, as an unpaid bank teller" (Ritzer 2004, p. 63), and with the emergence of internet communication technologies, companies find more innovative ways to extract free labor from their consumers (c.f. Terranova 2000). The concept of co-creation signifies the transfer of the McDonaldization logic of customer work from the sphere of production and process efficiency (c.f. Ritzer 2004) to that of new product development and innovation. In other words, "co-creation economy can be seen as driven by the need of capital to set up processes that enable the liberation and capture of large repositories of technical, social, and cultural competence in places previously considered outside the production of monetary value." In short, the co-creation economy is about experimenting with new possibilities for value creation that are based on the expropriation of free cultural, technological, social, and affective labor of the consumer masses (Zwick et al. 2008, p. 166). According to Holbrook (1996), value can be defined as "an interactive relativistic preference experience." This suggests the argument that experience defines what is valuable to a fan. This is an emergence of a new logic for value creation where value is embedded in personalized experiences. LEGO fans are increasingly savvy about the value created through their attention and engagement: "some are seeking ways to extract something in return for their creative co-creation and in recognition of the value they are generating" (Jenkins et al. 2013, p. 57). This emerging production ecology involves new kinds of distributed organizations and ad hoc platforms and epitomizes the drift of value (Hartley 2004) allowing us to understand how fan-oriented corporate innovative initiatives influence fans and vice versa. From this perspective, customers are configured as uniquely skilled workers who, for the production of value-in-use to occur, must be given full rein to articulate their inimitable requirements and share their knowledge (Prahalad and Ramaswamy 2004) as inputs to the manufacturing process. Online communication technology enables fans to participate in collective production, especially in the discourse on participatory culture (Schäfer 2011). Such participation demands acknowledgment of the fans' interests as fully legitimate elements of the design process (Simonsen and Robertson 2013). Maaike Lauwaert (2009), in this context, conceptualized the sum of all play practices, design, and discourses in terms of geography of play: "Within the LEGO geography, part of such activities are commoditized and used for innovation. This gives fans a more active role in the design of new products. Fans become to a certain extent co-constructors of new products and of the embedded design scripts and user configurations of these products (p. 70)." This represents the fundamental transcendence of the fans' role from being merely informants to being legitimate and acknowledged participants in the design process (Bødker et al. 2004).

9.5   Ideas and Companies in an Innovative Democratized Relationship

When von Hippel argued that innovation was being democratized, he meant that "users of products and services, both firms and individual consumers, were increasingly able to innovate for themselves. User-centered innovation processes offer great advantages over the manufacturer-centric innovation development systems that have been the mainstay of commerce for hundreds of years (von Hippel 2005, p. 1)." Companies, in this context, have expanded their reach to capture the talents of heretofore excluded groups of eccentrics and mentioned nonconformists. For example, after the premiere of The Lego Movie on February 7, 2014, the hero brought The Emmet Awards,[6] a series of monthly contests where participants can express whatever their imagination can create to everyone. Their imagination and building skills will be then tested and some of the creations awarded. In addition, fans co-created more than 100 unique 30 s stop-motion movies; five were used in the final version of the movie.

More ambitious project was launched in the fall of 2008, when the CUUSOO SYSTEM and the LEGO Group teamed up to launch the LEGO CUUSOO crowd-sourcing experiment. According to The Official LEGO® CUUSOO Blog, the promising results from the pilot LEGO CUUSOO platform led to the launch of the international LEGO CUUSOO beta site in the fall of 2011.

The partnership with CUUSOO SYSTEM had been such a success that LEGO decided to integrate the CUUSOO concept more closely into the LEGO experience. Now it is called: LEGO Ideas. All projects, supports, comments, profiles, and other data from LEGO CUUSOO were automatically migrated to LEGO Ideas. Now, ideas have value (Weiers 2014, p. 74). As the focus and emphasis on ideas shift, so does its value. Ideas are seen as the true sources of innovation. Richard Florida (2012) argued that creativity had become to be the most highly prized commodity, not being a "commodity." Accordingly, they should be rewarded. Ideas, according to the same author, will receive increasing credit and be rewarded for the innovation

---

[6] http://www.lego.com/en-us/movie/emmet-awards/

as the competition among implementation options, realization paths, and the range of actors increases.

Today, via crowdsourcing anyone can come up with a design, a slogan, or sell their photos, without being a professional designer, advertising specialist or photographer. Fans are recognized as a powerful source for generating new ideas, joining the exclusive domain of marketers, engineers, and designers. The actions of fans through crowdsourcing media platforms provide an important key for understanding the business models of the crowdsourcing as a driver toward value creation. The transformation of corporation from a manufacturer to a provider of platforms for user-generated content illustrates the extent to what the participation of fans is embedded in a business model where profit is being generated also by fans. This will intensify severely as ubiquitous competition not only within a professional stream but from anywhere will increase. "If we think of a contemporary of Edison – the ingenious Nikola Tesla, that is often considered the more brilliant inventor of the two, we cannot omit the fact that he is also the one who commercially fared even worse. His work includes amongst many others, pioneering work on wireless communication, the induction motor, x-rays, radar, energy weapons, weather control, and especially, long distance and wireless energy transmission. His many brilliant and often visionary inventions, as well as his profound scientific work are said to have helped "usher in the second industrial revolution. Yet, he never became a successful businessman himself. Good ideas require necessary skills and means to turn into successful products (Weiers 2014, p. 9)." The broader landscape, therefore, is shifting. Innovation became more effective and more democratic. It also became faster – and less a leisurely exercise. On the one hand, there are inventors. Now anyone invents. Anyone can come up with an idea, no matter the skills as a businessman, no matter the experience, no matter the employment situation, age, economic standing, or social origin. Ideas are democratic. Anyone can profit from their idea. "If innovation is indeed 1 % inspiration and 99 % perspiration, you too have to sweat it (Weiers 2014, p. 204)." Innovation becomes more effective as the competition increases, and the implementation process becomes more professionalized, better utilizing existing expertise, skills, and resources.

Crowdsourcing is the most recent approach to user-driven innovation. The term appeared for the first time in 2006, in Jeff Howe article "The rise of crowdsourcing," published in the online magazine Wired (Howe 2006). The word itself is a combination of two: crowd and outsourcing, which create the portmanteau – crowdsourcing – together. Jeff Howe defined crowdsourcing as follows: crowdsourcing is the act of taking a job traditionally performed by a designated agent (usually an employee) and outsourcing it to an undefined, generally large group of people in the form of an open call (Howe 2006). Jeff Howe did not invent the concept, but only the name and definition, which covers a very wide range of actions often differing in its essential features. As a form of user-driven innovation and co-creation, crowdsourcing is not simply a marketing promotion tool but a process through which companies can apply individuals' open innovation to their innovation efforts (Hopkins 2011), a form of "outside-in" collaboration in Chesbrough (2006) sense of the term. Despite the growing implementation of crowdsourcing practices in many companies in different sectors (Lego, Nike, Ideastorm, etc.), it remains little understood. With the overall shift to more open innovation, crowdsourcing is growing in importance. Although it is a powerful resource for companies, it is nonetheless very complex and gives rise to many questions (Hopkins 2011). Moreover, academic research on strategic management and media technologies has only recently begun to examine business models based on crowdsourcing. From the crowdsourcing, LEGO rewrote the rules of value co-creation. In the literature, co-creation is tightly related to crowdsourcing (Brabham 2008), co-innovation (Lee et al. 2012), or user innovation (Bogers et al. 2010). The source of new competitive advantage and the fertile ground for company's profitable growth lie in the strategic capital built by continuously interaction with its fans. Such collaboration involves enabling co-creative interactions so that individuals can have meaningful and compelling engagement experiences.

"Bringing the fans into the company marks a wider shift noticeable in many layers of society and culture, a shift based on the early philosophy of the internet: the many-to-many approach rather than the one-to-many approach (Lauwaert 2009)." Instead of having LEGO designers work in secrecy behind closed doors on new LEGO sets, the LEGO Company will invite the fans and the users to "sit at the table" with the designers and work together on future LEGO sets. "Increasingly, technology is at stake in toys, games and playing. With the immense popularity of computer games, questions concerning the role and function of technology in play have become more pressing. A key aspect of the increasing technologization and digitalization of both toys and play is the vagueness of borders between producers, consumers and players. In these so-called participatory cultures characterized by a many-to-many model, players do not play with a toy designed behind closed doors but become co-designers of their own toys (Lauwaert 2009, p. 8)." Participatory cultures are often hailed as a democratizing force, the ultimate means of consumer or user empowerment. "After all," Maaike Lauwaert argued: "one can now take on a more active role as consumer or user, be it as designer or co-designer of new products or product updates, as reviewer of consumer goods or as an expert helping out other users. These many-to-many or participatory options embody the promise that a more actively engaged relationship with traditionally remote processes is now possible, if not the actual democratization of certain consumerist processes. These changes are, needless to say, not restricted to consumerist processes but spread out into the domains of politics, knowledge creation and knowledge dissemination (p. 9)."

Significant efforts and much research have been put into an even more promising aspect of corporate innovation: accessing ideas outside the corporation. The possibilities to gain access to the vast spectrum of ideas outside the firm are being explored to take advantage of such broad innovation potential. The generation of ideas has become more democratic. A particular focus has been placed on users, which are argued to be "perhaps the most important developers of innovations." According to Weiers (2014), "as the generation of ideas becomes more and more distributed and democratized, they become increasingly likely to originate outside the corporation, with independent inventors, customers, suppliers, lead users, anyone really."

9.6   Conclusion

As companies allow an inflow of ideas from inventors outside of the corporate walls, an increasing division of labor will take place. This opens up an entirely new perspective on innovation. "An Idea Economy emerges where ideas are traded," Weiers argued. Anyone with an idea can approach a firma or gifted entrepreneur to realize the innovation together. Anyone can profit from their ideas even without the skills and resources to be an entrepreneur themselves. This new division of labor will lead to a new kind of innovation: cooperative innovation. This development has profound implication for the innovation process, it will reshape the nature of the firm, and will influence the way we think about innovation (ibid, p. 73).

LEGO set expectations and ensured win-win with its consumers while being reliable and inclusive. The Company ensured transparency and offered a fair compensation for the creators who contribute various platforms with their models. This new consumer-centric way of collaboration insured that the company which stayed inside the box has been registering the rise of profits for the past 5 years. Such a consumer-oriented development process is a fundamental parameter to the continued success so the LEGO Group continued its strong growth in 2013.

References

Antorini YM (2007) Brand community innovation: an intrinsic case study of the adult fans of LEGO community. PhD series 35.2007. Samfundslitteratur Publishers, Frederiksber

Baym N, Burnett R (2009) Amateur experts: international fan labor in Swedish independent music. Int J Cult Stud 12(5):433–449

Bødker K, Kensing F, Simonsen J (2004) Participatory IT design: designing for business and workplace realities. MIT Press, Cambridge, MA

Bogers M, Afuah A, Bastian B (2010) Users as innovators: a review, critique, and future research directions. J Manag 36(4):857–875

Bolton RN, Parasuraman A, Hoefnagels A, Migchels N, Kabadayi S, Gruber T et al (2013) Understanding generation Y and their use of social media: a review and research agenda. J Serv Manag 24(3):245–267

Brabham DC (2008) Crowdsourcing as a model for problem solving: an introduction and cases. Converg Int J Res New Media Technol 14(1):75–90

Bruns A (2008) Blogs, Wikipedia, Second Life, and beyond: from production to produsage. Digital formations, 45. Peter Lang, New York

Chesbrough H (2006) Open innovation: the new imperative for creating and profiting from technology. Harvard Business School Press, Boston

Chesbrough HW, Vanhaverbeke W, West J (2006) Open innovation: researching a new paradigm. Oxford University Press, New York

Deuze M (2008) Corporate appropriation of participatory culture. In: Nico C, De Cleen B (eds) Participation and media production: critical reflections on content creation. Cambridge Scholars Publishers, Newcastle, pp 27–40

Djelassi S, Decoopman I (2013) Customers participation in product development through crowdsourcing: issues and implications. Ind Mark Manag 42(5):683–692

Florida R (2012) Rise of the creative class — revisited: 10th anniversary edition — revised and expanded. Basic Books, New York

Hartley J (2004) The 'value chain of meaning' and the new economy. Int J Cultur Stud 7(1):129–41

Holbrook MB (1996) Customer value – a framework for analysis and research. Adv Consum Res 23(1):138–42

Hopkins R (2011) What is crowdsourcing? In: Sloane P (ed) A guide to open innovation and crowdsourcing. Kogan Page Ltd., London, pp 15–21

Howe J (2006) The rise of crowdsourcing. Wired 14(6) [online] Available at: http:// www.wired.com/wired/archive/14.06/crowds.html. Accessed 15 July 2014

Jenkins H, Ford S, Green J (2013) Spreadable media: creating value and meaning in a networked culture. New York University Press, New York

Koerner BI (2006) Geeks in Toyland. Wired 14:104–109

Lanier CD Jr, Fowler AR III (2013) Digital fandom: mediation, remediation, and demediation of fan practices. In: Belk RW, Llamas R (eds) The Routledge companion to digital consumption. Routledge, London

Lauwaert M (2009) The place of play: toys and digital cultures. Amsterdam University Press, Amsterdam

Lee SM, Olsen DL, Trimi S (2012) Co-innovation: convergenomics, collaboration, and co-creation for organizational values. Manag Decis 50(5):817–831

LEGO official Facebook page [online] Available at: https://www.facebook.com/LEGOGROUP. Accessed 27 July 2014

LEGO Annual Report (2000, 2003, 2005) [online] Available at: http://www.lego.com/en-us/aboutus/lego-group/annual-report. Accessed 15 July 2014

Papert S (1991) Situating constructionism In: Papert S, Harel I (eds) Constructionism. Research reports and essays, 1985–1990 by the Epistemology & Learning Research Group. Ablex Publishing Corporation, Norwood, pp 1–11

Plé L, Lecoq X, Angot J (2010) Customer-integrated business models: a theoretical framework. Management 13(4):226–265

Prahalad CK, Ramaswamy V (2004) The future of competition: co-creating unique value with customers. Harvard Business School Press, Boston

Ritzer G (2004) The McDonaldization of society, 4th edn. Pine Forge Press, Thousand Oaks

Schäfer MT (2011) Bastard culture! How user participation transforms cultural production. Amsterdam University Press, Amsterdam

Simonsen J, Robertson T (eds) (2013) Routledge international handbook of participatory design. Routledge, New York

Tapscott D, Anthony DW (2007) Wikinomics: how mass collaboration changes everything. Penguin, New York

Tapscott D, Williams A (2006) Wikinomics. Penguin, New York

Terranova T (2000) Free labor: producing culture in the digital economy. Social Text 18(2):33–58

The Lego Movie (2014) Directors: Lord Phil and Miller Christopher, Warner

Thomke S, von Hippel E (2002) Customers as innovators: a new way to create value. Harv Bus Rev 80(4):74–80

von Hippel E (2005) Democratizing innovation. MIT Press, Boston

Weiers G (2014) Innovation through cooperation: the emergence of an idea economy. Springer, Heidelberg

Zwick D et al (2008) Putting consumers to work: 'co-creation' and new marketing governmentality. J Consum Cult 8(2):163–196

Chapter 10
Communication in Crowdfunding Online Platforms

Gloria Gómez-Diago

10.1 Introduction

The internet is the media, or sum of media, which have probably provoked the most relevant revolution in the last decades. This revolution has utterance at different contexts of the citizens' lives. Searching a job, being in touch with people who are far away, being informed about issues of interest, streaming videos, listening to music, buying and or reading books and cocreating documents are all activities now performed online by most of the 40 % of the world population who have internet connection (Internet Live Stats, Internet Usage Statistics). Collective creation can be done with ease on the cyberspace by using any of the multitude of devices and options available. In another place (Gómez-Diago 2010, 2012), we have illustrated the suitability of virtual worlds such as Second Life® for working collaboratively online.

According to Stohl (2014) 'the crowds of today encapsulate new forms of political, economic, and creative power'. The ease with which users take part in social networks stimulates the creation of a social capital, the one that 'is result of the value of the connections among individuals and of the norms of reciprocity and trustworthiness that arise from them' (Putnam 2000).

An example of social capital produced on the net is free and open-source software, created under a methodology named The Bazaar by Raymond (1998) and which is characterised by the fact that being the source code available, many persons contribute to develop the software, to fix it and to improve it.

Free and open-source software is much more accessible than privative software which is unaffordable for most of the population, and more important, its use encourages citizens to program by allowing them to study its source code, to install the software in several computers, to update it, etc.

G. Gómez-Diago (✉)
Department of Communication Sciences II, Universidad Rey Juan Carlos, Madrid, Spain
e-mail: gloriagdiago@gmail.com; dpto.cc.ccII@urjc.es

© Springer-Verlag London 2015
N. Zagalo, P. Branco (eds.), *Creativity in the Digital Age*,
Springer Series on Cultural Computing, DOI 10.1007/978-1-4471-6681-8_10

Despite the ongoing development of free software and despite its availability through directories such as the free software directory, there are still a lot of people and enterprises that are slaves of privative software. This is caused mainly for two reasons. Firstly, because of piracy, which, as Bill Gates stated, has permitted him to reach a large long-term market, avoiding users from using free open-source software (Chopra and Dexter 2011). Secondly, privative software is used and promoted in the context of formal education. Sadly, we can find on the net syllabus of master courses that base its significance on the learning of a privative software package.

During the academic course 2011–2012, when teaching the privative software Illustrator® at the University of Vigo, we witnessed the problems encountered by most of the pupils (Gómez-Diago 2013a) through a pilot study underpinned by observant participation and by the realisation of open questionnaires; we ascertained how using privative software obstructs the learning process by restricting the learning environment to the classroom and by limiting the computer literacy.

Rushkoff (2010: 143) points out that due to the potential of technologies and networks to influence the economy, it is needed that many people participate in the design of the interaction patterns whereby the cyberspace is articulated. Educative institutions should empower students to create their own tools and to maintain their safety (Gómez-Diago 2014).

Development and accessibility of technology is helping people to create and to cocreate in a cyberspace where there are no physical barriers. Chatzimilioudis et al. (2012) highlight the role of smartphones in making collaboration easier and omnipresent, 'enabling new crowdsourcing applications by including capabilities, such as geolocation, light, movement, or audio and visual sensors'.

We can find examples of online collective creative works such as *Life in a Day*, a crowdsourced documentary produced by Ridley Scott and directed by Kevin Macdonald. The documentary, which debuted at the Sundance Film Festival and is free and available on the internet, comprises a selection made from 80,000 videos, which were uploaded to the YouTube platform by thousands of users, from 192 nations. These videos show part of the lives of the authors that occurred on July 24, 2010.

In this chapter we centre on crowdfunding, but it is important to highlight the relationship between crowdsourcing and crowdfunding. So, both concepts are bound to the collective effort of the crowd to achieve an objective. While in crowdsourcing participants contribute with their talent to a collective process of creation, in crowdfunding, the participation mainly implies funding a project for turning it into real. The success of this financial method reveals the interest of users around the world on contributing to the development of cultural actions, ideas and even political parties, which are being created with the help of crowdfunding actions. Since 2012, the online crowdfunding platform Kickstarter 'raises more money for the arts annually than the total funding provided through the US government-run National Endowment for the Arts' (Mollick and Nanda 2014).

10.2   Crowdfunding

Several examples of crowdfunding happened long before the appearance of the internet. Among them, we can cite the composers Mozart and Beethoven funding their concerts through advance subscriptions or the Statue of Liberty, which was funded by small donations from the American and French people (Hemer 2011). The campaign made by Joseph Pulitzer in 1885 (Davies 2013) is a successful crowdfunding example that occurred in a time where the internet did not exist. Seeing that city policymakers did not reach an agreement to fund the pedestal for the Statue of Liberty, in March 16, 1885, Pulitzer published a text in his own Journal, the *New York World*. He made a direct appeal to American patriotism and the working-class solidarity, encouraging people to respond to the gift made by the French working people. The effectiveness of the campaign was motivated by the emotive text but also by the reward method designed by Pulitzer. He created a section on his journal where he published the names of the donors and the quantity of money given by each one of them. By this action, Pulitzer generated transparency and rewarded the supporters, transmitting credibility, trust and engagement, three issues we consider central in the communication taking place in crowdfunding online platforms.

One hundred twenty-nine years after the campaign made by Pulitzer, the data provided by Statista website says that the number of crowdfunding platforms worldwide was 342 in 2012 and that the volume of funds obtained by crowdfunding platforms was around one and a half billion US dollars, in 2013.

Depending on the relationship established between creators and donators, we can distinguish four types of crowdfunding (Young 2012; De Buysere et al. 2012): donation-based crowdfunding, reward-based crowdfunding, debt-based crowdfunding and equity-based crowdfunding.

Donation-based crowdfunding is based on collecting funds from groups of people for specific projects or goals, and it does not require giving rewards to the pledgers.

Reward-based crowdfunding is the usual crowdfunding exerted by platforms such as Kickstarter or Indiegogo. The campaigns encourage people to donate so that a specific project can be done in exchange of rewards linked to the project itself. For example, filmmakers usually offer DVDs of their films, artists offer copies of their artwork, etc.

Debt-based crowdfunding, also named peer-to-peer lending (P2P) or social lending, is defined as a financial transaction between individuals, or 'peers', without a financial intermediary implicated.

Finally, equity-based crowdfunding offers the crowd the possibility to buy a piece of a business. They can invest in the company and receive shares in it.

Bellow, we identify the most important reasons that move creators and supporters to participate in crowdfunding actions.

10.3   Motivations of Supporters and Creators to Participate in Crowdfunding

To know how crowdfunding performs, it is important to understand the motivations that move creators and supporters to participate in this collective financing method. Helm (2011, cited by Damus 2014) identified factors for financially supporting crowdfunding projects by grouping them in three categories: intrinsic self-determined, extrinsic self-determined and foreign-extrinsic. She also indicates the weight and influence of each factor from 1, most relevant, to 9, less relevant.

Below we include a diagram (see Fig. 10.1) that illustrates how Helm understands the functioning of supporter's motivations.

By seeing the motivations expressed in Fig. 10.1, we perceive the active role of donors who, when funding projects, apart from helping people to develop their ideas, also perform actions such as being involved in a group or recognising and exerting a responsible action. To complete the proposal of Helm (2011), we summarise some of the motivations that creators and supporters have to participate in crowdfunding actions according to Belleflamme et al. (2010), Gerbner and Hui (2012) and Hemer (2011, cited by Willems 2013).

The motivations included on the table (see Table 10.1) comprise motives of creators and of donors to participate in crowdfunding projects. Studying the type of projects most funded could help to guess which type of creations users prefer. In this line, Jian and Usher (2014) analysed the behaviour of the donors in a crowdfunding journalism platform named Spot.Us. They found that users funded reports focused on news 'you can use', that is, news topics that are of immediate utility to them in daily living.

Creators and supporters who participate at crowdfunding projects share the interest on contributing in communities and/or in collective causes. This interest of being

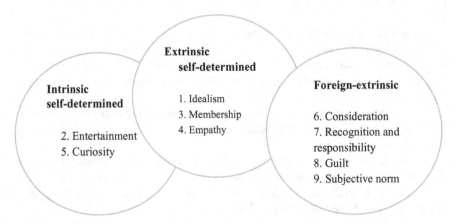

Fig. 10.1 Motivation factors for supporting crowdfunding projects, according to Helm (2011 cited by Damus 2014)

Table 10.1 Motivations for participating in crowdfunding projects. Creators and supporters

Motivations for participating in crowdfunding actions

	Creators	Supporters
1. The expectation of attracting founders	x	
2. Get an overall control over their works	x	
3. Helping testing, promoting and marketing their products, in gaining a better knowledge of their consumer's tastes and in creating new products or services altogether	x	
4. Being part of a network which have similar interests and forming connections	x	x
5. The chance to expand one's own personal network	x	x
6. Personal identification with the project's subject and its goals		x
7. Enjoying contributing to an innovation or being among the pioneers of new technology or business		x
8. Support a cause		x
9. To help others		x
10. Contribution to a societal important mission		x
11. To be rewarded with a material object or an experience		x

Based on Belleflamme et al. (2010), Gerbner and Hui (2012) and Hemer (2011 cited by Willems 2013)

part of something bigger than oneself can be considered one of the causes of the success of online crowdfunding platforms, environments where people around the world participate with ease in a collective aim.

10.4   Online Crowdfunding Platforms

There are a multitude of online crowdfunding platforms around the world that we can find easily by using a search engine or by utilising any directory such as global databases made by CrowdCafe or CrowdingIn, a directory created by the independent charity named Nesta, which facilitates individuals or organisations in the United Kingdom to choose the crowdfunding platform which better suits their project.

Crowdfunding platforms provide possibilities that are worth to know with detail when designing a project proposal. Depending on how creators use the space disposed for the projects, they will reach their objective or not. Mollick (2014: 8) identified quality indicators to predict the success of crowdfunding projects. Among them, he points out: the inclusion of video, doing quickly updates, not including spelling mistakes and having a reasonable number of Facebook friends.

Mollick and Nanda (2014) discovered a pattern regarding the characteristics of projects most liked by the crowds: they offer multiple tiers of rewards and provide more updates. To guide the design of crowdfunding support tools, Hui et al. (2014: 1) propose: '(1) to measure the size of support network, (2) to uncover motivations for different audiences and (3) to identify opportunities to build reputation'.

Yi and Gerbner (2012) consider that crowdfunding is an emerging creativity tool which supports collaboration in a community of users who share technical knowledge as well as monetary resources. According to the authors crowdfunding platforms encourage people to get their creative ideas shown, recognised, validated and supported. These platforms generate a pressure which gives discipline to the projects (Damus 2014) and which is exerted by delivering an idea online, sharing it with a critical mass, agreeing to a deadline to achieve the goal and accepting the all-or-nothing approach, that is, achieving the requested sum and receiving it or not getting anything.

This all-or-nothing approach is the only possibility in most of online crowdfunding platforms, but there are exceptions such as Indiegogo, which allows creators to choose a flexible project. If the authors do not meet the goal or purpose, they will obtain the money given by the donors until the last day of the campaign. In this case, Indiegogo will keep a 7 % of the amount obtained.

Shneiderman's Genex Framework, conceived to help human-computer interaction researchers and user interface designers to design effective tools to support creativity, proposes four activities representing the process of creative work – collect, relate, create and donate – defined by smaller tasks (Shneiderman 2000: 9) (see Fig. 10.2).

1. Collect: learn from previous works stored in libraries, the Web, etc.
2. Relate: consult with peers and mentors at early, middle and late stages.
3. Create: explore, compose and evaluate possible solutions.
4. Donate: disseminate the results and contribute to the libraries.

Aiming to identify the attributes of online crowdfunding platforms related to the creation process, Yi and Gerbner (2012) applied Shneiderman's Genex Framework, to the top three platforms – Kickstarter, RocketHub and Indiegogo – by grouping

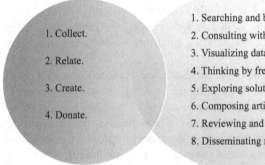

1. Collect.
2. Relate.
3. Create.
4. Donate.

1. Searching and browsing digital
2. Consulting with peers and mentors.
3. Visualizing data and processes.
4. Thinking by free associations.
5. Exploring solutions, what-if tools.
6. Composing artifacts and performances
7. Reviewing and replaying session histories.
8. Disseminating results.

Fig. 10.2 Genex phases and their related primary activities, according to Shneiderman (2000: 9)

some of their features in the four phases involved in the creation of a project according to Shneiderman.

Their proposal is very interesting because it approaches crowdfunding platforms as a creative tool, as an environment where creators carry out different actions involved in the creative process. Their perspective is situated between the creators and the platforms, so Yi and Gerbner focused on the elements of the cited platforms, which allowed achieving the actions needed to be completed in the creative process, according to Shneiderman's Genex Framework.

By applying Shneiderman's Genex Framework, they do not only link the features of the platforms to the activities included on the framework. They also identified the lack of features and/or tools of the platforms to perform the actions involved on the framework. Below we include a table elaborated by Yi and Gerbner (2012) to illustrate their work (see Table 10.2).

Table 10.2 Overview of crowdfunding platform design features as seen through the Genex Framework

Genex Framework		Implications to crowdfunding	
Phase	Activities	Design features on crowdfunding platforms	Crowdfunding platforms[a]
Collect	Search	1. Keyword search	KS, RH, IG
		2. Advanced search	IG
		3. Browsing by categories	KS, RH, IG
	Visualisation	4. Visualisation of steps of projects	Lack of visualisations of project info.
		5. Launch and project information	KS, RH, IG
Relate	Consult	1. Online contact form, e-mails	KS, RH, IG
		2. Updates, comments, blog	KS, RH, IG
		3. Discussion forum, real-time F & Q	IG
		4. Social networking tools	KS, RH, IG
		5. Online tutorials	KS, RH, IG
Create	Think	1. Visualisation tools to identify association of ideas	None
	Explore	2. Space for experimentation	None
	Compose	3. Exemplars from successful experience	None
	Review	4. Online sections of projects and funding records	None
Donate	Collect	1. Press media and social networking media	KS, RH, IG
		2. Listserv, digital library	None
		3. Recommendation and selective dissemination of info services	None

Yi and Gerbner (2012: 1603)

[a]Abbreviations of crowdfunding platforms: *KS* Kickstarter, *RH* RocketHub, *IG* Indiegogo

As we ascertain on the table (see Table 10.2), there are phases and activities of Shneiderman's Genex Framework, which have no design features at crowdfunding platforms. In this way, neither of the crowdfunding platforms studied have design features referred to the Create phase: (1) visualisation tools to identify association of ideas, (2) space for experimentation, (3) exemplars from successful experience and (4) online sections of projects and funding records. The same occurs with the features included in the Donate phase: (1) press media and social networking media; (2) Listserv, digital library; and (3) recommendation and selective dissemination of info services.

As we know, online crowdfunding platforms are evolving continuously. For this reason, when writing this chapter, the online crowdfunding platforms studied here, Kickstarter and Indiegogo, allow users to navigate around projects successfully funded, and it is also possible to see which campaigns are the most funded. On the other hand, Indiegogo has a newsletter to which users can subscribe.

The work of Yi and Gerbner is articulated from the perspective of a user who navigates the platform while creating or while thinking about creating an idea or a project, but it skips the fact that, apart from being oriented to creators, online crowdfunding platforms are targeted to donors, who will fund the projects. So, there are many elements that are mainstream in online crowdfunding platforms but not considered in their proposal.

In this context, we introduce this research. Taking into consideration that online crowdfunding platforms are environments intended to generate an interaction with users, and among users interested both in funding the projects and in submitting projects to be funded, we make an approach from a communicative perspective. This means that for identifying the features whereby Kickstarter and Indiegogo engender credibility, trust and engagement on the users, we take into consideration the different agents involved in the context of the crowdfunding platforms and the relationships that emerge between them.

10.5   Theoretical Framework and Method Employed

We agree with Rogers and Kincaid's approach (1981: 75), when placing communication as convergence assumption. They highlight the importance of studying how interaction takes place by pointing out that information sharing creates and defines a relationship between two or more individuals. In other words, it is in the interactions where meaning is placed (Marchiori and Buzzanell 2012).

Following Rogers and Kincaid, we consider that communicative behaviour should be studied as a dependent variable in communication research. The authors made their proposal in comparison with the research where communication was used as an independent variable to predict dependent variables indicating effects such as votes, consumer behaviour, violence, etc., variables which were taken by communication researchers from other disciplines such as political science, marketing or psychology.

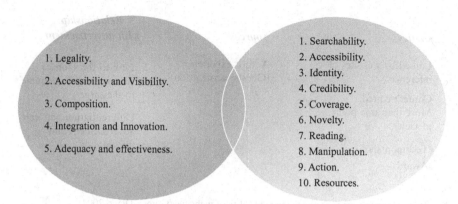

1. Legality.

2. Accessibility and Visibility.

3. Composition.

4. Integration and Innovation.

5. Adequacy and effectiveness.

1. Searchability.
2. Accessibility.
3. Identity.
4. Credibility.
5. Coverage.
6. Novelty.
7. Reading.
8. Manipulation.
9. Action.
10. Resources.

Fig. 10.3 Levels and criteria to evaluate the quality of web communication (Gómez-Diago 2004, 2005)

According to the investigators, 'until communication research begins to focus on the communicative behaviour rather than on the varied effects of communication in other behaviours, a consistent discipline of communication may not emerge'.

By approaching communication as something which is designed, we are applying the design concept in a way that enables to study the social world from the point of view of communication (Gómez-Diago 2013b). From this perspective, we conducted research oriented to propose and define through item criteria to evaluate the quality of the communication performed by websites (Gómez-Diago 2004, 2005). By analysing the features of the websites in hundreds of checklists proposed by libraries and by web festivals, we established five levels to evaluate the quality of websites which integrated issues that referred to content, to design and to technology. From these levels, we proposed ten criteria to evaluate the quality of web communication (see Fig. 10.3).

As we saw on the checklists studied and published by libraries to evaluate the quality of information web, credibility is a mainstream concept applied to determinate the quality of a website. By ordering all the elements proposed by the checklists studied, we reached to propose three criteria to determinate the quality of a website: sources, critics and relationship with advertisement. (see Fig. 10.4) Some of the items included in each of these criteria can be also applied to evaluate the credibility of a crowdfunding platform. This is the case of the items covered by the criteria named "critics": linked by websites of reference, testimonials and awards. These three items are related to the support that others give to a any website or to an online crowdfunding platform. They are very important to get more users. Both, testimonials and awards are items which can also be applied to any creative product in the physical context but on the Cyberspace testimonials are not made by famous people as happen in TV commercials. Users publish their comments about products, services, etcetera in the several range of platforms available, contributing to the "collective intelligence"; based on the users sharing their experiences to have more knowledge.

The approach presented is intended to analyse how communicative elements work for a certain purpose. We consider credibility, trust and engagement as dependent variables. From this perspective, we will be identifying the features and

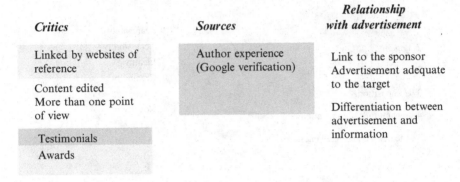

Critics	Sources	Relationship with advertisement
Linked by websites of reference	Author experience (Google verification)	Link to the sponsor
Content edited		Advertisement adequate to the target
More than one point of view		Differentiation between advertisement and information
Testimonials		
Awards		

Fig. 10.4 Three criteria to evaluate the credibility of websites (Gómez-Diago 2004)

elements which the online crowdfunding platforms Kickstarter and Indiegogo include for generating credibility, trust and engagement on users, that is, the elements of the cited crowdfunding platforms which are determinant to making them credible to their users, to be of trust and to make their users engaged in them.

10.6 Identifying Elements Which Generate Credibility, Trust and Engagement in Indiegogo and Kickstarter

We are interested in identifying how online crowdfunding platforms generate credibility, trust and engagement because we consider these three feelings to be central when convincing users to submit their projects to the platforms or when convincing users to fund one project.

Credibility, trust and engagement are concepts we know and manage at the physical world. When translating them to the virtual sphere, we are aware of how they acquire an active dimension motivated by the condition of the users, who, on the net, can obtain information with ease, test a tool or a device, check if data is real, etc. The three terms refer to three levels of an overall relationship between the user and the crowdfunding platform. The minimum level required for establishing contact is the credibility. Secondly, taking into account that these platforms are conceived to encourage users to donate money, it is needed to be of trust, and, finally, we situate the engagement as the condition to maintain users interested in using platforms.

Here we are identifying which elements of Kickstarter and Indiegogo online crowdfunding platforms contribute to generate credibility, trust and engagement. It would be possible to identify elements or features, which are not included in the framework here proposed; however, our aim in this chapter is not to include all the elements of the referred platforms, but to focus and analyse in depth only three of them.

10.6.1   *Credibility*

Credibility is given to us by others, meaning that it needs a context of interaction. The ways to obtain credibility depends on the context we have. Gradim (2009: 69) says that while old media obtained their credibility from authority and from a laboriously built brand name, in new media credibility and/or authority depends on the ongoing communicative process and of the quality of the collective intelligence that is generated. In the same line Benkler (2008: 54) states 'our old forms of assigning credibility and authority to a claim were closely aligned with the institutional origins of the claim. As information production becomes radically decentralized, new models of authority are seeking similar recognition'.

We could also add that to cyberspace, credibility can be tested. In this way the possibility we have to recover information published in the past, to find information published in other countries, to use search engines to localise information, etc., are mainstream.

Even more important is the fact that on the internet, users are part of a social network through which they can communicate easily, working as reporters from their own neighbourhoods, towns or countries. The points of view of users who are from different places around the world about a topic, a person or a project are very relevant to build credibility. We differentiate three levels on which Indiegogo and Kickstarter assemble elements that help to build credibility for users: support, identity and trajectory.

There are three dimensions of support, given by the online crowdfunding platforms: support based on alliances, support based on experience and support based on popularity. Firstly, support based on alliances means to have partners. Both crowdfunding online platforms, Indiegogo and Kickstarter, have partners. Indiegogo is supported by enterprises, organisations and institutions such as YouTube, UC Santa Barbara Technology Management Program or the American Red Cross. Among the partners of Kickstarter are Sundance Institute and The Guardian. Support based on experience is visible through testimonials of people who have achieved their goals. These testimonials are composed by the name and the surname of the creators and sentences expressed by them. Kickstarter includes also the quantity of money they raised, the number of backers who supported their project and the name of their projects. One example of testimonial from Kickstarter reads:

'Kickstarter creates a community of people interested in what you're doing, and the community that's created is important'. Braxton Pope. raised $159,015 from 1,050 backers for 'The Canyons'

One testimonial from Indiegogo says:

'With Indiegogo I found supporters for my film from around the globe. People who have not only become new collaborators but new friends' Anna Newman. Pinball Donut Girl.

Finally, support based on popularity refers to Twitter followers and to Facebook friends. Indiegogo Twitter account has 163,000 followers, and 235,427 persons

Table 10.3 Elements which generate credibility in Kickstarter and Indiegogo platforms

1. Credibility			
1.1. Support	Alliances	K, IG	Partners
	Experience	K, IG	Testimonials
	Popularity	K, IG	Number of Twitter followers and Facebook friends
1.2. Identity	Identity	K, IG	Section 'About us' where the members of the platform team are shown
	Trajectory	K, IG	Amount of money collected since its birth, number of projects funded
		IG	Two hundred and twenty-four countries and territories had a project. Manage five currencies and four languages

Note: Abbreviations of crowdfunding platforms: *K* Kickstarter, *IG* Indiegogo

have indicated they like it on their Facebook page. Kickstarter Twitter account has 892,000 followers and 974,000 likes users have liked it on their Facebook page.

The other two criteria that referred to credibility of platforms we have included are identity and trajectory. Identity refers to the fact that both Kickstarter and Indiegogo give information about the creators and the persons who manage the platforms. Indiegogo has a section called 'About us' where it is possible to see the photos, the names and phrases of three persons who work on the platform. Kickstarter is much more transparent than Indiegogo in presenting their team. They include the name and surname of the 89 people based in Greenpoint, Brooklyn, who work in the platform.

To share their trajectory, the platforms publish data that referred to the amount of money collected by them, and also they publish data that referred to the number of projects funded. Kickstarter states that since 2009, 6.9 million people have pledged one billion dollars, funding sixty-eight thousand and one hundred creative projects.

Indiegogo does not include on their website the data about the money collected or about the projects successfully done. Highlighting their international vocation, they refer to the fact that 224 countries and territories have developed one project by using this platform. In the same line, they point out that the platform manages five currencies and four languages (see Table 10.3).

10.6.2　Trust

Credibility is a characteristic attributed to individuals, institutions or their communicative products. Nevertheless, we do not only trust individuals or organisations but also technical and sociotechnical systems. Belsky et al. (2010) explain that 'trust in computer science is used to characterise the success of a system that removes the possibility of human defection or error. That is the purpose of trusted computing platforms. When used, thus, trust is not a design level at all but rather a description of the outcome of a system, which signifies confidence in its performance'.

Choi and Scott (2012) carried a research whereby they found that the social network sites' usage intensity is positively linked to some of the aspects of users' relational social capital (trust and identification), which have a positive effect on electronic word-of-mouth quality.

Trust at crowdfunding platforms is highly needed because the mainstream motivation of these websites is to get people funding the projects, and that means users making online payments. Reimink (2014) identified eight factors which may be important for the intention to invest in a crowdfunding initiative: 'quality of the project, amount of money, rewards, geography, network involvement, shared values, trust and duration'.

Brogan and Smith (2012: 215) elaborated a formula which should help to calculate trust in a virtual environment: 'C (credibility)$\times$R (reliability)$\times$I (intimacy)/S (self-orientation)'. The formula says that 'the more credible and reliable a person appears, and the lesser I am in doubt about his altruism, the more I will trust him or her'.

To generate trust, both platforms, Kickstarter and Indiegogo, state clearly the conditions that they impose to creators and to donors. Furthermore, they have a tracking income system, which is visible and updated immediately to let users see the changes that occurred in the project's state. This tracking income system is central to these online platforms because it permits users to dispose of the funding data immediately, creating an environment where all is done with transparency. If a person funds any project, he or she can see how the money is automatically added to the chosen project. This improves notably the method created by Pulitzer, which consisted on publishing on his newspaper the name of the donors and the quantity they had given. It is possible to know immediately the changes that occurred in the state of a project, seeing the quantity of money received, the number of donors and even the quantity given by each donor.

Kickstarter and Indiegogo state clearly which are the fees they keep and also explain the payment methods that supporters can use. Kickstarter obtains 5 % from the amount of money if a project is successfully funded. Indiegogo permits users to choose a flexible option which means that in case the project does not achieve the goal aimed, the creators still receive the money that the donors gave to them until the last day of the campaign. In this case, the platform will keep 7 % of the amount collected.

Both platforms indicate how to do the payments and also refer to their security servers and to the possession of certificates certifying trust on the operations. It is important to highlight that, as it is explained at the platforms, there are payment processing fees of 3 or 5 % (see Table 10.4).

Table 10.4 Elements which generate trust in Kickstarter and Indiegogo online crowdfunding platforms

2. Trust			
2.1. Conditions	Fees	K	If a project is successfully funded, 5 % of the total amount of money. No fees if a project is not successfully funded
		IG	It permits flexible funding. If goal is not reached, creators keep the money collected and the platform keeps 7 % of the amount obtained
	Intellectual property	K, IG	Authors retain the intellectual property
	Payment method	K	US-based projects: Amazon payments. Non-US projects: third-party payment processor. Payment processing fees: 3–5 %. Credit card and prepaid card
		IG	PayPal and credit card
	Security	K	Transactions through secure server. Software protocol Secure Sockets Layer Secure
		IG	Trusted Certified Privacy and BBB Accredited Business
2.2. Tracking income		K, IG	It is possible to know immediately the changes of a project: quantity of money received, number of donors and quantity given by each donor

Note: Abbreviations of crowdfunding platforms: *K* Kickstarter, *IG* Indiegogo

10.6.3   Engagement

According to Goodman (2012, in Paykacheva 2014: 14), 'engagement process mainly consists of providing customers with a memorable experience that would encourage the consumers to spread the word of mouth about the company's products. Essentially, it generates a special connection between the company and its customers, thus, providing the customers with additional value to the products'. She describes an engagement marketing cycle as having the following phases: providing service experience, entice to stay in touch, engaging into communication and customer endorsement.

Thinking about crowdfunding online platforms, engagement consists on providing users with a memorable experience, which encourages them not just to support projects, or to submit them, but to participate in comment threads and to spread the content provided in the platforms by the creators of the projects. These are the usual expectations of creators to raise awareness about the project.

Platforms generate engagement with the user through different elements. Firstly, it is needed to have a usable interface design. Secondly, platforms must introduce the use and the link to social media whereby the users can be connected and can generate social participation. Ta Lu et al. (2014) carried a research intended to analyse how the use of social media contributes to the success of a crowdfunding project. From their empirical work, they concluded that promotional activities on social media have positive impacts on the crowdfunding projects. They also found that the results of a project are much more correlated to the early promotional activities on social media rather than to its own characteristics such as project duration or fundraising goal, and they demonstrated that promotion in social media must be combined with the performance of actions outside the social media because while promotion to friends increases the size of a group, the external actions through different channels expose the project to more groups.

Moisseyev (2013: 17) points out that crowdfunding backers support projects not only by providing funds but also by using social seals of approval. After studying several successful crowdfunding projects, the author states 546 Facebook likes as a number of 'likes' that a project is supposed to have in order to achieve its goal.

According to the author, the index of social media seals of approval has a direct connection with the fund obtained and with the number of supporters of the projects. His research also concludes that the number of social media followers has a direct relation with the index of social media seals of approval.

The researcher concludes that the connection between fundraising total and 'likes' shows that, without enough 'likes', the project will not reach its objective. Following this idea, he states that even if an author has a social profile with few 'friends', it is better to include it because social media can rapidly transform real-life connections into social media followers.

We grouped in eight criteria the features of Kickstarter and Indiegogo platforms referred to engagement: (1) accessibility, (2) navigation, (3) networking, (4) feedback, (5) source of information, (6) time constraint, (7) applications and (8) freedom (see Table 10.5). Each of this criterion is responsible for the overall engagement developed with platform, but essentially with each project: (1) accessibility contains the features, which refer to the coverage of the platforms and how to access them; (2) navigation helps also to engage users. In this criteria we include the features oriented to facilitate the navigation through the platforms: (3) networking embraces the social networks where platforms have presence; (4) feedback cover forms to establish asynchronous and synchronous communication through the platforms; (5) source of information refers to the elements included in the platforms intended to help creators to use them; (6) time constraint, as its name indicates, refers to the time established as maximum to reach the amount of money stated as needed by the creators; (7) applications concern tools and devices oriented to facilitate the use of the crowdfunding platforms; (8) finally, freedom refers to the possibility that donors have to contribute to the projects anonymously.

10.7 Conclusions

In a context where the difficulties that people find to have a job are pushing them to their limits, a collective interest on helping others and on sharing things, time and effort is visible on the cyberspace through the existence of a multitude of online

Table 10.5 Elements which generate engagement in Kickstarter and Indiegogo online crowdfunding platforms

3. Engagement			
3.1. Accessibility	Coverage	K	To launch a project, it is needed to be within the United States, United Kingdom, Canada, Australia and New Zealand
		IG	Anybody can launch a project
	Registration	K, IG	It is possible to enter with a Facebook account
3.2. Navigation	Searcher	IG	Advanced search engine. Localise projects by geographic area and by categories
	Categories	K	Art, comics, crafts, dance, design, fashion, film and video, food, games, journalism, music, photography, publishing, technology and theatre
		IG	Art, comics, community, dance, design, education, environment, fashion, film, food, gaming, health, music, photography, politics, religion, small business, sports, technology, theatre, transmedia, video/web, writing
3.3. Networking	Social networks	K	Twitter, Facebook, Tumblr, Instagram, Vine
		IG	Facebook, Twitter, Instagram, LinkedIn, Google+
3.4. Feedback	Asynchronous	K, IG	Forum which is answered in 24 h
	Synchronous	IG	Offers 'DIWO Live! Service' every Friday at 12 pm. It brings users the possibility to ask questions in real time, receive tips from the founders and learn from other members
3.5. Source of information	Periodical	K, IG	Weekly newsletter blog
	Non-periodical	K, IG	Creator Handbook (Kickstarter)
			Indiegogo Playbook
3.6. Time constraint		K, IG	Sixty days as maximum to fund a project
3.7. Applications		K, IG	App for I phone
3.8. Freedom		K, IG	Possibility to fund without being registered as donor, that is, anonymously

Note: Abbreviations of crowdfunding platforms: *K* Kickstarter, *IG* Indiegogo

platforms whereby users share cars, houses and even lend money in exchange of interests which usually are lower than required by the financial system.

The success of online crowdfunding platforms takes place in this context where users are interested in being part of projects, in participating in the building of our society and of our environment; this is specially clear in the case of the named civic crowdfunding platforms, whereby users who live in the same neighbourhood or village contribute with their money to repair and/or to install or create any element of their surroundings.

It is important to highlight the role that crowdfunding is playing in the political arena. New political parties are emerging thanks to the money collected from the crowd, fostering a political renovation in different countries. Even when some governments around the world are defining regulations intended to reduce the capability of crowdfunding, this financial method seems unstoppable.

Online crowdfunding platforms, similarly as free software, are a great example of creative technologies. They do not work only as tools but as environments where it is possible to perform actions that in another space could be more difficult, or even impossible, to achieve. Crowdfunding platforms, in a technological dimension, allow users to propose projects to be funded. From a social perspective, they are contributing to generate a kind of template to present creative projects, which can be useful to develop innovative projects to attract the interest not only of the users but also of the industry. So, a new industry might be developed. In this way and as an example of how crowdfunding projects, and indirectly their supporters, are being introduced in the industry, we point out the Oscar for Best Documentary Short 2013 was won by 'Inocente', a movie funded with $52,527 through Kickstarter, on a goal of $50,000.

References

Belleflamme P, Lambert T, Schwienbacher A (2010) Crowdfunding: an industrial organization perspective. Paper presented at digital business models: understanding strategies conference held in Paris on 25–26 June 2010. Retrieved from http://economix.fr/pdf/workshops/2010_dbm/Belleflamme_al.pdf

Belsky L, Kahr B, Berkelhammer M, Benkler Y (2010) Everything in its right place: social cooperation and artist compensation, 17 Mich Telecomm Tech Law Rev 1 (2010). Retrieved from http://www.mttlr.org/volseventeen/belsky.pdf

Benkler Y (2008) The university in the networked economy and society: challenges and opportunities in the tower and the cloud: higher education in the age of cloud computing. In: Katz RN (ed) EDUCAUSE. Retrieved from https://net.educause.edu/ir/library/pdf/PUB7202f.pdf

Brogan C, Smith JS (2012) The impact equation: Are you making things happen or just making noise? Penguin, New York

Chatzimilioudis et al. (2012) Crowdsourcing with smartphones. IEEE Internet Computing. Published by the IEEE Computer Society, September–October 2012, pp 36–34. Retrieved from http://staff.frederick.ac.cy/com.ca/AndreasConstantinides/Docs/ieeeIC12.pdf

Choi JHE, Scott J (2012) Electronic word of mouth and knowledge sharing on social network sites: a social capital perspective. Retrieved from http://www.scielo.cl/pdf/jtaer/v8n1/art06.pdf

Chopra S, Dexter S (2011) Free software and the economics of information justice. Ethics Inf Technol 13:173–184. doi 10.1007/s10676-010-9226-6

Crowdfunding Platforms Database. The crowdcafe. Retrieved from http://www.thecrowdcafe.com/crowdfunding-platforms/database

Crowdfunding Platforms: Global Database. The crowdcafe. Retrieved from http://www.thecrowdcafe.com/crowdfunding-platforms/database/

CrowdingIn. Crowdfunding in the UK. Retrieved from http://crowdingin.com/about

Damus M (2014) Crowd funding. Developing concepts for supportive instruments beyond the funding phase. Universität Bremen. Hochschule Bremerhaven. Institut for Kommunication in sozialen Medien. Retrieved from http://www.epubli.de/shop/buch/37608/excerpt

Davies R (2013) Civic crowdfunding from the statue of liberty onwards. Retrieved from http://rodrigodavies.com/blog/2013/02/19/civic-crowdfunding-from-the-statue-of-liberty-to-now.html

De Buysere K, Gajda O, Kleverlaan R, Marom D (2012) A framework for European crowdfunding. Retrieved from vhttp://www.europecrowdfunding.org/files/2013/06/FRAMEWORK_EU_CROWDFUNDING.pdf

Gerbner E, Hui J (2012) Crowdfunding: motivations and deterrents for participation. Retrieved from http://egerber.mech.northwestern.edu/wp-content/uploads/2012/11/Gerber_Crowdfunding_MotivationsandDeterrents.pdf

Global List of Crowdfunding Sites. The Soho Loft. Retrieved from http://thesoholoft.com/global-list-of-crowdfunding-sites/

Gómez-Diago G (2004) Una perspectiva evaluadora de documentos web desde la Ciencia de la Comunicación/A perspective for evaluating web documents from communication science. Razón y Palabra. Retrieved from http://www.razonypalabra.org.mx/anteriores/n40/ggomez.html

Gómez-Diago G (2005) Tres criterios para evaluar la calidad informativa en Internet: Credibilidad, Cobertura, Novedad/Three criteria for evaluating the quality of information on the Internet: credibility, coverage, novelty. Global Media J. Retrieved from http://gmje.mty.itesm.mx/articulos4/gomez_g.html

Gómez-Diago G (2010) Brainflowing, virtual/physical space and the flow of communication: an explanatory approach to the metaverse through a tool designed for brainstorming. Metaverse Creat 1(1):49–65. Retrieved from http://dx.doi.org/10.1386/mvcr.1.1.51_1

Gómez-Diago G (2012) Cyberspace and cyberculture. In: Kosut M, Golson JG (eds) Encyclopedia of gender in media. SAGE Reference Publication, Thousand Oaks

Gómez-Diago G (2013a) Identificación de Consecuencias negativas de incluir la enseñanza y/o aprendizaje de software privativo en el aula universitaria. Estudio Piloto./ Identification of Negative effects of include learning of privative software in the university classroom. Pilot Study. Razón y Palabra 82. Retrieved from. http://www.razonypalabra.org.mx/N/N82/V82/28a_Gomez_V82.pdf

Gómez-Diago G (2013b) Aplicando el concepto de diseño de la comunicación para realizar investigación aplicada. Dos posibles vías: Diseñando herramientas de comunicación y metodologías de diseño. Brainflowing/Applying the concept of communication design for applied research. Two possible routes: designing communication tools and design methodologies. Brainflowing, pp 1019–1029. National conference on research methodology in communication. Spanish Association of Communication Research. Segovia, 2–3 May 2013. Retrieved from http://dialnet.unirioja.es/descarga/articulo/4230554.pdf

Gómez-Diago G (2014) Emancipative technology in formal education: the case for free and open source software (FOSS). In: Stochetti M (ed) Media and education in the digital age. A critical introduction. Peter Lang, Frankfurt am Main/Berlin/Bern/Bruxelles/New York/Oxford/Wien

Goodman G (2012) Engagement marketing: how small business wins in a socially connected world. Wiley, Hoboken

Gradim A (2009) Digital natives and virtual communities: towards a new paradigm of mediated communication. Estudos em Comunicação no 5:53–73 Maio. Retrieved from http://www.ec.ubi.pt/ec/05/pdf/03-gradim-digital.pdf

Growth of Crowdfunding Platforms Worldwide. Statista. Retrieved from http://www.statista.com/statistics/251567/growth-r-of-crowdfunding-platforms-worldwide/

Helm M (2011) Träume finanzieren 2.0 Eine quantitative Befragung zu den Motivationen der finanziellen Projektunterstützung auf deutschsprachigen Crowdfunding-Plattformen, Master thesis, Institute of Media and Communication Studies, Technical University of Ilmenau, Germany

Hemer J (2011) A snapshot on crowdfunding. Working papers firms and region, No. R2/2011. Retrieved from https://www.econstor.eu/dspace/bitstream/10419/52302/1/671522264.pdf, https://www.facebook.com/LYNCHthree

Hui J, Gerbner E, Gergle G (2014) Understanding and leveraging social networks in crowdfunding: implications for support tools. Retrieved from http://collablab.northwestern.edu/pubs/DIS2014_HuiGerberGergle.pdf

Internet Live Stats. Internet users in the world. Retrieved from http://www.internetlivestats.com/internet-users//

Internet Usage Statistics. The internet big picture. World internet users and population stats. Retrieved from http://www.internetworldstats.com/stats.htm

Jian L, Usher N (2014) Crowd-funded journalism. J Comput-Med Commun 19:155–170. doi:10.1111/jcc4.12051

Life in a Day (Documentary Film). Retrieved from https://www.youtube.com/user/lifeinaday

Marchiori MR, Buzzanell MP (2012) Communities of interaction. A Brazilian NGO sustainability case study. European Group for Organizational Studies, 28th EGOS Colloquium 2012. Aalto University & Hanken School of Economics, Helsinki, Finland, 5–7 July 2012. Retrieved from http://www.uel.br/grupo-estudo/gefacescom/images/EGOS_2012_n77Fg_MARCHIORIBUZZANELL_FINAL_PAPER.pdf

Moisseyev A (2013) Effect of social media on crowdfunding project results. Retrieved from http://digitalcommons.unl.edu/cgi/viewcontent.cgi?article=1043&context=businessdiss

Mollick E (2014) The dynamics of crowdfunding: an exploratory study. J Bus Ventur 29:1–16, Retrieved from http://www.sciencedirect.com/science/article/pii/S088390261300058X

Mollick E, Nanda R (2014) Wisdom or madness? Comparing crowds with expert evaluation in funding the arts. Harvard Business School Entrepreneurial Management, Working paper No. 14–116. Retrieved from http://papers.ssrn.com/sol3/papers.cfm?abstract_id=2443114

Paykacheva V (2014) Crowdfunding as a customer engagement channel. Thesis Kajaani University of Applied Sciences, School of Business and Administration Degree Program in International Business. Spring 2014. Retrieved from https://www.theseus.fi/bitstream/handle/10024/72731/Paykacheva_Valeriya.pdf?sequence=1

Percentage growth of crowdfunding platforms worldwide between 2008 and 2012. Retrieved from http://www.statista.com/statistics/251567/growth-r-of-crowdfunding-platforms-worldwide

Putnam R (2000) Bowling alone: the collapse and revival of the American community. Simon & Schuster, New York

Raymond ES (1998) The cathedral and the bazaar. First Monday 3, No. 3. Retrieved from http://www.firstmonday.org/issues/issue3_3/raymond/

Reimink M (2014) Crowdfunding in Dutch small and medium enterprises: an empirical analysis of factors influencing the intention to invest in a crowdfunding initiative. Retrieved from http://essay.utwente.nl/65168/1/Reimink_MA_MB.pdf

Rogers E, Kincaid DL (1981) Communication networks: toward a new paradigm for research. Free Press, New York

Rushkoff D (2010) Program or be programmed. Ten commands for a digital age. OR Books, New York

Shneiderman B (2000) Creating creativity: user interfaces for supporting innovation. ACM Trans Comput-Human Interact 7(1):114–138. Retrieved from http://hcil2.cs.umd.edu/trs/99-01/99-01.pdf

Stohl C (2014) Crowds, clouds, and community. J Commun. doi: 10.111/jcom.12075. Retrieved from http://onlinelibrary.wiley.com/doi/10.1111/jcom.12075/pdf

Ta Lu, Chun Xie, Sihonh, Kong, Xiangnan, Yu, Philip S (2014) Inferring the impacts of social media in crowdfunding. In: WSDM '14 proceedings of the 7th ACM international conference on web search and data mining, pp 573–582. ACM, New York. doi 10.1145/2556195.25562.51. Retrieved from http://users.wpi.edu/~xkong/paper/wsdm14_lu.pdf

The Free Software Directory. Retrieved from http://directory.fsf.org/wiki/Main_Page

Willems W (2013) What characteristics of crowdfunding platforms influence the success rate? Kunst- & Cultuurwetenschappen, 30 August. Retrieved from http://hdl.handle.net/2105/15182

Yi Kuo, Pei & M. Gerbner, Elizabeth (2012) Design Principles: Crowdfunding as a Creativity Support Tool. CHI 2012, May 5–10, 2012, Austin, Texas, USA. Retrieved from http://www.researchgate.net/profile/Pei_Yi_patricia_Kuo/publication/261360075_Design_principles_crowdfunding_as_a_creativity_support_tool/links/00463533f733865c48000000.pdf

Young Elliott T (2012) The everything guide to crowdfunding. Adams Media, Avon

Part IV
Makers and Players

Chapter 11
Fabricating Futures: Envisioning Scenarios for Home Fabrication Technology

Joshua G. Tanenbaum and Karen Tanenbaum

11.1 Introduction

11.1.1 *If You Aren't a Maker Yet, You Will Be Soon*

Making and Maker culture are growing at such prodigious speed that there are very few people whose lives aren't touched by them, even if they don't realize it. The scope of activities and practices that fit under the heading of Maker Culture is vast: woodworking, electronic prototyping, robotics, urban farming, software development, fire-art, weaving, circuit-bending, citizen science, prop-making, cosplay, reenactment, soapbox racer rallies, home genetic sequencing, bio-art, homesteading, knitting, rocketry, and many other more obscure practices all fit inside the "tent" of Making. Making is many things: it is a practice, a set of values, a culture and a community, a return to the past, an embracing of the future, and a new mode of production and consumption. While much of the best making involves a return to lost handcrafts and traditional "boutique" production techniques, one cannot underestimate the impact of recent innovations in small-scale fabrication technologies. Machines that used to only be available at industrial scales, at prices that could only be borne by large corporations, are now becoming accessible to the home Maker. And some machines, like 3D printers, are creating new workflows and prototyping processes that defy traditional industrial production methods.

J.G. Tanenbaum (✉) • K. Tanenbaum
Department of Informatics, Donald Bren School of Information and Computer Sciences,
University of California-Irvine, Irvine, CA, USA
e-mail: tanenbaj@uci.edu

© Springer-Verlag London 2015
N. Zagalo, P. Branco (eds.), *Creativity in the Digital Age*,
Springer Series on Cultural Computing, DOI 10.1007/978-1-4471-6681-8_11

In this chapter we explore the role that home fabrication technology might play in our future by examining how fabrication technology has been imagined in popular culture and science fiction and by envisioning several near-future scenarios of our own. We situate these scenarios within the emergent space of *design fiction*: a form of envisioning that combines design thinking with fictional imaginings about a desired (or feared) future.

11.1.2 The Rise of Maker and DIY Culture: A New Kind of Industrial Revolution

The idea that do-it-yourself (DIY) practices could be seen as a cultural movement is relatively new. In a sense, DIY was the only option available for most of human history: in order to survive, one must be capable of some sort of "making," whether it be the production of food, or the creation of tools, or the construction of shelter and clothing. The majority of humans, for the majority of the time that we have been on the earth, survived by making. The first industrial revolution changed all of this in the late 1700s, in Great Britain. Characterized by a radical growth of manufacturing capability, it brought with it radical changes to the quality of life of those living in industrializing areas: infant mortality dropped, population increased, our life spans lengthened, and, for the first time in history, wealth spread beyond the confines of the aristocracy. It really wasn't until the first industrial revolution and the sudden emergence of a literate, urban, educated, moneyed middle class that large portions of the population were released from making-to-survive and afforded the affluence and leisure time to indulge in making-for-pleasure. In the mid-1800s, before the dust had even settled on this new world, a *second* industrial revolution was underway. Advances in metallurgy, transportation, and petroleum refinement once again reshaped the world, leading to some of the signature industrial innovations of that period including the assembly line, the railroad, and the automobile.[1] While the changes wrought by industrialization resulted in sweeping social change, the first two industrial revolutions are generally considered to be the result of large-scale technological innovation and infrastructural development, rather than the actions and practices of a small subculture of individuals. The same cannot be said about the revolution that is currently underway, which has its origins in a return to the small- and mid-scale practices that had been in decline in the era of mass production.

Chris Anderson argues that there are three characteristics of the current Maker movement:

1. People using digital desktop tools to create designs for new products and prototype them ("digital DIY").
2. A cultural norm to share those designs and collaborate with others in online communities.

---

[1] For a more detailed discussion of the history of industrial culture as it relates to Maker culture, see (Anderson 2012).

3. The use of common design file standards that allow anyone, if they desire, to send their designs to commercial manufacturing services and to be produced in any number, just as easily as they can fabricate them on their desktop. This radically foreshortens the path from idea to entrepreneurship, just as the Web did in software, information, and content (Anderson 2012, p. 21).

Anderson's triad of characteristics is focused on the impact of digital creation tools and the spread of common standards, all of which are crucial for the rise of a mode of production that is diffuse rather than concentrated. Taking his list as a starting point, we would argue for the inclusion of several environmental factors as well: the recent explosion in electronic waste and cheaply available high-technology surplus, a growing environmental consciousness and desire for sustainable material goods, and the growth of institutions that support Making and/or thrive on it. Perhaps the most well known of these, MAKE magazine and the affiliated small and large Maker Faires across the globe, have highlighted the explosive growth of home- and garage-based activities that combine art, technology, craft, and science. Local Maker spaces and fab labs, along with an explosion in Maker-oriented education and summer camps, are creating safe places for making across all ages and socioeconomic classes. At the same time, the platforms for experimenting with robotics, microcontrollers, wireless networks, and other high-tech tools are rapidly democratizing: dropping in price, increasing in capability, and becoming much more accessible to hobbyists and young Makers through more abstracted programming languages and simplified electronics platforms. Taken altogether, these conditions and practices can be seen as a "third industrial revolution" (Anderson 2010, 2012).

There has also been an explosion of new technologies that radically augment the industrial production capabilities of the individual or small group. Chris Anderson calls particular attention to the rapid growth of 3D printer technology as the basis for this new industrial revolution. The sales of 3D printers for personal use increased over 35,000 % between 2007 (66 printers sold) and 2011 (23,265 printers sold),[2] and there has also been an explosion of homemade 3D printers, spearheaded by the RepRap project [Fig. 11.1]. We would expand the set of home fabrication technologies to include laser cutters, CNC mills, and other industrial fabrication machinery that is rapidly becoming available at the hobbyist scale. With the proliferation of home fabrication technology, the production loop from concept to prototype to product can take place in a single garage or community hacker space, without employing the large-scale industrial machineries that were previously necessary to develop a new technology. The third industrial revolution takes the technological capabilities of industrial society and blends them with the individualized modes of production of preindustrial society to create a distributed set of local practices that simultaneously subvert and rely upon the economies of scale developed during the modern era.

---

[2] http://www.bloomberg.com/news/print/2012-10-24/personal-3-d-printer-sales-jump-35-000-since-2007.html

Fig. 11.1 (*Left*) A homebuilt RepRap 3D printer. "RepRap" is short for "*Rep*licating *Rap*id proto-typer" (http://reprap.org/wiki/RepRap) (Picture under GNU Free Documentation license, http://www.gnu.org/copyleft/fdl.html). (*Right*) The MakerBot Replicator 2. One of the flagship commercial 3D printers for the hobbyist market (http://www.makerbot.com/) (Picture under Creative Commons Attribution License: https://creativecommons.org/licenses/by/2.0/)

11.1.3   Maker Motivations: Pleasure, Utility, and Expressiveness

While many of those who identify as capital-M Makers pursue their practice largely as a personal creative outlet, there are also elements of making-to-survive present in the movement. In earlier work, we analyzed current Maker motivations in terms of three principles: pleasure, utility, and expressiveness (Tanenbaum et al. 2013a), which we will briefly revisit here.

People make things for a variety of reasons. Many are driven purely by the joy of learning a new skill and the pride of having created something with their hands. Examples of playful making can be found at large venues such as Maker Faire and Burning Man as well as within the practices of smaller maker subcultures, such as the Steampunk movement. For many Makers, there is a pleasure to be had in the use of a particular material or technique: practitioners develop emotional relationships with woodworking, blacksmithing, glass blowing, or book binding because of the rich material properties of the medium. Maker and hacker cultures also offer an imagined vision of what the world could be if personal and creative production of design artifacts was spread democratically across individual creators. Nostalgic movements like urban homesteading or needlework/knitting communities suggest a different way of approaching the future of food and textile production by revisiting past ways of making. In these cases, the potentially abstract envisioning of a different past or future is supported by the physical practice of making. In these practices of playfulness, material engagement, and embodied cultural imagination, we can find an underlying concern with pleasure.

However, it would be inaccurate to characterize Maker practices as being solely motivated by pleasure: much Making is undertaken in pursuit of a specific practical

Fig. 11.2 (*Left*) A urine powered generator developed by 14-year-old Duro-Aina Adebola, Akindele Abiola, Faleke Oluwatoyin, and 15-year-old Bello Eniola. Shown at Maker Faire Africa in 2012 (http://makerfaireafrica.com/2012/11/06/a-urine-powered-generator/) (Picture under a Creative Commons Attribution License: https://creativecommons.org/licenses/by/2.0/). (*Right*) A machine for processing sisal into rope by Alex Odira Odundo at Maker Faire 2010 (http://www.matchamaker.info/maker15.php) (Picture under a Creative Commons 3.0 license: https://creative-commons.org/licenses/by/3.0/us/)

goal or to address a particular local need. In many cases, Making is motivated by a need to repair something broken or to modify something to better suit the needs of the Maker. Still other Makers are participating in crowd-funding platforms like Kickstarter and IndieGoGo and start-up accelerators like Haxlr8r to transform their handcrafted vision into a small business. There is also a growing discourse around DIY in non-Western contexts, especially with the rise of Maker Faires in China and Africa in recent years. Many of the projects on display at Maker Faire Africa reflect a marriage of the playful and the pragmatic, such as the urine powered generator (Fig. 11.2, left), or the Sisal Processing Machine of Alex Odira Odundo (Fig. 11.2, right) that is reminiscent of the Spinning Jenny, one of the earliest and most important inventions of the first Industrial revolution. The diversity of the works on display makes a strong argument for utilitarian and pleasure-oriented motivations coexisting.

Finally, we have found that many Makers are motivated by a desire for self-expression. Making is often deeply enmeshed with other ideological positions such as a critique of consumer cultures of mass production (in the case of many Steampunk Makers (Tanenbaum et al. 2012), a desire for radical self-reliance (in the case of many makers within the Burning Man community[3]), or a commitment to sustainable practices of repair and reuse. Making is, in many ways, a political act: by repairing rather than replacing broken items and by creating material goods within home workshops and maker spaces, Makers are opting out of the supply chains and industrial processes that underlie the economies of the nineteenth and twentieth centuries. We therefore consider expressiveness to be a third significant motivation for Maker practice.

---

[3] http://www.burningman.com/preparation/event_survival/radical_self_reliance.html#.
UkXbRsZ498E

While there is much more to be said about Maker practice, we feel that this brief introduction provides a good grounding in the movement. The remainder of the chapter will explore potential paths that this exponential growth of home fabrication and making processes might take, using the framework of design fiction as an analytical tool.

11.2   Envisioning and Design Fiction

The notion of design fiction is a relatively new one. Bruce Sterling coined the term in his 2005 book *Shaping Things,* where he distinguished it from other forms of science fiction as being more concerned with the realities of design than with the "grandeur of science" (Sterling 2005). The term was later picked up and expanded in a presentation given by Julian Bleecker at the Engage Design conference in 2008, where he discussed the ways in which "science, fact, and fiction are all knotted up," i.e., influencing one another (Bleecker 2008). Bleecker's talk was given in response to an unpublished paper by Paul Dourish and Genevieve Bell entitled "Resistance is Futile: Reading Science Fiction Alongside Ubiquitous Computing" (Dourish and Bell 2014). In this article, the authors perform parallel analyses of design trends in science fiction television during the period from 1963 to 1989 and developments in ubiquitous computing in the 1980s. They show how science fiction stories in movies and books play a significant role in shaping the general public's understanding of science fact and even contribute directly to inspiring the scientists and technologists who engage in turning fiction into fact.

David Kirby uses the term diegetic prototypes to "account for the ways in which cinematic depictions of future technologies demonstrate to large public audiences a technology's need, viability and benevolence" (Kirby 2010). Both Kirby and Bleecker provide the gestural interface from the film Minority Report as an example of a fictional realization of a technology that went on to broadly inform public opinion (and design practice) about interactive technologies. A more recent work by Bleecker explores how actual design and science as practices intersect with the imagined futures of science fiction narratives (Bleecker 2009). There is certainly a rich body of evidence connecting representations of technology in fiction to actual innovations. Nathan Shedroff and Chrostopher Noessel dedicate an entire book to tracing the connections between science fictional interfaces and interaction design; one of their more striking observations is the similarity between the flip-open communicators of the original Star Trek television show and the immensely popular Motorola StarTAC phone, which was the first cellular phone to flip open and closed (Shedroff and Noessel 2012).

In a recent interview, science fiction author Bruce Sterling redefined design fiction, in light of the evolution of the concept in these other venues, describing it thusly:

> It's the deliberate use of diegetic prototypes to suspend disbelief about change. That's the best definition we've come up with. The important word there is diegetic. It means you're thinking very seriously about potential objects and services and trying to get people to

concentrate on those rather than entire worlds or political trends or geopolitical strategies. It's not a kind of fiction. It's a kind of design. It tells worlds rather than stories. (Bosch and Sterling 2012)

Stories, on the screen or the page, are a powerful vehicle for exploring the ramifications of potential new technology and the practices that surround it. These stories expose our hopes and fears for the future, examining how specific pieces of technology might change us for better or worse. Stuart Reeves positions design fiction within the broader heading of *envisioning*, a term which he uses "to refer to a broadly future-oriented aspect of technology design which mixes fictions, forecasts, extrapolations or projections into societal visions for technological progress" (Reeves 2012). Mark Weiser, in his seminal work *The Computer for the 21st Century,* described the imagined life of "Sal," the heroine of his near-future scenario that defined many of the core principles for ubicomp (Weiser 1991). While this scenario had many of the hallmarks of science fiction literature, Mark Blythe points out that the Sal scenario, and those like it, often omit *conflict,* which he claims is "the basic foundation of all narrative" (Blythe 2014). Blythe argues that an understanding of narrative (and the techniques of literary theory and criticism) is becoming more and more important to the development of new technologies. One very interesting recent example of this is a paper by Kirman et al. entitled "CHI and the future robot enslavement of humankind: a retrospective" (Kirman et al. 2013). Written from the perspective of "robots from the future," the paper presents itself as a historical document outlining how a number of contemporary trends in the field of human-computer interaction were manipulated in order to allow robot overlords to fully enslave the human race. These types of envisionings are crucial in exploring all of the possible ramifications of new technology, and they serve an important role in how we imagine our technological future.

11.3 Design Fictions of Fabrication in Popular Culture

In this section, we look at several existing design fictions of the future of fabrication, drawn from popular science fiction books, TV, and comics. We show how these specific pieces of media approach fabrication and what role it plays in the imagined society that surrounds it. By looking at these specific visions, we can uncover some of the common anxieties and desires surrounding home fabrication and think about possible trajectories for its development. Following the analysis of existing works of design fiction, we purpose two scenarios of our own, one utopic and one dystopic, as lenses for contemplating the potential of home fabrication technologies.[4] Throughout this section we refer to a number of resources and works created by participants in the fan communities surrounding these design fictions. These "vernacular criticisms" provide a rich body of insight into these works that greatly

---

[4] A much more comprehensive list of the appearance of matter replication in media can be found here: http://tvtropes.org/pmwiki/pmwiki.php/Main/MatterReplicator.

exceeds that produced in formal scholarship, a point that has been made quite rigorously in the work of Henry Jenkins (Jenkins 1992, 2006a, b).

11.3.1 Star Trek: *The Replicator*

In 1987 Gene Roddenberry launched the first television sequel to *Star Trek*, his legendary science fiction series. *Star Trek: The Next Generation* (TNG) updated the look and feel of the sci-fi classic and introduced a number of new fictional technologies including the holodeck and the matter replicator. In the world of TNG, matter replication is an extension of the teleportation technology introduced in the original series. Described in some detail in a fan wiki,[5] the replicator is capable of materializing (and dematerializing) matter according to a set of preprogrammed "templates" stored in its memory. Replicators are also programmed with safeguards to prevent them from producing anything poisonous and are capable of filtering out contaminants and "cleaning up the dishes" by dematerializing them back into their "pattern buffers."

Star Trek sets out to depict a utopian future: a post-greed, post-disease, post-poverty society where most conflict arises from encounters with the unknown universe, rather than from human factors. Humans are depicted as having overcome many of their flaws and failings in order to pursue more noble lives of scientific exploration. Perhaps because humans have overcome the need or desire to acquire wealth and material goods, the world depicted by the show is often quite sterile and minimalistic: life aboard a starship is shown to be almost ascetic in nature. For much of the show, the replicator is relegated to the background, an enabling technology that provides for most of life's necessities including food, water, and clothing. Although replication can conceivably create any material object, it is most often seen serving drinks (Fig. 11.3). Jean Luc Picard, the captain of the starship Enterprise, is frequently shown ordering "Tea, Earl Grey, Hot," from the replicator,[6] although it is worth noting that the first instance of this order—in Season 2 Episode 11: *Contagion*—is met with a malfunction: the replicator provides him with a potted plant in a teacup. Indeed, when replication technology *does* surface from the background, it is often because there is some sort of problem with it, as in the case of the first episode of Season 3: *Evolution*. When a science experiment involving medical nanotechnology goes awry, a number of malfunctions afflict the starship Enterprise, including a faulty replicator.

In a fan-made reedit of scenes from this episode[7], the ship's doctor gets in a verbal sparring match with a malfunctioning replicator "food slot," resulting in a

---

[5] http://en.memory-alpha.org/wiki/Replicator

[6] "StarTrek—Picard"Tea,EarlGrey,Hot"Clips": http://www.youtube.com/watch?v=R2IJdfxWtPM

[7] "Crusher oses battle with replicator": https://www.youtube.com/watch?feature=player_embedded&v=YgR_ySkR1fo

Fig. 11.3 A replicator materializes a mug of coffee in Star Trek: Voyager (http://www.startrek.com/database_article/replicator)

Fig. 11.4 The faulty food slot in Star Trek TNG, Season 3, Episode 1 (http://en.memory-alpha.org/wiki/File:Food_slot_malfunction_evolution.jpg)

brilliant vernacular critique of how science fiction envisions technology. The video goes as follows:

"Computer, fix the food slot," Dr. Crusher demands. "The food slot is functioning properly," the computer replies. The replicator continues to visibly malfunction, spilling liquid out of a glass and onto the floor [Fig. 11.4]. "Well, check it again!" insists Crusher. "The food slot is functioning properly," the computer retorts, in what is clearly a lie. "Computer, deactivate the food slot," she tries, but the malfunction continues. "The food slot is functioning properly," the computer says. Crusher continues to throw commands at the system, hoping that one will work, but seems to be caught in a loop. Finally, frustrated, she begins to walk way. The food slot deactivates when her back is turned. She returns, and the malfunction immediately begins once more. Crusher rolls her eyes and walks off in a huff.

This type of diagnostic frustration is one that is familiar to anyone who has used a piece of technology that isn't working properly. While the struggle with the replicator in the video in question is exaggerated for comic effect well beyond the circumstances of the original episode, the sentiment that it expresses highlights a fundamental truth about our relationship to technology, especially when we don't understand the underlying systems that we interact with. Replicators in Star Trek are "black boxes"—their functions are opaque and almost magical most of the time. It also highlights an important property of matter replication which we will see recurring throughout all of our considered design fictions: that physical making has nontrivial consequences that cannot be ignored. An error in a piece of software that governs a digital system of some sort can be put aside until one is ready to deal with it. An error in a replication system creates a material problem that must be dealt with immediately, lest it spiral out of control and threaten one's safety in the physical world.

In the "post-scarcity" economy of Star Trek, matter replication has taken the place of most other industrial processes. The world includes portable replicators, replication parlors, and industrial sized replicators, capable of creating large-scale components for starships and other vehicles. At the same time, the replicator appears to have reduced the need for designers: seldom do we see someone programming a new design into the replicator. The central computer of the ship seems capable of instructing the system to create any object that might not already exist in the system's database, with only minor verbal specifications from a human interlocutor. The only real limitation of the replicator seems to be whether or not it can be provided with adequate energy to operate properly: in one of the sequels to TNG—*Star Trek: Voyager*—replicator access is rationed due to an energy shortfall when the ship finds itself stranded far from home.[8] Unsurprisingly, the reintroduction of scarcity into the world of Star Trek results in a return to previous economic tropes including black markets and gambling for replicator ration cards.

11.3.2 Transmetropolitan: The Maker

A stark contrast to the optimistic minimalist utopia of *Star Trek*, Warren Ellis describes a disturbingly familiar, far-future dystopia in *Transmetropolitan*. Ellis's graphic novel follows the exploits of Spider Jerusalem: a futuristic Hunter S. Thompson-esque journalist whose commitment to ferreting out the truth earns him the ire of the city's immensely corrupt police department and sociopathic political administration. Part sociopolitical commentary, part gonzo reporting, and part post-humanist rumination, Transmetropolitan envisions a future of radical technological body modification, rampant consumption, and hedonistic abandon where nothing is too shocking or too extreme. Against this landscape, Ellis explores

---

[8] http://en.memory-alpha.org/wiki/Replicator_ration

Fig. 11.5 The introduction of Spider Jerusalem's drug addicted maker in Transmetropolitan, Issue #1 (Ellis and Robertson 1997)

a wide-ranging assortment of common science fiction tropes, including the home replicator, or "Maker."

Makers in Transmetropolitan are marketed and sold by "Godti": a branch of the mafia, whose advertisements proudly exclaim "Live like a Don….or Sleep with the Fishes"! In Issue #1 of Transmetropolitan (Fig. 11.5), Spider Jerusalem's Maker introduces itself, saying:

> *I AM A GODTI 101 MAKER: I RECOMBINE MATTER INTO ANY OF TWENTY-FIVE THOUSAND DIFFERENT FORMS. I AM FUELED BY A BASE BLOCK OF SUPERDENSE NEUTRAL MATTER SUSPENDED IN A DRIFT VISE, ALSO HOLDING THE FUEL CONVERSION THAT ALLOWS ME TO USE GARBAGE OR OTHER UNWANTED MATTER…AND I AM NOT YOUR FUCKING ASHTRAY.* (Ellis and Robertson 1997, p. 20)

Makers in Transmetropolitan have personalities and opinions: When Spider Jerusalem orders a pair of "live-shades," his maker produces a set of glasses with mismatched red and green lenses. Jerusalem discovers that the machine intelligence embedded in his Maker is high on a synthetic "hallucinogen simulator for live machinery" (Fig. 11.5). Even after Spider Jerusalem removes the machine's "drugs," it continues to manufacture and install new ones, and at one point, when he tries to "junk" the machine, he wakes up with a horse's head in his bed, courtesy of the

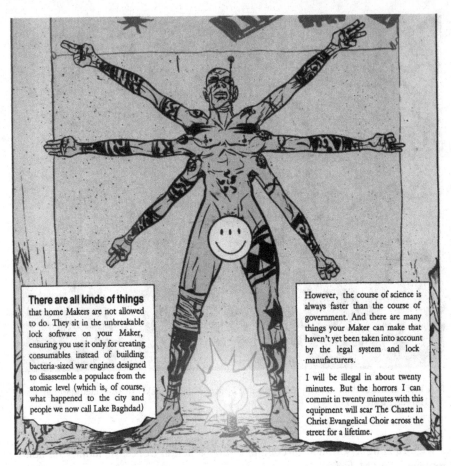

There are all kinds of things that home Makers are not allowed to do. They sit in the unbreakable lock software on your Maker, ensuring you use it only for creating consumables instead of building bacteria-sized war engines designed to disassemble a populace from the atomic level (which is, of course, what happened to the city and people we now call Lake Baghdad)

However, the course of science is always faster than the course of government. And there are many things your Maker can make that haven't yet been taken into account by the legal system and lock manufacturers.

I will be illegal in about twenty minutes. But the horrors I can commit in twenty minutes with this equipment will scar The Chaste in Christ Evangelical Choir across the street for a lifetime.

Fig. 11.6 An "excerpt" from one of Spider Jerusalem's columns, in which he discusses the legal and illegal uses of home Makers (Ellis et al., Ellis and Pope 2001)

Mafia. In spite of these dystopian elements, the Maker in Transmetropolitan demonstrates a variety of unique capabilities that are not seen in other fictional home fabrication devices: it can scan and evaluate its surroundings and it is capable of recycling household garbage.

The Maker is like a genie in a bottle, with extensive restrictions on what it can and cannot produce (Fig. 11.6).

There are all kinds of things that home Makers are not allowed to do. They sit in the unbreakable lock software on your Maker, ensuring you use it only for creating consumables instead of building bacteria-sized war engines designed to disassemble a populace from the atomic level (which is, of course, what happened to the city and people we now call Lake Baghdad).

However, the course of science is always faster than the course of government. And there are many things that your Maker can make that haven't yet been taken into account by the legal system and lock manufacturers (Ellis and Pope 2001, p. 13).

This highlights the very real challenges that home fabrication poses to contemporary industrial regulation, when faced with the emergence of small-scale manufacturing centers that are neither willing nor able to comply with the many safety and environmental regulations that have been developed for factories and industrial centers. In a fictional world where the most popular beverage is "Ebola Cola…you drink it…it eats you!" the fact that home replication is heavily regulated at the engineering level stands out as a significant commentary on the possible dangers of this technology.

The technology underlying the fabrication system results in different companion technologies within a design fiction. Makers in the world of Transmet rely on nanoscale reconfiguration in order to operate—they take raw material and rearrange its molecules to create new things. In contrast, the replicators in Star Trek rely on energy-to-matter conversion to create physical objects from energy templates. Related technologies in Star Trek are the teleportation systems and the holodeck, both of which use variations of this technique. Because making in Transmetropolitan relies on nanotechnology, the possible related design fictions are very different. Perhaps the most interesting additional use for nanotech in Transmet is a "post-singularity" scenario where humans upload their consciousness to clouds of nano-technological "Foglets." These post-human consciousnesses exist distributed across millions of microscopic robots, which are capable of manipulating other matter at the atomic level, in essence turning people into sentient "Maker Clouds" (Fig. 11.7).

Unlike the replicators of Star Trek, the Maker does not result in a post-scarcity economy. While Makers *can* recycle garbage, it is indicated that they operate much better if fueled by "base blocks." In Transmetropolitan Issue #9, Spider Jerusalem's neighbor demands the exorbitant fee of two base blocks in exchange for agreeing to watch Jerusalem's mutated two faced chain-smoking cat (Ellis and Robertson 1998). Rather than becoming *less* materialistic, people in Transmet are portrayed as becoming more concerned with material pleasures than can be easily imagined.

11.3.3   The Diamond Age: *The Feed*

Occupying something of a middle ground between the future worlds depicted in Star Trek and Transmetropolitan, Neal Stephenson's 1995 novel *The Diamond Age* takes place in a future version of earth revolutionized by nanotechnology advances that permit commonplace matter replication at both the domestic and industrial level (Stephenson 1995). Matter compilers are connected to "the Feed," a stream of configurable matter organized like the current day electrical grid, powered by centralized "Sources" which deconstruct air and water into constituent molecules for the raw Feed material.

> Source Victoria's air intakes erupted from the summit of the Royal Ecological Conservatory like a spray of hundred-meter-long calla lilies…The lilies sprouted from a stadium-sized cut-crystal vase, the Diamond Palace, which was open to the public. Tourists, aerobicizing pensioners, and ranks of uniformed schoolchildren marched through it year in and year out,

Fig. 11.7 A "Foglet Human" manufactures a flower from molecules in the air (Ellis and Robertson 1998)

peering through walls of glass (actually solid diamond, which was cheaper) at various phases of the molecular disassembly line that was Source Victoria. Dirty air and dirty water came in and pooled in tanks. Next to each tank was another tank containing slightly cleaner air or cleaner water. Repeat several dozen times. The tanks at the end were filled with perfectly clean nitrogen gas and perfectly clean water.

The line of tanks was referred to as a cascade, a rather abstract bit of engineer's whimsy lost on the tourists who did not see anything snapshot-worthy there. All the action took place in the walls separating the tanks, which were not really walls but nearly infinite grids of submicroscopic wheels, ever-rotating and many-spoked. Each spoke grabbed a nitrogen or water molecule on the dirty side and released it after spinning around to the clean side. Things that weren't nitrogen or water didn't get grabbed, hence didn't make it through. There were also wheels for grabbing handy trace elements like carbon, sulfur, and phosphorus; these were passed along smaller, parallel cascades until they were also perfectly pure. The immaculate molecules wound up in reservoirs. Some of them got combined with others to make simple but handy molecular widgets. In the end, all of them were funneled into a bundle of molecular conveyor belts known as the Feed, of which Source Victoria and the other half-dozen Sources of Atlantis/Shanghai, were the fountainheads (Stephenson 1995, pp. 7–8).

The Sources, and by extension the Feed, are controlled by one particular cultural group, the Neo-Victorians. Basic versions of food, water, and shelter can be compiled for free, yielding a post-scarcity world in which work is not really strictly necessary. As with many science fiction dystopias, however, this freedom from the burden of simple survival does not create a world of only intellectual and creative explorers, but rather a large, illiterate population focused on consuming low-brow entertainment. One of the main characters of the book, a young girl named Nell, grows up in this environment, living in a high-rise apartment she never leaves, receiving all toys, food, and clothing from the MC (matter compiler) in the kitchen, about which she knows only that "mites" inside the machine create the items that emerge. At one point, her older brother comes home from a scavenging mission in the outside world with a ragged piece of fabric he found washed up on a beach, coming from the high-class compound of the Neo-Victorians, who do not rely solely on MC-created goods. Nell and Harv investigate the strange material:

Harv gripped the end of the thread beneath his thumbnail and pulled. It looked quite short, but it lengthened as he pulled, and the fuzzy edge of the piece of fabric waffled too fast to see, and then the thread had come loose entirely. He held it up for inspection, then let it drift down onto a heap of others just like it.

'How many does it have?' Nell said.

'Nell', Harv said, turning to face her so that his light shown into her face, his voice coming out of the light epiphanically, 'You got it wrong. It's not that the thing has threads in it— it is threads. Threads going under and over each other. If you pulled out all of the threads, nothing would be left.'

'Did mites make it?' Nell asked.

'The way it's made—so digital—each thread going over and under other threads, and those ones going over and under all the other threads—' Harv stopped for a moment, his mind overloaded by the inhuman audacity of the thing, the promiscuous reference frames. 'It had to be mites, Nell, nothing else could do it'. (Stephenson 1995, p. 55)

The children are unable to comprehend how human effort could produce something like the intricacy of tightly woven cloth fabric. Later in the book, Nell encounters an enclave of craftspeople who still maintain the knowledge of making things by hand, but the only purchasers of their goods are the wealthy Neo-Victorians who value such things in a way that is both moral and aesthetic. One of the central conflicts of the book is around the covert development of a competing version of nanotechnology, "the Seed," which decentralizes the Feed system, providing more anarchic access and creating economic disruption.

The ability to easily fabricate anything one can imagine reconfigures how wealth and social status are construed in this world. In an early chapter, a character is traveling by "airship" to a birthday party for the granddaughter of one of the Neo-Victorian "Equity Lords."

> The hierarchy of staterooms on _Æther_ matched the status of its passengers perfectly, as these parts of the ship could be decompiled and remade between voyages. For Lord Finkle-McGraw, his three children and their spouses, and Elizabeth (his first and only grandchild so far), the airship lowered a private escalator that carried them up into the suite at the very prow, with its nearly 180-degree forward view.
>
> Aft of the Finkle McGraws were a dozen or so other Equity Lords, merely earl- or baron-level, mostly ushering grandchildren rather than children into the class B suites. Then it was executives, whose gold watch chains, adangle with tiny email-boxes, phones, torches, snuffboxes, and other fetishes, curved round the dark waistcoats they wore to deemphasize their bellies...
>
> ...John Percival Hackworth was an engineer. Most engineers were assigned to tiny rooms with fold-down beds, but Hackworth bore the loftier title of Artifex and had been a team leader on this very project, so he rate a second-class stateroom with one double bed and a fold-out for Fiona (Stephenson 1995, p. 13).

Where Star Trek imagines a world where fabrication and freedom-from-want result in a reduction in the trappings of status and wealth, The Diamond Age instead suggests how such technologies could reify social hierarchies. The Neo-Victorians appear to have combined corporate structures with the notions of "Peerage" that dominated British society in the nineteenth century. There is, however, evidence of some meritocratic systems in place: the society also values design sufficiently to reward those with talent and skill, such as Hackworth. On the airship _Æther_, the most valuable commodity is space, and so the subdivision of space becomes far more significant as a status representation than other elements such as the materials for the construction of the staterooms or other aspects of ornamentation that might have previously represented affluence. _Time_ and _effort_ are also things to be valued, as seen in the previous example, where the use of handwoven cloth is preferred by the Neo-Victorians over a nanotechnologically fabricated material. Affluence and wealth aren't about access to rare materials (such as gold or diamond, both of which can be fabricated as cheaply as any other object), but instead about access to other things that are in short supply: particular skills and expertise.

11.3.4 Makers: _The Ride and "Disney in a Box"_

Our last example is set in the much more immediate future and deals with the implications of today's home fabrication technologies and of the explosion of electronic waste. Cory Doctorow's novel _Makers_ explores a potential near future of the Make movement in general and 3D printing in particular.[9] (Doctorow 2009). In a not-too-distant future, an economic downtown has created rampant unemployment. Two genius tinkerers, Lester and Perry, help create an era of "New Work," where rapid fabrication techniques allow for fast-paced innovation and creativity. Small, local collectives of Makers create scads of crazy new inventions and throw them on the open market, knowing at least one will succeed and fund the next cycle of innovation. "New Work" is fun and successful for about a decade, but eventually its bubble pops under the weight of lawsuits, knockoffs, and poor business decisions by the not-business-inclined inventors. As a lark, Perry and Lester build a "ride," a golf-cart navigable theme park depicting the glory days of New Work, highlighting all the wacky inventions of those years. Over time, the ride becomes crowd sourced as people contribute new items to it and vote on what should and shouldn't be included as they ride through. The next innovation comes when Lester suggests "franchising" the ride, by opening new locations across the country. Networked together online, armed with 3D printers and small assembly bots, each ride is updated nightly with new additions and rearrangements. Narrative and evocative scenes start to appear instead of just collections of objects and are replicated across the country. Everything seems great until pieces of a recently dismantled Disney attraction are "contributed" to the ride and Disney cracks down, suing for copyright infringement. While legal (and physical battles) are waged, a Disney executive named Sammy comes up with an idea inspired by the ride's use of 3D printing and robotics: Disney in a Box (DiaB), a Disney-made 3D printer that produces miniature versions of the park attractions, assembled by small robots in people's homes. Each day a new miniature set is released and printed using Disney's proprietary printers and proprietary "goop."

> [Sammy] outfitted [his office] with fan photos of their DiaB shrines in their homes, with kids watching enthralled as the day's model was assembled before their eyes. The hypnotic fascination in their eyes was unmistakable. Disney was the focus of their daily lives, and all they wanted was more, more, more…One model a day was all. Leave them wanting more. Never breathe a hint of what the next day's model would be—oh, how he loved to watch the blogs and the chatter as the models self-assembled, the heated, time-bound fights over what the day's model was going to be (Doctorow 2009, p. 327).

Of course, in Doctorow's world this type of closed system demands liberation, and so Perry and Lester do exactly that, hacking the printers to accept non-Disney-licensed designs and use non-Disney-provided feedstock. In doing so, Lester expresses one of the core tenets of the Maker movement:

> So here's this stupid thing which Disney gives you for free. It looks like a tool, like a thing that you use to better your life, but in reality, it's a tool that Disney uses to control your life. You can't program it. You can't change the channel. It doesn't even have an *off switch*. That's what gets me exercised. I want to redesign this thing so it gets converted from something that controls to something that gives you control (Doctorow 2009, p. 342).

Unlike the previous three design fictions we've looked at, *Makers* was written with the values and practices of today's Maker and DIY cultures in mind. Fabrication

---

[9] The entire novel is available under a creative commons license here: http://craphound.com/makers/download/

is much less "magical" and the issues surrounding it map to some of the major concerns of today's Maker communities: how does the technology subvert or reify existing industrial infrastructures (and the systems of power that rely on them)? How can intellectual property law stretch to deal with the rapid growth of open-source hardware and software movements and the decentralization of manufacturing? These are questions that we have asked in some detail in some of our previous work (Tanenbaum et al. 2013a), and so we will not get into in detail here. In *Makers*, Doctorow explores these types of political questions by envisioning shantytowns that emerge in response to the slow economic collapse of the USA. These ad hoc communities become natural allies for Perry and Lester and the other fringe makers of the New Work movement, so when the one near their workspace is burned down, they invite the residents to rebuild inside their abandoned factory workspace.

> The squatter village was a shantytown, but it was no slum. It was a neighborhood that could be improved. And the boys are doing that: having relocated the village to their grounds, they're inventing and remixing new techniques for building cheap and homey shelter fast (Doctorow 2009, p. 84).

The result is an unregulated community in which invention and innovation are put to work solving immediate local problems, like housing and transportation, without reliance on larger industrial infrastructures.

11.4   Analysis

Each of the four design fictions we have considered takes a different perspective on the nature of fabrication technology, and each results in a very different view of the future. The ways in which these scenarios converge and diverge reflect broadly how the future of fabrication has been imagined. Of critical importance is the underlying structural mechanics of the technology that each scenario envisions:

- *Star Trek* materializes objects and food from energy templates, which are freely available to all.
- *Transmetropolitan* uses home appliances to break down garbage and "base blocks" into raw materials which are recombined into goods.
- *The Diamond Age* envisions a "server → client" relationship in which raw materials (refined atoms) are distributed to remote fabrication terminals.
- *Makers* envisions slightly more advanced 3D printers, combined with home automation technologies.

These different approaches mean that each scenario has a different set of dynamics in place, in terms of the relationship between raw materials and manufactured goods, in terms of production and distribution, and in terms of the economics of fabrication. The infrastructures of *The Diamond Age* parallel our current industrial model of production and distribution, whereas the isolated Makers and replicators of *Transmet* and *Star Trek* reflect two different takes on decentralization of what are essentially "black boxes." *Makers* takes these decentralized super-local solutions and positions them in relationship to more traditional industrial infrastructures, arguing for the value of cracking open the black box in order to escape the restrictions of global manufacturing. Encoded within these technological systems are four different value systems about the impact of fabrication on society:

- *Star Trek* optimistically imagines that freedom-from-want will result in a more egalitarian distribution of goods to all.
- *Transmetropolitan* argues that people are just waiting for an excuse and an opportunity to indulge themselves in the extremes of hedonism, something made much easier by the home Maker.
- *The Diamond Age* sees replication technology as a way to reinforce social hierarchies, making the livelihood of the "crass lower classes" dependent upon the advances of the upper crust. The plot pivots around the introduction of a disruptive, decentralized fabrication technology.
- *Makers* argues that fabrication technology can free one from dependence on systems of production, provided one has the skill and wherewithal to hack together a solution.

It is clear that when we envision the future of fabrication and replication, our visions are intimately bound up in how we feel about the economics of scarcity. Small-scale fabrication is seen as a way of circumventing the dynamics of supply and demand. Whether or not this results in liberating us from greed and materialism (Star Trek), reinforcing class distinctions and hierarchies (The Diamond Age), freeing us to desire more outlandish and extreme things (Transmetropolitan), or casting us into a frontier of radical self-sufficiency (Makers) is a matter of perspective.

Each of these fictions also reflects some interesting fears about the negative implications of fabrication technology. Paramount among these is the fear that, left unregulated, fabrication could be extremely dangerous. Both Star Trek and Transmetropolitan include safeguards on what their fabricators are allowed to produce. Interestingly, both of these design fictions also assign a certain degree of autonomy to their fabrication control systems—the central computer, in the case of Star Trek, and an AI personality, in the case of Transmet. The presence of a synthetic intelligence underlying the technology in both of these worlds also minimizes the presence of a human designer: objects are requested in broad strokes ("Tea, Earl Grey, Hot"), but the details are left up to the machine. In contrast, both The Diamond Age and Makers envision societies where the ability to modify, design, and program is a source of prestige and power. Both of these scenarios argue for the value of a decentralized, democratized, relationship with fabrication technology, and both position their characters in opposition to a larger, more traditional industrial infrastructure.

11.5   Fabrication Scenarios

Envisioning the future of fabrication is not the same thing as predicting the future. Design fiction is about imagining the implications of a technology in a potential future setting, rather than predicting the specific future of a new technology. The remainder of this chapter is devoted to some imagined scenarios of our own that we believe can inform our understanding of the possible futures of home fabrication.

11.5.1   The Horizon of Home Fabrication: The Next Decade

Our scenarios require that we make some educated guesses about what the future of fabrication will look like. These guesses are at least partially extrapolated from current trends and trajectories that we have observed in the development of home fabrication appliances. However, some of these conditions are less grounded in the current technology and more grounded in what we imagine would need to happen in order for our fictional scenarios to come to pass. We suggest the following five conditions as likely advances over the next 10 years:

1. *3D printers as household appliance:* In order for 3D printers to spread beyond hackers and hobbyists, they need to become cheaper and easier to use and maintain. Fortunately, this appears to be happening already. The same cannot be said for laser cutters and other more industrial fabrication solutions (such as lathes and CNC mills). In our imagined future, 3D printers and other fabrication technologies are common, affordable, and well on the way to ubiquity. It also seems reasonable to imagine that the home fabricator of the future will be a networked device, connected to the other computers and media devices in the home, and able to exchange information with them.
2. *Closed loop between "feedstock" and "product":* One factor that limits the usefulness of 3D printers is that they require raw feedstock in various materials and colors to produce objects. Over time the cost of this feedstock can exceed the cost of the printer (similar to the cost of cartridges for ink-jet printers). Further, one drawback of ubiquitous 3D printing is a potential proliferation of fabricated "junk" in people's lives. Unlike data (which can be accumulated without any meaningful material footprint in the home) fabricated objects take up nonnegotiable physical space. If we wish to imagine fabrication being used more widely and frequently, we must solve both of these problems. To do so, we envision an integrated recycling solution[10] that closes the loop between input and output by allowing us to fuel our replicators with household waste and previously printed objects.
3. *Wider range of printable materials and colors:* As 3D printing has evolved, the technology has moved from the slow creation of low-resolution plastic parts to

---

[10] Similar to the Filabot: http://filabot.com/

systems that can print in metal, ceramic, paper, and other materials, at high resolutions, often very quickly. In the last few years, the MakerBot "Replicator" has evolved from a single to a dual extrusion system capable of printing multiple colors of material simultaneously. In our envisioned future scenario, we extend this trend to imagine home 3D printing with a wide spectrum of simultaneous colors and materials, including the ability to print with biological material.[11] We also expect home fabricators with larger printable areas which can support larger-scale projects.

4. *Improved tools for designing, scanning, and recombining physical items into digital models:* One of the major bottlenecks for creating unique 3D printed objects is the learning curve needed to produce a 3D model that is suitable for printing. Many online services, such as Thing-a-Verse, offer premade models for a small price or even for free under open-source licensing. However, as home fabrication technologies grow, so too must grow the resources for creating usable digital source files of things to be printed. 3D scanning technology is rapidly becoming more accessible, following a similar trajectory to 3D printers. One notable system, "FabScan," is open source and can be built for less than $100,[12] making it a spiritual cousin to the RepRap project and the DIY Makerbots.

5. *Hybrid fabrication systems that blend different methods:* 3D printing is an "additive" fabrication method which sets it apart from the more commonly used "subtractive" systems such as laser cutting and CNC milling. We envision home fabrication appliances that combine both of these methods, resulting in a much broader range of potential outputs.

These five advances set the stage for our scenarios, as we try to imagine some of the new applications for home fabrication as a communications platform.

11.5.2 Utopian Scenarios: Fabrication as Communication and Tool

Although we have identified at least three motivations for Making above, when we look at how current Maker culture discusses home fabrication, in many cases the discourse seems focused solely on the utilitarian motivations, with very little attention paid to pleasure and expressiveness. Consider that in each of the four design fictions we have examined, design is something that is done by a computer (Star Trek and Transmetropolitan) or an expert (The Diamond Age) or a genius (Makers). None of these scenarios see home fabrication technology as a creative platform for

---

[11] Already, we have seen medical research use 3D printing to grow a human ear (http://lifesciences. ieee.org/articles/feature-articles/332-printing-body-parts-a-sampling-of-progress-in-biological-3d-printing) and the Burritobot project suggests that 3D printed food is not too far off (http://vimeo.com/41461637).

[12] http://hci.rwth-aachen.de/fabscan

regular people, and perhaps consequentially, none of these scenarios imagine a role for home fabrication outside of filling a set of already well-understood utilitarian needs.

It shouldn't be surprising that many of our visions of the future of fabrication are focused on utilitarian applications. Home fabrication allows people to rapidly iterate prototypes, to easily replace damaged parts, and to facilitate hands-on learning and create communities of Makers. These are significant capabilities, and they have the potential to be highly disruptive. The history of the personal computer followed a similar trajectory, with computers initially being viewed through primarily utilitarian lenses. However, we believe that there is a lot of room for our other two motivations— pleasure and expressiveness—to play out in home fabrication, in ways that haven't been fully envisioned yet. In this scenario we explore one possible future for expressive and pleasurable home fabrication.

Throughout *Makers*, Doctorow champions the fabrication system of the Ride as a source of *emergent* meaning: he cultivates a political stance in which outsider communities built on ingenuity and appropriation are morally superior to mainstream consumer culture. A narrative can be found within the ride, but it is explicitly an emergent, non-authored one, coming out of the "collective unconscious" of the Maker community who builds it piece by piece, vote by vote. Bottom-up phenomena like the ride and hacked replicators are shown to be superior to the empty corporate-entertainment complex embodied by Disney. In this regard, he is faithful to the values arising in contemporary Maker communities. But by characterizing (and valorizing) replication technology as a tool, Doctorow is ignoring a much more interesting role for this technology. Relegating the *Disney in a Box* system to the status of tool is like relegating a book to being only an instruction manual and not a novel; it is like saying that computers are only good for engineering, math, and science but not art, games, or communication.

The core insight of Doctorow's *Disney in a Box* example is that the objects that it creates carry meaning—that it is a system for telling stories. The fabricators he envisions regularly produce new models for their users—models that convey a story designed to be communicated and distributed through the medium of fabrication. Networked fabricators can be used to syndicate material objects—to communicate stories through material objects. When viewed in this light, 3D printers are not just a tool: they are a new communications platform. Home fabrication technology isn't just a powerful tool: it's also a medium.

Understanding 3D printers, laser cutters, and home milling machines as communication technology is a profound leap away from the utilitarian and towards the playful and the aesthetic. This is a critical step in the evolution of home fabrication, in the same way that playful and artistic uses of computers were critical to the growth of personal computing in the 1970s and 1980s. While Makers, hackers, designers, engineers, and artists already have a myriad of uses for home fabrication technology, it is still hard to make a case for the everyday use of these devices among the general public. This parallels the ways in which early computers were of critical importance to scientists, mathematicians, and engineers, but of little use in the home. The powerful number crunching capabilities of computers could not drive a consumer market, but the development of desktop publishing, digital games, graphical user interfaces, and networked communication expanded the role of the personal computer in the home by transforming the number crunching machine into a platform for communication, creativity, and entertainment.

Disney in a Box illustrates one possible future for home fabrication as a communications and media platform, but it relies on some advances in fabrication that are still far off, such as the ability of 3D printers to create small functional automata to perform simple tasks. We need not look so far into the future of this technology, however, to envision a world in which home fabrication can be used as a meaningful distribution and syndication platform.

11.5.3 Storytelling Objects

To understand the origins of these scenarios, one must first be familiar with some of our earlier work in interactive storytelling (Tanenbaum and Tanenbaum 2010, 2011; Tanenbaum et al. 2011, 2013b). We created a storytelling system called *The Reading Glove* that used RFID tagged objects and a custom-built digital glove to tell a story through tactile interaction. To read the story, one must pick up physical objects, triggering audio narration that relates the experiences of a British spy in French-occupied Algiers at the turn of the nineteenth century, who is betrayed by his agency and forced to flee. The project is part of a larger ongoing investigation into Tangible Ubiquitous Narrative Experiences, or TUNE (Fig. 11.8).

While there are many wonderful things about working with physical objects for storytelling—they have tactile and structural affordances, they activate embodied memory, they create playful opportunities for interaction, etc.—one of the major drawbacks is that we could not easily disseminate our story in the form that it was meant to be experienced in. Authors, filmmakers, and game designers all are able to publish and distribute their narratives to broad audiences with relative ease, but telling stories with objects is materially more difficult to communicate to an audience. It was against this backdrop of personal creative frustration that we envisioned these scenarios.

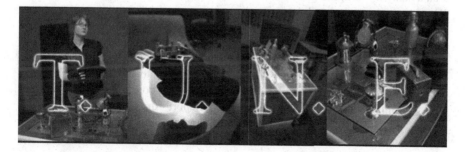

Fig. 11.8 Images of the reading glove

11.5.4 Fabrication as Syndication

David loves new types of stories and has been excited about a project that he read about online recently that takes advantage of his home Maker. He navigates to the website of the author and registers as a new reader. He fills out a brief questionnaire about himself, his preferences, and his favorite books and movies, before being given a selection of titles and genres to choose from. He is in the mood for something "magical," so he selects a story titled "The Sorcerer's Legacy," in the Fantasy genre, and hits the "download" button. Next to his computer, the Maker whirrs into life. Slowly an object begins to take shape: it is a floppy wizard hat in blue velvet, with silver and gold stars. A tag attached to it reads "Wear Me!" The clear protective dome over the print bed pops open to indicate that the hat is finished, and David is quick to put it on. His webcam registers that he is wearing the hat and captures a quick 3D scan of his likeness. Within moments, the Maker is printing a new item: a magic wand! An animated version of David is casting spells on the screen, and David follows along with his new wand, conjuring items from the "aether" which appear in the bed of his Maker. Each item is a clue—a fragment of a puzzle that he must solve to access the next fragment of the story...

Imagine that instead of downloading an e-book version of a story, you download an encrypted set of instructions for your 3D printer. You run the program, and slowly, each object takes shape before you, like an artifact in an archaeological dig site, being carefully revealed. These objects are a material record: a collection of artifacts pregnant with narrative meaning. You pick them up and turn them over in your hands, looking for a clue about where to begin. Each object triggers a fragment of media playback associated with it (for our The Reading Glove project we used RFID to accomplish this, but it could be done with fiducial markers, camera vision, or a host of other technologies). As you play with the objects, you find yourself embodying a character in the story who also interacted with them. Some of the objects have particular physical affordances, inviting embodied interactions that communicate meaning by evoking muscle memory and somatic awareness. Others combine to form new objects, which unlock hidden narrative content.

We can take this idea even farther. In *Makers*, Doctorow has Disney selling subscriptions to a "model of the day" that prints out each morning, enthralling children as they try to figure out what it will be. We can imagine a scenario where the 3D printer is part of a much larger media ecosystem: where the objects it produces are a small part of a much bigger experience that spans digital games, traditional narratives, and physical play. This notion is inspired in part by the success of the Skylanders system, which uses a combination of action figures, digital games, and collectible cards to create an experience that extends into both the physical and digital realms.[13] The core conceit of this system is the "Portal of Power"—a near-field communication device that is used to "teleport" the action figures into the digital game. Each figure has its own onboard memory, allowing players to develop

---

[13] http://www.skylanders.com/giants/whatyouneed-new

them through play on their own game consoles or in collaboration/competition with their friends. At least partially in response to the success of Skylanders, Disney has recently released "Disney Infinity"[14]—a game using the entire Disney catalog of intellectual property that combines digitally augmented physical toys with a large virtual toybox that is reminiscent of Minecraft or Little Big Planet.

Imagine a serialized story with a weekly release schedule. Every Sunday afternoon a new model is released and immediately pushed out to the printers of all subscribers. This model might be an action figure of a major character in the story or a piece needed to solve a secret puzzle at the end of the previous week's episode. This is a black box: you don't know what the model will look like until it is printed. Subscribers get preferred access to the models, while nonsubscribers have to wait for (or pirate) their copies later. Having the model gives you additional capabilities needed to succeed in the next level of the digital game, and the models are cool toys in their own right. On Monday the week's new episode is broadcast, both as a television show and as a new playable component of a digital game. This new episode incorporates Sunday's printed item in some meaningful way, providing the subscriber with a tangible piece of the narrative world that is also a key to deeper levels of the narrative and the game play.

In this situation, the 3D printer and its objects become part of a broader set of interlocking narratives and interactions. It becomes another channel for communicating information about the story, as well as a means of rewarding and reinforcing players in the game. Storytellers might use this to build suspense by releasing a mysterious artifact or create surprise by delivering an innocuous seeming object that takes on narrative significance later. Storytellers can foreshadow important moments or create a series of interlocking objects that slowly interconnect to reveal additional narrative information over the course of a season.

A final element that we'd like to consider in this section is the role that expressiveness plays in this context, specifically the ability to customize physical objects to the particular user's preferences. Now let's imagine a version of the above system where you download an action figure and it has a face that you designed, or is wearing an outfit that you selected, or is even a miniature version of yourself as a character in the story. Or perhaps your participation in this system allows you to craft a profile of your own preferences. Personalization means that you can participate in a shared media experience, but that your participation reflects something about you. So perhaps you and all of your friends have subscribed to the same story, but each of you receives an object that is slightly different and tailored to your preferences.

These scenarios begin to explore the possibilities of 3D printing and home fabrication for purposes beyond the utilitarian. Our next set of scenarios consider some of the ways that these technologies could become intrusive and problematic in the future.

---

[14] https://infinity.disney.com

11.5.5 Dystopian Scenarios: Fabrication, Spam, Hacking, and Biological Warfare

While we are likely a long way off from matter replicators capable of creating nanomachines that can convert entire cities into dust (Transmetropolitan), there are still plenty of potentially harmful effects that we can imagine on our horizon of home fabrication. Already we are starting to have to deal with the legal and ethical issues that 3D printed handguns are raising.[15] Untraceable, unregistered, plastic firearms are just the tip of the iceberg when it comes time to envision the dark future of these technologies; however, for this discussion we would like to first consider a more mundane (and we believe much more likely) annoyance.

11.5.5.1 3D Printed Spam

Elena is woken up in the middle of the night by the sound of her Maker as it whirrs away on an elaborate print job. "Did I forget to disconnect it before bed?" she asks herself. This is not the first time this has happened, but she had hoped that her new message filters would prevent the machine from wasting power and feedstock on these things. She stumbles out of bed and pads down the hall to her home office, where the printer is steadily churning away. On the print bed she can already see the inevitable object taking shape and she rolls her eyes in annoyance. It is a comically oversized set of male genitals. Emblazoned along one side is a web address and a message (in broken English) informing her that she too could satisfy the ladies in her life, if she orders this secret herbal formula today! The printer dome pops open, and she removes the fabricated penis. Sighing she tosses it into a bin under the desk marked "Recycle," where it joins a half dozen similarly priapic items in various rainbow hues. "How the hell did I get onto this list?!" she wonders, as she heads back to bed. Tomorrow she will need to upgrade her spam filters.

There is no reason to think that 3D printing will not be subject to the same unwanted commercial messaging as every other networked technology. In the 1980s, as fax machines proliferated, the practice of sending "Junk Faxes" became a common annoyance. Spam e-mails have existed as long as there have been computer networks. We can imagine a future where networked home fabrication systems fall victim to a whole host of creative intrusions. As we considered in our example of the malfunctioning replicator "food slot" in Star Trek, unwanted and uncontrolled fabrication isn't a problem that can be easily ignored. There is no harm to allowing spam e-mail messages to build up in your inbox, but allowing a growing pile of physical objects to build up in your office can become a serious problem, especially when you consider that each object requires physical materials to construct and represents a significant time and energy investment.

---

[15] One of the most prominent of these is the Defense Distributed *Liberator* pistol: http://defdist. org/. As of writing this, however, the download page for the CAD plans is offline.

11.5.5.2   3D Printers as a Vector for Hybrid Physical/Digital Attacks

A common form of digital attack today is the distributed denial of service (DDoS), in which a network of infected computers is directed to rapidly overwhelm a server with requests. These attacks are a simple, brute force method of bringing down an unwanted website or service, and while they can be incredibly disruptive to the targeted individual or organization, they don't present any physical risk. Consider how the same scenario would play out if the target was an office building with a 3D printer on every desk. Employees arrive in the morning to find the floor of the office covered in spiked metal caltrops, which have spilled out of every 3D printer like popcorn in an air popper, with more spitting out every few seconds. No one can sit down, or even reach their seats, until the mess is cleaned up. As long as the feedstock holds out, so does the mess. An attack like this could bring an entire business to a halt, with serious costs to productivity mounting up alongside the maintenance costs to operate so many printers simultaneously.

11.5.6   3D Printing and Biological Warfare

There are clearly even more frightening scenarios on the horizon once we consider what could be done with a home fabricator capable of fabricating sophisticated biological and chemical outputs. Once home fabricators are capable of creating food, then it stands to reason that they are also capable of creating poisons. It is not a huge leap to then imagine the power (and danger) of a home replicator that serves as a small-scale home pharmacy, capable of fabricating medicine or narcotics. Imagine a scenario where an unsecured bio-printer is hacked and instructed to produce clouds of toxic gas which fill an apartment building or a scenario where a bug in a piece of program code results in the synthesis of a virulent strain of fungus. While this might seem alarmist and far-fetched, it is in keeping with both the imagined futures of home replication envisioned by Star Trek and Transmetropolitan and with the current trajectory of the technology.

11.6   Conclusion

The present state of home fabrication technology is quickly converging with the imagined futures of science fiction, driven by an enthusiastic community of Makers and the rapid development of 3D printing technology. Much like personal computing led to a revolution in communications technology, it seems like 3D printing (and its associated technologies) are poised to lead to a new world of small-scale, distributed manufacturing. In this chapter we have considered some of the potential futures that have already been envisioned for this technology and have also argued that there are more varied and interesting possibilities than have been imagined. Home fabrication is going to force us to reimagine some of our most basic assumptions about material culture and not just because it is a new industrial tool. We will also have to grapple with the social implications of it as a communications platform and as a networked device with potential outputs that are much harder to ignore than those of any previously networked system. The future we imagine for home fabrication depends largely on our own ideological commitments about the future: how will people act when presented with a technology with so much capability for both "good" and "evil"? To what extent can (or should) we anticipate and regulate dangerous uses of this technology? How does this technology disrupt or reinforce existing hierarchies and systems of authority? What type of playful new possibilities exist when traditional barriers to small-scale fabrication are removed? These questions don't have answers yet, but as home fabrication continues to grow in capability and as the ethos of the Maker movement continues to spread, we can draw on them to orient ourselves to the possibilities of this fast-approaching future. Through the lens of fictional scenarios and stories, we can ground these abstract ideas in concrete visions that make it easier to work out the implications and possibilities these technologies raise.

References

Anderson C (2010) In the next industrial revolution, atoms are the new bits. Wired 18(2):58–67, 105–106

Anderson C (2012) Makers: the new industrial revolution. Crown Business, New York

Bleecker J (2008) Design fiction: a short slideshow on design, science, fact and fiction. Slideshare.net. Retrieved September 2011, from http://www.slideshare.net/bleeckerj/design-fiction-a-short-slideshow-on-design-science-fact-and-fiction

Bleecker J (2009) Design fiction: a short essay on design, science, fact and fiction. Near Future Laboratory. Retrieved September 2, 2011, from http://www.nearfuturelaboratory.com/2009/03/17/design-fiction-a-short-essay-on-design-science-fact-and-fiction/

Blythe M (2014) The hitchhiker's guide to ubicomp: using techniques from literary and critical theory to reframe scientific agendas. Pers Ubiquit Comput 18(4):795–808

Bosch T, Sterling B (2012) Sci-fi writer Bruce Sterling explains the intriguing new concept of design fiction. Future Tense. Retrieved December 13, 2012, from http://www.slate.com/blogs/future_tense/2012/03/02/bruce_sterling_on_design_fictions_.html

Doctorow C (2009) Makers: TOR

Dourish P, Bell G (2014) "Resistance is futile": reading science fiction alongside ubiquitous computing. Pers Ubiquitous Comput 18(4):769–778

Ellis W, Pope P (2001) Transmetropolitan: filth of the city. DC Comics, Vertigo, New York

Ellis W, Robertson D (1997) Transmetropolitan, vol 1. DC Comics, Vertigo, New York

Ellis W, Robertson D (1998) Transmetropolitan: lust for life, vol 2. DC Comics, Vertigo, New York

Jenkins H (1992) Textual poachers: television fans & participatory culture. Routledge, New York

Jenkins H (2006a) Convergence culture: where old and new media collide. New York University Press, New York

Jenkins H (2006b) Fans, bloggers, and gamers: exploring participatory culture. New York University Press, New York

Kirby D (2010) The future is now: diegetic prototypes and the role of popular films in generating real-world technological development. Soc Stud Sci 40:41–70

Kirman BTK, Linehan JC, Lawson SF, O'Hara D.-d (2013) CHI and the future robot enslavement of humankind; a retrospective. Paper presented at the CHI'13 – extended abstracts on human factors in computing systems, Paris, France

Reeves S (2012) Envisioning ubiquitous computing. Paper presented at the CHI'12, Austin, TX

Shedroff N, Noessel C (2012) Make it so: interaction design lessons from science fiction. Rosenfeld Media, New York

Stephenson N (1995) The Diamond Age. Bantam Spectra, New York, NY.

Sterling B (2005) Shaping things. MIT Press, Cambridge, MA

Tanenbaum J, Tanenbaum K (2010). The reading glove: designing interactions for object-based tangible storytelling. Paper presented at the international conference on the augmented human, Mageve, France, 2–3 April 2010

Tanenbaum J, Tanenbaum K (2011) Getting your hands on electronic literature: exploring tactile fictions with the reading glove. J Int Digital Media Assoc J (iDMAa) 8(2):46–57

Tanenbaum K, Tanenbaum J, Antle AN, Bizzocchi J, Seif El-Nasr M, Hatala M (2011) Experiencing the reading glove. Paper presented at the international conference on tangible and embedded/embodied interaction (TEI '11), Funchal, Portugal, 23–26 January 2011

Tanenbaum J, Tanenbaum K, Wakkary R (2012) Steampunk as design fiction. Paper presented at the CHI'12, Austin, TX, USA, 5–10 May 2012

Tanenbaum J, Williams A, Desjardins A, Tanenbaum K (2013a) Democratizing technology: pleasure, utility, and expressiveness in DIY and maker practice. Paper presented at the CHI'13, Paris, France

Tanenbaum K, Hatala M, Tanenbaum J, Wakkary R, Antle AN (2013b) A case study of intended versus actual experience of adaptivity in a tangible storytelling system. User Modeling User-Adapt Interact, 1–43. doi: 10.1007/s11257-013-9140-9

Weiser M (1991) The computer for the 21st century. Sci Am 265(3):94–104

Chapter 12
Play Platforms for Children's Creativity

Cristina Sylla, Clara Coutinho, and Pedro Branco

12.1 Introduction

Children's imagination and their natural need for exploration and discovery can be stimulated when they are in contact with rich contexts and environments (Van Scoter et al. 2001; Van Scoter 2008); this inherent tendency offers an enormous opportunity for researchers and designers to develop tools that unleash children's potential, involving them in creating meaningful projects (Papert 1993). Research on this field has highlighted that well-design technological tools for children need to be compelling, support exploration, encourage creativity, develop curiosity and promote interaction and collaboration with peers while being simple and intuitive to use (Plowman et al. 2012; Resnick et al. 2005; Resnick and Silverman 2005).

However, despite a move from virtual to physical as the focus of digital interaction (Ishii and Ullmer 1997), which is leading to a diversification of interaction contexts, objects and applications, opening new possibilities for the creation of innovative interactive artefacts, discussions about the use of technology for young children have disclosed that technology often fails to exploit the affordances of the medium, by merely transposing traditional materials to the corresponding electronic format (Plowman et al. 2012).

Aiming at developing an authoring and sharing tool for children, which empowers them to collaboratively create interactive content and share it with others, this study describes the design and development of an interface for tangible narrative

C. Sylla (✉)
Centre for Child Studies, University of Minho, Braga, Portugal
e-mail: sylla@engagelab.org

C. Coutinho
Institute of Education, University of Minho, Braga, Portugal

P. Branco
Department of Information Systems, University of Minho, Portugal

© Springer-Verlag London 2015
N. Zagalo, P. Branco (eds.), *Creativity in the Digital Age*,
Springer Series on Cultural Computing, DOI 10.1007/978-1-4471-6681-8_12

creation. The process, which extended for a period of 3 years, involved six classes of 5-year-old preschoolers and six preschool teachers. From the conception to the development of the final product, several design iterations were carried with the children, in which the research team tried to understand how to design an engaging and compelling tool, for children to play around and experiment with story elements, creating their own narratives. The design of the digital tool was based on the assumption that narrative construction should be centred on the playful character of language and the pleasure in dealing with words through playful experimentation, where children are "players rather than spectators" (Bruner 1966: 95).

12.2 Materials for Exploring the World

Using objects to promote exploration and spark imagination has a long tradition that can be traced back to Friedrich Fröbel – the creator of the world's first kindergarten in Germany, in 1840. Fröbel developed a curriculum for young children where they could engage in *self-activity* and *self-expression* through play (Fröbel 1909: vi). Core to his approach were the *gifts*, a collection of 20 physical objects that included balls, strings, sticks and blocks and were used as play materials to help children think about and express their ideas. The concept behind the *gifts* was that the manipulation of familiar forms, present in everyday life and in nature, facilitates the comprehension of abstract concepts (Brosterman 1997).

Like Fröbel, Maria Montessori highlighted the importance of using objects and actively engaging in exploring the environment. Montessori's method, based on the *Didactic Materials*, addressed the stimulation of every sense (Montessori 1912), and the design principle behind each of the objects from the *Didactic Materials* set was to raise children's interest and curiosity.

12.2.1 Digital Manipulatives

Recent technological developments made it possible to embed computational technology in objects, creating a new interaction paradigm with digital technology. Digital manipulatives[1] (Resnick et al. 1998) also referred to as tangible user interfaces (TUIs) (Ishii and Ullmer 1997) or tangible systems provide a more natural interaction, stimulating sensory and whole body perception giving users freedom of movements while creating richer experiences. Research has shown that physical

---

[1] The term digital manipulatives has been coined by Resnick and the lifelong kindergarten at the MIT Media Laboratory, Cambridge, MA, referring to a new generation of computationally enhanced manipulative materials that enable children to interact with digital information (Resnick et al. 1998). In the scope of this work, we will use the terms digital manipulatives, tangible user interfaces (TUIs), or tangible systems as synonyms.

manipulation greatly improves comprehension (Glenberg 2010; Glenberg et al. 2011) and that digital manipulatives have the potential to expand the range of concepts that children understand (O'Malley and Fraser 2005; Zuckerman et al. 2005), promoting peer collaboration and negotiation (Hornecker 2005; Hornecker and Buur 2006; Zuckerman et al. 2005) and particularly supporting exploratory and expressive learning activities (Marshall 2007).

Zaman et al. (2012: 368) summarise the affordances of digital manipulatives as follows:

- Specificity of input devices, which reduces modality on the interface
- Improved accessibility of the interaction, building on everyday skills and experiences of the physical world
- Employment of bimanual and haptic interaction skills
- Facilitation of spatial tasks through the inherent spatiality of TUIs
- Tight coupling of control of the physical object and the manipulation of its digital representation

Resnick and colleagues (2005; Resnick and Silverman 2005) suggest *Design Principles for Tools to Support Creative Thinking*, placing the emphasis on promoting exploration and creativity:

- Support exploration
- Low threshold, high ceiling and wide walls
- Support many paths and many styles
- Support collaboration
- Support open interchange
- Make it as simple as possible – and maybe even simpler
- Choose black boxes carefully
- Invent things that you would want to use yourself
- Balance user suggestions, with observation and participatory processes
- Iterate, iterate – then iterate again
- Design for designers

12.3   Exploring the Design of Digital Manipulatives with Children

Previous research has shown that one of the most effective ways of designing child-centred technology is to involve children in the design process. In fact, children's participation in the evaluation of technology goes back to the 1970s, where children were involved as users in the development of new technology (Papert 1977). Today this is a common practice, and based on the relation that children and the research team have, as well as the stage at which children integrate the design process, children can be users, testers, informants or design partners (Druin 1999, 2002).

12.3.1   Context of the Study

The study presented here took place in a Portuguese preschool, involving six classes of preschoolers, of 5-year-olds, and six preschool teachers, for a period of around 3 years (Sylla 2013; Sylla et al. 2011, 2013b). Although the teachers were always the same, the team worked every year with two new groups of children, namely, the class attending the last preschool year, just before entering primary school the year after. During this period, the research team carried several cycles of rapid prototyping, trying a variety of different approaches and materials, prototyping, testing, gathering information and redesigning again. These various iterations led to the development of several prototypes, some of which evolved into more finished products, such as *t-words*, an interface that received the Golden Award for the Best Demo at ACE 2012 (Sylla et al. 2012) and the World Technology Award 2013[2] in the category Entertainment.

12.3.2   Initial Explorations

In the first design iterations, the team wanted to assess how children create stories using tangible props. To gather information on this aspect, the researchers used a low-fi prototype that consisted of a set of cards with drawings representing animals, objects, places and nature elements (Table 12.1) and a large-format book, with a grid of rectangular marks drawn on it for placing the paper cards. Following a Wizard-of-Oz technique,[3] using a small programme developed in Processing,[4] by pressing a certain key on the computer, the researchers simulated audio feedback for each card that children placed on the prototype.

The syntax of the objects was linked to the verbs that support the action related to it, e.g. the audio of the card representing a "ball of yarn" was "plays with the ball of yarn", the card "bowl of milk" was "drinks a bowl of milk", and so on. By placing the picture cards on the book, children could create very simple narratives, such as:

Table 12.1 Cards used to test the audio interaction			
Cat	Ball of yarn	Meadow	Sun
Dog	Bowl of milk	House	Moon
Mice	Piece of cheese		
	Bone		

---

[2] http://www.prweb.com/releases/2013/11/prweb11342067.htm

[3] Wizard of Oz defines a technique in which users interact with a technological system that they believe to be autonomous but which is actually being operated or partially operated by a person who simulates the system responses to the user's input.

[4] Processing: http://www.processing.org/

Fig. 12.1 Children creating and changing their stories

"The sun is shining, the cat drinks a bowl of milk at the meadow". The prototype was tested in two following days during class with small groups of three children each, and each session lasted about one hour (Fig. 12.1).

The researchers explained to the children that each card had an audio identification and that they could create a story by placing the cards on the paper "platform". The children could create variations of the narrative, according to the sequence of cards that they placed. The children were enthusiastic about the prototype and surprised about the interaction and the audio feedback. They placed the cards on the "book", dealing with each other, while trying to create stories. Children personalised and extended the narratives, adding their own ideas to the very simple stories they were hearing.

12.3.2.1   Reflections on the First Design Iterations

The sessions with the children showed that the use of tangible picture cards generated ideas for the creation of narratives, promoting a very dynamic peer interaction. Relative to using speech with the cards, it seemed that it constrained children's imagination and consequently their narratives, and indeed, children seemed to prefer to create their own spoken version of the stories. Following those observations, the researchers decided to remove the speech in future versions of the prototype, giving children more freedom in the creation of the stories.

Further, the observation of children's use of the prototype showed that the tangible cards promoted peer collaboration, greatly increasing children's motivation. Definitely part of children's involvement and enthusiasm was generated by hearing each other contributions (Wood and O'Malley 1996) and handling with each other which cards they should use. One idea or a comment generated another one, moving the story forward and involving the children in collaboratively creating different variations of the narrative. Additionally, children exchanged opinions about which cards would make sense to place, exchanging ideas about the cards they wanted to use. For instance, in one of the groups, there was a conversation between the children about when they ought to use the card picturing a moon, as one child stated that the moon should be placed to finish the story. Such kind of argument illustrates how children reflected about the sequence and structure of stories, which they were able to verbalise and discuss with their peers.

12.3.3 Follow-Up

After the initial design explorations, the team wanted to gather more detailed information about how children would use tangible cards to create a story. Therefore in the following iterations the researchers used a paper prototype that consisted of an A4 cardboard to simulate an electronic platform and a set of picture cards with drawings representing characters, places and actions. In two following sessions, with the duration of one hour each, the team tested the prototype with four groups of three children each. The sessions took place in the preschool's painting room with the children and one researcher (Fig. 12.2).

The children sat in groups of three around a table, where the picture cards were scattered, each child was given a cardboard, and the researcher proposed them to create and tell a story using the cards. All the children used the "platform", creating a total of 30 stories. The content of the cards was in general very clear to them. Some of the children took the cards they liked and began to place them on the "platform"; others took time to reflect about what they wanted to tell and looked for very specific cards. Most children began to place the cards on the "platform" aligning them horizontally, some on the top, others on the bottom of the "platform". Three of the children used the "platform" like a drawing, placing the sun, the clouds and a flying bird on the top and the characters on the bottom (Fig. 12.2 middle row right).

Fig. 12.2 Children interacting with the second paper prototype

Almost all the children filled the paper "platform"; most of them felt the need to align the cards, arranging them in straight lines while telling the story. Very often the children spontaneously removed some cards from the "platform", replacing and adjusting them to the narrative that they were creating.

12.3.3.1   Reflections on the Follow-Up Iteration

Observing the children placing the cards in rows on the paper "platform" and noticing that many of them were concerned with their alignment suggested that having slots to place the cards would facilitate children's task, offloading extra cognitive processes, as children would not have to worry about alignment issues.

Relatively to the size of the platform, some children felt compelled to fill the complete cardboard with the cards, clearly showing the need to reduce the size of the platform. Given that the children used the space differently – e.g. some began to place the cards on the top-left side, others on the bottom-right side, others placed the cards on the middle of the "platform", and some used the space as a drawing – the system needed to identify three things:

- The content of each card
- Its location
- The order each card entered the system

This would allow users to place a card on the bottom of the platform and then continue placing the next card on the middle of the platform, jumping back and forth as they created their story. Additionally the system needed to support connections between cards, or groupings of cards.

12.3.4   Functional Prototype

The next design stage was to explore the development of a prototype that recognised physical content and displayed it digitally, generating an environment for the creation of narratives, as well as to define the physical interaction with the digital content.

12.3.4.1   Physical Manipulation

The manipulation of the digital content needed to be intuitive and direct, placing the emphasis on the interaction between the users and the task (Djajadiningrat et al. 2004; Forlizzi and Ford 2000; Hornecker and Buur 2006), creating a direct mapping between input and output (Anderson and Shattuck 2012; Antle et al. 2011). Outgoing from the idea of using picture cards, the team chose blocks for defining and manipulating the story elements. Blocks are simple, intuitive objects, familiar to every child, and easy to handle, manipulate and store and represent a very natural means to support complementary strategies (Antle et al. 2011; Kirsh 1996). A complementary strategy can be defined as "any organizing activity, which recruits external elements to reduce cognitive loads" (Kirsh 1995: 212).

Additionally, blocks allow multiple users to simultaneously manipulate the content, supporting peer collaboration and "facilitating communication and "transparency" of interaction between multiple collocated users" (Ullmer and Ishii 2001: 12), providing "multiple access points" (Hornecker 2005).

The design of the interaction followed three development principles: visibility, rapidity and reversibility of actions (Shneiderman and Plaisant 2004). Following these principles, the tangible blocks make the interaction explicit and open (Hornecker 2005; Ullmer and Ishii 2001) and give rapid feedback of the performed actions (placing a block on the platform immediately displays its digital content), and every performed action is reversible by simply removing the block from the platform, a feature particularly relevant for content exploration (Hourcade 2008).

12.3.4.2 Detection of the Physical Content

Having defined the physical manipulation, the researchers considered several methods for the detection of the blocks, ranging from optical recognition, radio identification, physical properties to embedded circuitry (Fig. 12.3). The first electronic prototype consisted of a platform and a small number of blocks with printed

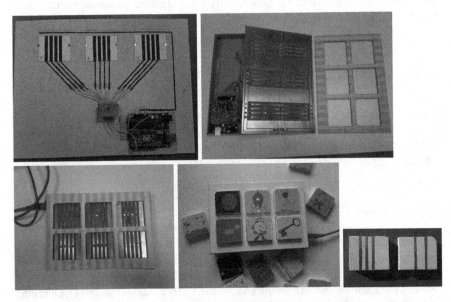

Fig. 12.3 Proof of concept (*top left*); first functional electronic prototype (*bottom left*); prototype with blocks (*bottom centre*) and backside of two blocks (*bottom right*)

stickers on the upper side, representing fantasy characters, objects and settings. The platform had an electronic circuit with six slots to place the blocks; each block had an ID on the backside, created by different patterns of conductive aluminium. Placing a block on a slot closed the electronic circuit on the board according to the block's ID and displayed the corresponding animation on the computer screen. To indicate the right placement of the blocks, the slots on the electronic platform and the blocks were square shaped with the left corner cut off.

This prototype was tested with small groups of two children each, in the pre-school's painting room. To assess how intuitive the system was for the children, the researcher briefly explained the functioning to the first group and remained in the background, observing how children used it. Children immediately appropriated the prototype, placing the blocks on the platform and exploring the content, and when the following group came in the room, the children were excited and eager to show the functioning to the newcomers.

12.3.4.3   Reflections on the Functional Prototype

The feedback from the children was very positive, and in general the system was easy to use, as the observation from children's interaction revealed; however, some refinements of the prototype were still needed. The connection between the slots and the blocks was designed following a puzzle principle, which did not provided a smooth interaction. Indeed, the placement of the blocks had to be easy, direct and quick. Also, there were some problems with the recognition of the block's IDs due to the oxidation of the contacts; therefore, a different technical solution had to be implemented.

12.3.5   TOK: Touch, Organize, Create

After testing several solutions for the detection and considering different forms for the blocks, the final prototype uses capacitive sensors for the detection of the blocks. Each block has a sticker with a picture of what it represents on the upper side and a conductive pattern on its base, which is detected by capacitive sensors located on the platform base. The final system is composed of an electronic platform with six or eight slots, which connects to a computer or a tablet through USB or Bluetooth, a microphone and 23 physical blocks to manipulate the digital content. In the current implementation, the system can read up to 250 different blocks, but that number can be extended.

The backside of the blocks as well as the electronic platform have magnets on their surface that correctly snap the blocks to the platform (instead of the puzzle approach), making it easy for the users to place the blocks while simultaneously assuring a stable contact between the blocks and the platform. The size of the blocks $4.5 \times 4.5 \times 1$ cm gives children a good grip and easy manipulation (Fig. 12.4).

Fig. 12.4 Children interacting with the system; block, front and backside (*bottom right*)

Placing a block on the platform displays the corresponding digital content on the screen, creating a direct mapping between input and output; the sequence of blocks placed on the platform unfolds a narrative. Outgoing from the observations gathered during the design iterations with the children, the system presents the content of the picture blocks on the screen following the order in which they are placed, enabling the placement of the blocks on the slots without having to follow any order. Similarly, when a block is removed from the platform, it disappears from the screen.

Following suggestions from the teachers, the blocks represent classical scenarios and actants from narratives for children – basically, heroes and opponents (Greimas 1973; Propp 1928) – and are composed of characters, objects and nature elements (Fig. 12.5).

The familiarity of the characters allows recreating narratives, variations from the original stories or creating completely new stories. Five different scenarios (a castle landscape, a forest, a desert, the woods and a circus) allow locating the stories in different settings (Fig. 12.6).

The narrative unfolds according to the sequence of blocks placed on the platform; as such there are no predefined stories, a characteristic that sets the interface apart from other tangible storytelling systems (Budd et al. 2007; Hunter et al. 2010). We will illustrate this with an example: when children place the combination of blocks as pictured on Fig. 12.7 (*witch, fairy, princess*), the witch attacks the princess and the fairy tries to help her.

Fig. 12.5 Some of the characters and objects

Fig. 12.6 Some scenarios that can be used to place the story in different settings, a scenario placed together with the moon, which makes the night appear (*bottom right*)

Fig. 12.7 Children creating a narrative with the digital manipulative, setting the story at different times of the day (by placing the *moon* block)

Fig. 12.8 Automatically generated snapshots of a narrative

As the fairy alone is not strong enough to defeat the witch, the princess dies. However children can use different strategies to change the plot, e.g. by placing an extra character to help the fairy, placing a house for the princess to hide, removing the princess or the witch from the platform or trying to hit the witch with the caldron.

The design of the interface placed a "high priority on tinkerability", stimulating children to explore different possibilities, encouraging them "to try out multiple alternatives, shift directions in the middle of the process, to take things apart and create new versions" (Resnick et al. 2005). The system, which was named TOK – Touch, Organize, Create – allows children to change the scene, mix and remix the characters, try out different solutions, shift direction and start all over again. Further, as there is only visual feedback (except for the ambient sounds), children can imagine and create their own spoken narratives.

To extend the interaction beyond the interface itself and share the storytelling experience with others, pressing the Enter key in the computer keyboard (or an icon on the tablet version) generates snapshots of the created narratives, saving them as digital images (Fig. 12.8), which are automatically sent to a blog and also stored in a special folder in the computer. These representations, which look like a comic book, can be visualised together, printed and shared with family and friends, involving them into a collaborative storytelling experience.

12.3.6 Modelling the Story World

To define the relations between the story elements and to achieve a certain degree of unpredictability, the story world was modelled through behaviour trees (BTs). BTs describe general actions of entities, thus each entity interacts with the environment according to a set of predefined rules that define its behaviour. Since the behaviour triggered for each entity depends on the other entities that are also present in the scene, and the properties of those entities, for instance, their level of health, there is a certain degree of unpredictability in the outcome of a given situation.

The principle followed in the design of the BTs was to model a world that would be understandable for young children, by creating a set of rules that they know from traditional story plots. As before mentioned, there are four types of entities: scenarios, elements, objects and characters. Scenarios represent the background image where the action occurs. The elements (day, night and wind) interact with the objects and the characters, bringing a dimension of change and unpredictability to the story.

The objects and characters are classified in good, bad or neutral; bad characters attack the good ones; good characters defend the neutral and help each other. Both good and bad characters can join forces to defend or attack their opponents. Specific objects like a caldron or a flowerpot can be used to knock down bad characters and defend the good ones. A bad object – like a poisoned apple – diminishes the health of a character; on the contrary, a good object – like a carrot – increases the health of a character.

The nature elements allow the configuration of the story settings, e.g. the use of the moon turns the day into night, or the cloud blows everything away from the scene. Additionally, there are ambient sounds according to the different scenarios, e.g. birds singing in the forest at dawn, frogs croaking or an owl singing at dusk.

Each entity has a BT, which defines a number of actions for that entity. In case some specific rules or actions are needed, they can be added to the entities' BT. In case it becomes necessary to add a new object or character to the story engine, it only has to be associated with the corresponding BT and include the corresponding animations, as well as the picture block. The new entity will automatically interact with the other entities. The BT's interaction model rules each class and subclass; basic indicators of the class are, e.g. health, velocity or symbiosis (entities that belong to the same class join forces to achieve a common goal) (Chart 1).

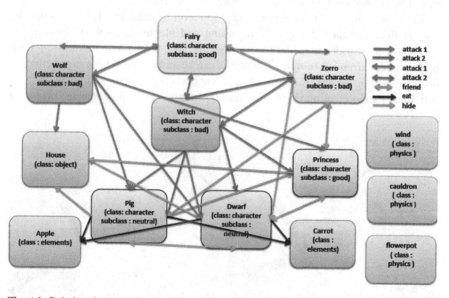

Chart 1 Relations between the entities

When users place the blocks on the platform, the BT gets the inputs of the entities that are present (we refer to the blocks placed on the platform as the state of the world). Regularly at a predefined time stamp, the BT performs updates about the state of the world and checks the defined priorities before triggering any actions. As a result, there are no predefined stories nor a linear narrative. The users create their own narratives according to the sequence of blocks and the order in which they place them on the platform.

12.4 Trying Out Different Ways of Involvement

12.4.1 The t-words Interface: Tangible Words

A second interface that resulted from the various design sessions with the children is the *t-words* interface (Sylla et al. 2012, 2013a), which emerged out of the idea of exploring and experimenting with narratives, focusing on the audio aspect. Children no longer just use the content that they have at their disposal but are empowered to create their very personal audio materials. Inspired by other tangible systems like Telltale (Ananny 2001), StoryMat (Cassel 2004; Cassell, and Ryokai 2001) or Jabberstamp (Raffle et al. 2007), t-words consists of a set of rectangular blocks that can record and play sounds, words or sentences, enabling users to record and store audio, as well as to play the recorded sounds (Fig. 12.9). Each block has an audio recorder with a 4GB storage card, an audio player with an embedded speaker and magnetic connectors on each side to connect to the other blocks.

Each block has a button to start and stop recording and an LED that gives the user feedback about the action of recording and playing the sound. To play the recorded audio, users snap the blocks together, and the recorded audio sequence begins to play from left to right. The blocks can be arranged and rearranged creating different audio sequences. The interface supports a variety of language-related activities such as creating rhymes; recording sounds, words or sentences; inventing

Fig. 12.9 The t-words prototype

and playing language games; exploring tongue twisters; or creating narratives. Additionally, users can customise the blocks by drawing on top of their surface; the drawings can be wiped out and new ones can be drawn again.

12.5   Assessing How Children Use the Interfaces

12.5.1   The t-words Interface

The researchers had the opportunity to carry two workshops with the t-words interface at the "Entertainment Kids Workshops", which were part of the ACE 2012[5] conference held in Kathmandu, Nepal. The theme of the conference was "Entertainment for the Whole World" (Cheok et al. 2014), and the Kids Workshop proposed to *engage with local young children with the aim of exploring concepts such as creativity, experience and "cool" ways of creating entertainment media and ways of expanding children's understanding of entertainment computing and its potential* (ACE 2012). Additionally the workshops were hoped to act as seeds for further research.

The workshops were held in two schools – the Rudrayanee School and the Ullens School (Fig. 12.10). Children liked to record their own voices into the t-words boxes

Fig. 12.10 Children in Kathmandu recording audio in the t-words blocks (*top*) and children drawing on their blocks (*bottom*)

---

[5] 9th International Conference on Advances in Computer Entertainment Technology http://aceconference.tumblr.com

and to play around experimenting different audio sequences by just changing the order of the boxes. They used the boxes to record words, stories and messages but also songs and a variety of sounds that they improvised with objects they found at hand. The workshops revealed that simple technology, which does not need a computer or any developed content, but instead gives users space to play around and explore with different audio recordings, creating their own content, is a powerful engaging tool, freeing users and developers of language constraints (Chisik et al. 2014).

12.5.2 The TOK Interface

Following the development of TOK, the researchers had the opportunity to carry two interventions at the preschool. The first intervention involved 24 pairs of 5-year-old preschoolers who interacted with the interface during free-play time for a period of 4 months; the second intervention involved 27 pairs of preschoolers who also interacted with TOK during free-play time for a period of 6 months. The first intervention investigated how children used the system after the novelty aspect had faded away, as well as the kind of activities in which they involved, the challenges they faced and how they solved them. The second intervention investigated aspects of children's embodiment in the creation of narratives (Sylla et al. 2014). Both interventions disclosed that the sharing of the input devices (blocks and microphone) promoted children's embodiment of the stories they created, fostering their immersion in the story world. The microphone, initially used to capture children's verbalisations during their interaction with the interface for later analyses, turned out to be an important feature of the interface. Children immediately appropriated the device, using it when they were speaking and creating their stories, and the microphone became a powerful motivating tool for children to verbalise their ideas.

Children used their voice as an expressive tool (Collins 1999: 82; White 1954), changing the intonation and playing different voices for the various characters, sang songs or mimicked ambient sounds; they often spoke with the story elements addressing them with direct speech. Children expressed their feelings of enthusiasm (e.g. when their favourite characters managed to win against their opponents or when they successfully used the objects to knock down certain characters) and anxiety (e.g. when a character was in danger) standing up from their chairs, waving their arms or jumping joyfully (Fig. 12.11).

The tangible blocks, with the different story elements, stimulated children's imagination, triggering new ideas for the creation and development of narratives. Children created their own personal narratives, using different strategies to achieve their goals, such as placing characters to help others when they were fighting (e.g. the *fairy* to help *Zorro* fight the *wolf*) or removing characters from the platform to help others or to escape danger (e.g. they removed the *witch* when she was attacking the *princess* or removed the *little pigs* when the *wolf* was attacking them); children used objects to knock down characters and lifted the blocks to bring characters again to life. The collaboration with peers was a strong motivating factor.

Fig. 12.11 Children gesturing and standing up, rejoicing and simulating movements of their characters

12.6   Overall Reflections on the Design Process

Having the possibility of carrying several design iterations and evaluating their use for an extended period of time gave the researchers an insight into children's world, allowing the team to understand some of their needs, preferences, likes and dislikes. Some ideas and prototypes created along this process slowly evolved into more developed products that underwent several optimisation cycles. Many of the initial ideas were left behind and several paths proved unpromising due to various reasons. However, they were part of the design process and helped to clear ideas towards what was important and not and which approach worked or not. Some important design solutions emerged just by chance, as, for instance, the use of a microphone.

The observations from the interventions at preschool strongly support the *Design Principles for Tools to Support Creative Thinking* (see Sect. 12.2.1) proposed by Resnick et al. (2005; Resnick and Silverman 2005). The very simple and intuitive setup of the interface, as well as its robustness, made it easy for children to start, supporting different approaches and different levels of interaction, promoting exploration and experimentation while sparking children's creativity.

A certain degree of unpredictability of the stories (which depend from the sequence of blocks placed on the platform and the order they enter the system), generated by the integration of a plot- and character-based approach, nurtured children's motivation and engagement. They located their stories in different settings and combined the characters and the objects in numerous ways, always creating original stories. In fact, children not only created their stories by adding elements to the platform, they also recurrently applied different creative strategies to achieve a specific goal, such as removing certain elements from the scene, revealing that they understood the functioning of the underlying system and that they were able to subvert its rules.

The sharing of the input devices gave children equal control of their performance being another strong motivating factor. Children often verbalised that it was more fun to use the tools with their peers, and when creating stories together, they built on each other's contribution. These joint activities generated fun, ideas, experimentation, change of experiences and sometimes discussion, which in turn generated reflection over their actions. According to Fischer and Shipman (2011) "Environments that support the interaction of different skilled participants, encouraging "all voices to be heard" and combining different perspectives are a potential source for learning" (cited in Eagle 2012: 48). Eagle adds to this that the extent to which the artefact is capable of promoting social interactions and an active, engaged, participation with the learning subject is decisive (Eagle 2012). The importance of the social environment and the benefits of collaborative learning environments have long been acknowledged (Bruner 1966; Eagle 2012; Lave and Wenger 1991; Vygotsky 1978).

Further, touching and manipulating the tangible objects, whether the TOK or t-words blocks, gave children a sense of ownership over their creations, acting as an additional motivational factor (Buur and Soendergaard 2000).

12.7   Conclusions

While it is still difficult to measure creativity, it seems consensual that longitudinal studies with active users in real world settings are a valid method to gain valuable insights about how the tools impact users in the long term (Yarosh et al. 2011: 143) and which features are relevant for triggering creativity (Resnick et al. 2005). Research has emphasised the importance of developing tools that encourage authentic, creative and meaningful opportunities for learning (Plowman et al. 2012; Yelland 1999; Van Scoter 2008). Indeed, although technology has the potential to create experiences that go beyond what is possible in the real world, nonetheless technology is useless if it does not meet children's needs (Van Scoter 2008). It is by creating that people become creative (Resnick et al. 2005).

While t-words gives children absolute freedom to create their own personalised content, focusing on the audio component, TOK is like a stage where children take over multiple roles, becoming authors, directors, scripters, performers and narrators, thus creating multiple layers of interaction (Sylla et al. 2014; Wright 2007). The versatility of tangible interfaces and their appropriateness for carrying child-centred activities, fostering exploratory and collaborative tasks, indeed show their potential for supporting a new paradigm, shifting from an instructional towards an exploratory model, where the use of well-designed technology can open up a space where active intrinsic learning may take place.

Acknowledgements We would like to express our thankfulness to the Colégio Teresiano, Braga, and give a very special thank you to all the preschool children, their parents and preschool teachers, who creatively helped us developing and testing this project in all its various development phases. This work is funded by FEDER through the Operational Competitiveness Factors Programme (COMPETE) and by National Funds through the FCT – Portuguese Foundation for the Science and the Technology – within the Projects PTDC/CPE-CED/110417/2009 and the Doctoral Grant SFRH/BD/62531/2009.

References

ACE (2012) International conference on advances in computer entertainment technology. http://aceconference.tumblr.com

Ananny M (2001) Telling tales: a new toy for encouraging written literacy through oral storytelling. In: Proceedings of the Biennale Conference Society for Research in Child Development, Minneapolis

Anderson T, Shattuck J (2012) Design-based research: a decade of progress in education research. Educ Res 41(1):16–25

Antle AN, Wise AF, Nielsen K (2011) Towards Utopia: designing tangibles for learning. In: Proceedings of the international conference on interaction design and children. ACM Press, New York, pp 11–20

Brosterman N (1997) Inventing kindergarten. Harry N. Adams Inc., New York

Bruner JS (1966) Towards a theory of instruction. Belknap/Harvard, Cambridge/London

Budd J, Madej K, Stephens-wells J, De Jong J, Katzur E, Mulligan L (2007) PageCraft: learning in context a tangible interactive storytelling platform to support early narrative development for young children. In: Proceedings of the 6th IDC international conference on interaction design and children. ACM Press, New York, pp 97–100

Buur J, Soendergaard A (2000) Video card game: an augmented environment for user centred design discussions. In: Proceedings of DARE. ACM Press, New York, pp 63–69

Cassel J (2004) Towards a model of technology and literacy development: story listening systems. J Appl Dev Psychol 25:75–105

Cassell J, Ryokai K (2001) Making space for voice: technologies to support children's fantasy and storytelling. J Pers Technol 5(3):203–224

Cheok A, Nijholt A, Romão T (eds) (2014) Entertaining the whole world. Human–computer interaction series 2014. Springer, doi: 10.1007/978-1-4471-6446-3

Chisik Y, Antle A, Birtles B, Márquez E, Sylla C (2014) The Kathmandu children entertainment workshops. In: Nijholt A, Romão T, Reidsma D (eds) Entertaining the whole world. Human–computer interaction series 2014. Springer, pp 5–21. doi: 10.1007/978-1-4471-6446-3

Collins F (1999) The use of traditional storytelling in education to the learning of early literacy skills. Early Child Dev Care 152(1):77–108

Djajadiningrat WS, Frens J, Overbeeke K (2004) Tangible products: redressing the balance between appearance and action. J Pers Ubiquitous Comput 8(5):294–309

Druin A (1999) Cooperative inquiry: developing new technologies for children with children. In: Proceedings of the conference on human factors in computing systems. ACM Press, New York, pp 592–599

Druin A (2002) The role of children in the design of new technology. Behav Inf Technol 21(1):1–25

Eagle S (2012) Learning in the early years: social interactions around picture books, puzzles and digital technologies. Comput Educ 59:38–49

Fischer G, Shipman F (2011) Collaborative design rationale and social creativity in cultures of participation. Human Technol Interdiscip J Humans ICT Environ 7:164–187

Forlizzi J, Ford S (2000) The building blocks of experience: an early framework for interaction designers. In: Proceedings of the designing interactive systems conference. ACM Press, New York, pp 419–423

Fröbel F (1909) Pedagogics of the Kindergarten. D. Appleton and Company, New York

Glenberg AM (2010) Embodiment as a unifying perspective for psychology. WIREs Cogn Sci 1:586–596. Wiley.

Glenberg AM, Goldberg AB, Zhu X (2011) Improving early reading comprehension using embodied CAI. Instr Sci 39:27–39. doi:10.1007/s11251-009-9096-7

Greimas AJ (1973) Actants, Actors, and Figures. On Meaning: Selected Writings in Semiotic Theory (trans: Perron PJ, Frank HC). Theory and history of literature 38. University of Minnesota P, Minneapolis, pp 106–120, 1987.

Hornecker E (2005) A design theme for tangible interaction: embodied facilitation. In: Gellerseen H et al (eds) Proceedings of the ninth European conference on computer-supported cooperative work. Springer International Publishing, Zurich, pp 18–22

Hornecker E, Buur J (2006) Getting a grip on tangible interaction: a framework on physical space and social interaction. In: Proceedings of the conference on human factors in computing systems. ACM Press, New York, pp 437–446

Hourcade JP (2008) Interaction design and children. J Found Trends Human–Comput Interact 1(4):277–392. doi:10.1561/1100000006

Hunter S, Kalanithi J, Merrill D (2010) Make a riddle and teleStory: designing children's applications for the siftables platform. In: Proceedings of the 9th IDC international conference on interaction design and children. ACM Press, New York, pp 206–209

Ishii H, Ullmer B (1997) Tangible bits: towards seamless interfaces between people, bits and atoms. In: Proceedings of the conference on human factors in computing systems. ACM Press, New York, pp 234–241

Kirsh D (1995) Complementary strategies: why we use our hands when we think. In: Moore JD, Lehman JF (eds) Proceedings of the seventeenth annual conference of the cognitive science. University of Pittsburgh, Carnegie Mellon, Pittsburgh, pp 212–217

Kirsh D (1996) Adapting the environment instead of oneself. J Adapt Behav 4(3):415–452

Lave J, Wenger E (1991) Situated learning: legitimate peripheral participation. Cambridge University Press, Cambridge

Marshall P (2007) Do tangible interfaces enhance learning? In: Proceedings of the 1st international conference on tangible and embedded interaction. ACM press, New York, pp 163–170

Montessori M (1912) The Montessori method: scientific pedagogy as applied to child education in the "children's houses". R. Bentley, Cambridge, MA

O'Malley C, Fraser DS (2005) Literature review in learning with tangible technologies. NESTA Futurelab Report, 12

Papert S (1977) A learning environment for children. In: Seidel RJ, Rubin M (eds) Computers and communication: implications for education. Academic, New York, pp 271–278

Papert S (1993) Mindstorms: children, computers, and powerful ideas, 2nd edn. Harvester, Wheatsheaf, New York

Plowman L, McPake J, Stephen C (2012) Extending opportunities for learning: the role of digital media in early education. In: Suggate S, Reese E (eds) Contemporary debates in child development and education. Rutledge, London

Propp V (1928) Morphology of the Folktale (trans: Laurence Scott), 2nd ed. University of Texas Press, Austin

Raffle H, Vaucelle C, Wang R, Ishii H (2007) Jabberstamp: embedding sound and voice in traditional drawings. In: Proceedings of the international conference on computer graphics and interactive. ACM Press, New York, pp 137–144

Resnick M, Silverman B (2005) Some reflections on designing construction kits for kids. In: Proceedings of interaction design and children conference. ACM Press, New York

Resnick M, Martin F, Berg R, Borovoy R, Colella V, Kramer K, Silverman B (1998) Digital manipulatives: new toys to think with. In: Proceedings of the conference on human factors in computing systems. ACM Press, New York, pp 281–287

Resnick M, Myers B, Nakakoji K, Schneidenman B, Pausch R, Selker T, Eisenberg M (2005) Design principles for tools to support creative thinking. Institute for Software Research, Paper 816

Shneiderman B, Plaisant C (2004) Designing the user interface: strategies for effective human-computer interaction, 4th edn. Addison-Wesley, Boston

Sylla C (2013) Designing a long term study evaluating a physical interface for preschoolers. In: Proceedings of TEI '13, 7th international conference on tangible embedded and embodied interaction. ACM Press, New York, pp 363–364. doi:10.1145/2460625.2460695

Sylla C, Branco P, Coutinho C, Coquet ME, Škaroupka D (2011) TOK- a tangible interface for storytelling. In: Proceedings of the conference on human factors in computing systems. ACM Press, New York, pp 1363–1368. doi:10.1145/1979742.1979775

Sylla C, Gonçalves S, Branco P, Coutinho C (2012) T-words: playing with sounds and creating narratives. In: Nijholt A, Romão T, Reidsma D (eds) Proceedings of the 9th international conference on advances in computer entertainment. Springer International Publishing, Lecture Notes in Computer Science, Zurich, pp 565–568. doi: 10.1007/978-3-642-34292-9

Sylla C, Gonçalves S, Branco P, Coutinho C (2013a) Peter piper picked a peck of pickled peppers – an interface for playful language exploration. In: Proceedings of the conference on human factors in computing systems. ACM Press, New York, pp 3127–3130. doi:10.1145/2468356.2479627

Sylla C, Gonçalves S, Brito P, BrancoP, Coutinho C (2013b) A tangible platform for mixing and remixing narratives. In: Reidsma D, Katayose H, Nijholt A (eds) Proceedings the 10th international conference on advances in computer entertainment, ACE 2013, LNCS 8253. Springer International Publishing, Zurich, pp 630–633

Sylla C, Coutinho C, Branco P (2014) A digital manipulative for embodied "Stage-narrative" creation. Entertainment Computing, Elsevier. doi: 10.1016/j.entcom.2014.08.011

Ullmer B, Ishii H (2001) Emerging frameworks for tangible user interfaces. In: Carroll JM (ed) Human-computer interaction in the new millennium. Addison-Wesley, Reading, MA, pp 579–601

Van Scoter J (2008) The potential of IT to foster literacy development in Kindergarten. In: Voogt J, Knezek G (eds) International handbook of information technology in primary and secondary education, Part I. Springer, London, pp 149–161

Van Scoter J, Ellis D, Railsback J (2001) Technology in early childhood education: finding the balance. Northwest Regional Educational Laboratory, Portland

Vygotsky LS (1978) Mind in society. Harvard University Press, Cambridge, MA

White D (1954) Books before five. Whitcomb and Tombs, Christchurch

Wood D, O'Malley C (1996) Collaborative learning between peers: an overview. Educ Psychol Pract 11(4):4–9

Wright S (2007) Graphic-narrative play: young children's authoring through drawing and telling. Int J Educ Arts 8(8):1–27

Yarosh S, Radu I, Hunter S, Rosenbaum E (2011) Examining values: an analysis of nine examining values: an analysis of nine years of IDC. In: Proceedings of the international conference on interaction design and children. ACM Press, New York, pp 136–144

Yelland N (1999) Reconceptualising schooling with technology for the 21st century: images and reflections. Inf Technol Child Educ Annu 1:39–59

Zaman B, Vanden Abeeleb V, Markopoulos P, Marshall P (2012) The evolving field of tangible interaction for children: the challenge of empirical validation. Pers Ubiquit Comput 16:367–378. doi:10.1007/s00779-011-0409-x

Zuckerman O, Arida S, Resnick M (2005) Extending tangible interfaces for education: digital montessori – inspired manipulatives. In: Proceedings of the conference on human factors in computing systems. ACM Press, New York, pp 859–868

Chapter 13
Game Design with Portfolios and Creative Skills

Daniela Reimann and Simone Bekk

13.1 Introduction

The project combines art education approaches and portfolio work to develop artistic processes with digital media technology. A new concept to support digital media literacy of young people is developed, tested and evaluated. It brings together art and technology education accompanied by a specific mentoring concept including portfolios. The project realizes an education-through-art approach to technology in five thematic media modules such as robotics, interactive light installation, smart textile, sound as well as games. The latter will be described in the context of the GamesLab ON/OFF, realized at ZKM with student mentors and young people. The GamesLab ON/OFF approach encourages the participants to develop, design and perform their own game concept using the Web, a variety of media, technologies and the physical learning space of the ZKM media museum.

Digital technologies determine today's everyday life. They are used by the younger generation as a matter of course in their daily life. Pupils love to play games, especially if they are linked to computers and digital media. Furthermore, they like the idea of developing a game by themselves, according to their own imagination as we came up with in earlier projects developing mixed reality games (Reimann and Blohm 2007). However, in the research project MediaArt@Edu (Acronym), we intend to address a special mix of on- and offline game scenarios to introduce game design in a wider sense than screen based, including performative activities and expressions in physical space and the integration of the urban environment. The media education approach integrates different tools (such as Makey Makey, Dead drop as well as iPads and a QR code generator) to support complex design processes of shaping technology as a space for aesthetic experiences. The

D. Reimann (✉) • S. Bekk
Karlsruhe Institute of Technology, Institute of Vocational and General Education,
Karlsruhe, Germany
e-mail: daniela.reimann@kit.edu; simone.bekk@kit.edu

© Springer-Verlag London 2015
N. Zagalo, P. Branco (eds.), *Creativity in the Digital Age*,
Springer Series on Cultural Computing, DOI 10.1007/978-1-4471-6681-8_13

245

Fig. 13.1 Performative activities supporting an electronic circuit through body connections

aims of the project are as follows: firstly, to realize an artistic media education approach including a scenario to support social and core skills through creative project work in team-based arrangements. Secondly, the mentoring of such processes with university students is a goal to aspire to. In the paper, we look at examples developed in the GamesLab workshop. The projects presented are based on 3-day workshop settings which were developed, realized and applied with education students who collaborate with students of technological subjects (e.g. such as electronical engineering, computer science, architecture as well as machine engineering) who attain so called key qualification/transferable skills[1] in the framework of a seminar at university level (Fig. 13.1).

The qualitative research methodology is based on the continuous observations of lessons by the mentors as well as on feedback rounds and semi-structured group interviews with the participants. As a result, the workshop scenario as well as projects developed by the young people are introduced in the following. In conclusion, the paper looks at the lessons learned through artistic game education as didactic tool for unlocking creativity in vocational preparation.

The project aims to scrutinize artistic approaches to media design and mentoring concepts and to enable students to accompany game development projects in creative contexts. It brings together game design and portfolio practice to reflect and

---

[1] The German term of Schlüsselqualifikationen.

visualize the processes by the learners themselves, following a constructivist and artistic learning approach. In order to improve media literacy of the young participants, the project aims to support them to shape their own vocational biography towards the development of a vocational identity in the future.

In Germany, vocational preparation is organized separately both at school and out of school in vocational preparation measures. An uncoordinated and confusing variety of offers exist for the young people to deal with. However, most measures do not lead to a profession according to the German dual system. Young people are prepared for work or advised to take up formal vocational apprenticeships. They are placed in a transit situation, hoping to enable their employment in future.

The project is based on the idea of integrating the target group of young people in vocational preparation who usually are characterized by having experienced negative learning situations and failure in their school careers. Most of them are holding leaving certificates of the secondary school (Hauptschule) or middle school (Realschule) with bad grades. Some even miss any leaving certificates. They are aged 15–21. The young people compete on the labour market with the increasing number of school leavers of academic secondary schools holding the A levels (Abitur), so that there is poor school to work transition for them. The number of such disadvantaged youngsters is increasing not only in Germany. However, it is the main pedagogical aim of the project to focus on their creative capacities, which can be defined as processes of developing and designing original ideas which have value (Robinson 2001), in order to enable them to investigate their own strength, and interests through developing and designing integrated on- and offline games.

The integration of the physical environment and technology was realized by equipping the young people with tools and media in order for them to experiment with it, to develop interest and to explore their own resources, rather than to focus on updating technical and job-related skills and competences. By developing a project, based on their own ideas and negotiations in the teams, they are expected to deal with their own concepts, to find solutions and to develop responsibility towards the realization of the game. Summing it up, they imagine an idea and give life to it, passing all processes of production, design as well as construction, testing, redesigning and problem solving.

13.2   Creative Game Development in Education and the 'GamesLab ON/OFF' Approach

Games represent activity systems in which the subjects act and communicate on the basis of using game specific tools according to the given rules. The latter is an overall agreement by the players. Activity theory can be perceived as an overall theoretical approach analysing human actions which are mediated by the tools used as well as the cultural environment wherein the subjects and objects of activity are operating and develop meaning (Engeström 1987; Reimann and Blohm 2007). The concept of play and the games developed in our culture constitute a special sort of activity system. Kafai (1995) has highlighted the significance of game design in education to make pupils teach fractions to other kids of lower grade. She introduced the 'designer notebook' for kids to develop the story board and document the design processes and revisions. It stems from the tradition of constructivist pedagogy and *constructionist* technology education introduced by Papert, which were employed for development purposes in the project and considered in the light of the project goals. Following an integrated approach of constructionist technology and art education, in our project, the designer notebook as well as the art education idea of process development was taken into account when developing the design process oriented by MediaArt@Edu project portfolio.

However, rather than constructing virtual worlds or augmented reality applications, this paper looks at a particular concept of creative game development, that is, the invention and design of on- and offline games using different sorts of tools, materials and media, such as Makey Makey (MIT), an Arduino-based technology to turn everyday objects into computer keys and use the tangible physical objects of the environment as a computer keyboard. It was inspired by the do-it-yourself (DIY) and maker movement. Further, the art project 'Dead drop', a shared offline data store in public space to engage people in participating in it, and the software iMovie which comes along with the iPad were introduced.

We use the term of the GamesLab ON/OFF, which addresses the linking of the physical and the digital world in a wider sense, bringing together a variety of levels of reality to virtual spaces of the computer. Imagination, analogue and digital media as well as the physical bodies of the players, as well as the issue of motion, are considered the basis of our human existence. Different to the typical and widely spread screen-based computer games, our approach is not focusing on the construction of virtual worlds but on the game concepts embedded in the physical world, the objects, bodies, materials required as well as shaping and communication processes between the learners. Our online-offline game design approach also differs from new edutainment applications, which extend and augment the space of physical acting (augmented/mixed reality, as described in the context of mixed reality learning spaces (Reimann 2006). Rather than developing computer-based systems, we intend to make them invent complex game conceptions, which bring together digital and physical space and media in rather unusual, new ways to them.

As kids love to play computer games, such media serve as motivators to learning, that is, the activation of young people as learners in vocational preparation. In our education scenario, we support the processes of game invention in cooperation with education students. Jenkins has introduced 'play' as relevant skill for the twenty-first century, defined as 'the capacity to experiment with the surroundings as a form of problem solving' (Jenkins 2009).

The students in the project act as mentors and researchers who scientifically observe the design and learning activities of the young people. The mentoring concept aims to support all processes of creativity, such as the conception, the development of a narrative, that is, the storytelling and game flow, as well as the interface design and the technical realization. The processes include basic social, communicative and collaborative activities, practised in team-based arrangements.

Fig. 13.2 Portfolio process supporting the game development

However, as we found, most of the participants have little or no awareness about their own capacities, the skills practised as well as the learning contents attached to it, nor do they have an idea about the meaning of such team experiences for future jobs and employment requirements. Additionally to the invention of a game, in order to improve the participants' awareness concerning their own learning processes, the project portfolio was introduced. It serves not only as a tool for visualizing the abstract idea of the game towards a clear structured story with different parts and tasks for the players to fulfil. It was intended to accompany the processes and to become a familiar practice of design and reflection (Fig. 13.2).

13.3 Game Design ON/OFF Linking Physical and Digital Spaces

The GamesLab ON/OFF module combines games and media, reality and virtuality. In the 3-day workshops, the participants are asked to develop and design games that are played with the help of digital media on the Web, on the computer tablet and in the offline world.

The workshop participants are given the opportunity to deal with digital media on a level other than that of their experience, i.e. at the interface of digital and ana-

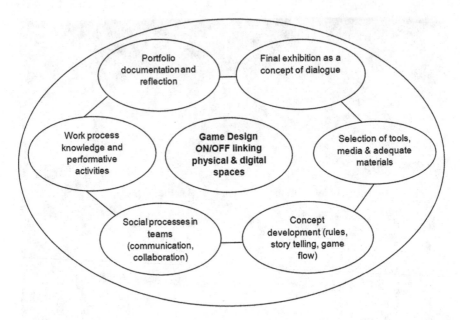

Fig. 13.3 Activities and learning contents practised in the game development process of the GamesLab ON/OFF workshops

logue – reality and virtuality. For this purpose, the GamesLab ON/OFF workshop module was designed and organized at the KIT, Karlsruhe Institute of Technology, and ZKM, Karlsruhe Center for Art and Media. The four workshops of 3 days' duration each were directed by a media pedagogue, whose scope of tasks covered both workshop design and technical aspects.

The workshop modules focus on multidisciplinary competencies needed by the participants to prepare for their profession rather than on job-specific competencies. The module and the associated learning objectives will be explained in more detail below (Fig. 13.3).

13.3.1 Selection of Tools, Media and Adequate Materials

The workshop started with a presentation of the tools available, i.e. the hardware and software, according to the principle of 'learning by doing'. This means that the tools were tested in practice by the participants before the game development. The four following tools were available for selection: the Makey Makey (MIT), an Arduino-based technology to turn everyday objects into computer keys and use the tangible physical objects of the environment as a computer keyboard. It is inspired by the do-it-yourself (DIY) and maker movement. Further, the art project 'Dead drop', a shared offline data store in public space to engage people in participating in it,[2] and the software iMovie which comes along with the iPad (in particular for videos and photos taken, Stop-Motion production and audio recordings) were introduced as well as Google Maps. In addition, single-lens reflex cameras were used for photography, encoded zip files were generated and QR codes were generated with a QR code generator to link to videos recorded and stored on, for example, YouTube.

The tools were selected since they met the following criteria: They supported the flexible and mobile use in the learning environment of the museum (e.g. the continuous exhibition ZKM_Gameplay[3]) as well as in the public space (such as iPads). They were either available on the Web (such as Google Maps or free apps), as open source (such as 'Dead drops'), or came along with the hardware (such as iMovie), or low budget (such as 'Makey Makey').

The participants' own skills were incorporated into the project, such as film cutting and programming. Presentation of the tools was aimed at developing an understanding of the technology and its potentials by direct application. Every tool was discussed theoretically and with respect to games and game development.

13.3.2   Concept Development (Rules, Storytelling, Game Flow)

After the presentation of the media and tools available, the participants were asked to choose some tools (or an individual tool or medium) and to design in working groups a game at the interface of online and offline. This general task definition resulted in various approaches to game development pursued by the working groups. While one group applied a technical approach by identifying technically feasible options, other groups decided in favour of a content-related approach by developing the background story of the game. In general, free working was highly appreciated by the workshop participants. This is also obvious from the interviews and online questionnaires. One participant commented: 'We were free and we could decide what to do, which is much more fun. Otherwise, we would have been caught in a type of labyrinth'. And another participant added: 'Free work allows to be more creative and to contribute own skills'.

For every game, instructions had to be written for the future players to know what the rules are and what the objective of the game is. For this purpose, the participants had to analyse their game on a meta-level and to assume the role of a future player in order to decide which information and aid might be helpful and how the game has to be explained for playing it.

---

[2] Website: http://deaddrops.com/blog [20.6.2014].

[3] "ZKM_Gameplay is the new permanent exhibition on the theme of video games and experimented forms of play. Since its opening in 1997, numerous computer games have been presented at the ZKM | Media Museum in Karlsruhe, since these reflect an essential part within modern society heavily influenced by digitalized realities of life. For centuries new artistic, experimental, media-reflective as well as 'serious' games have evolved. The cultural and economic power of digital games and gameplay have experienced and continuous growth. This has made the games an important object of the ZKM." http://on1.zkm.de/zkm/stories/storyReader$8340 [20.6.2014]

13.3.3 Social Processes in Teams (Communication, Collaboration)

Two working groups were formed with up to three participants in the vocational preparation workshop and one student mentor each. The group had to jointly develop and plan a game concept. Hence, the group members interacted. In the planning and development phase, social skills, such as the ability to work in a team, the ability to establish contacts, the ability to solve conflicts and the ability to become accepted, were required in particular. The workshop trained the participants' ability to cooperate and to agree on a game idea by making compromises as well as the ability to solve conflicts and technical problems arising.

In addition, the groups had to plan the work and time. Accordingly, the working group members also had to share the work to reach the defined objective. In this case, individual work was required and observed. The workshop focused on aspects such as the perception and defence of own interests, the ability to work under pressure, own responsibility and the ability to reach decisions.

13.3.4 Work Process Knowledge and Performative Activities

In the following table, the game design and learning contents are summarized (Fig. 13.4).

In order to present the variety of different game concepts developed, the following examples are presented.

13.3.4.1 The Game 'Fresh Air GMDC'

The game 'Fresh Air GMDC' combines virtuality and reality. For instruction purposes, a video was produced. It included photos of objects and drawings together with the spoken explanation of the game flow and the objective of the game. This tutorial leads the player to the first level, a game station. A beamer transmits the computer game onto a big screen, and the player can play the game with the feet or the hands via two metal plates connected with the computer by Makey Makey. Depending on the score reached, the player has to repeat the game, is asked a riddle that has to be solved and is given a hint or the direct coordinates of the next game station. This station is located outside of the ZKM. There, Dead drops can be found at various points (park bench, staircase, a wall of the building). These are USB storage media that are publicly accessible. On these storage media, a self-generated audio file is found. It explains level 2 and poses the next task. A riddle has to be solved. The solution is password and a hint where the next Dead drop can be found. There, the password can be used to open a new self-generated audio file. This audio file contains another password. At the

Activities of the pupils	Learning contents
Working methods (single person working, team based working)	• Work planning • Self-dependent • Commitment • Accuracy • Concentration and endurance • Social role in the team • Team communication and agreements • Collaborative problem solving • Collaboration
Media design and use	• Material and media selection • developing ideas and game concept (on and offline) according to one's mental model • realisation of concepts • Testing the concept of the game using the prototype • Improving the games • Use of hard-and software • Exploration of the tools • Creativity • Dealing with the unknown / unpredictable • artistic acting and means • research of media and material
Portfolio practise	• Aesthetic appeal • Accuracy • Self dependency • Portfolio structure

Fig. 13.4 Game design activities and learning contents

next Dead drop, an extension of the browser game is to be played (which was not possible during the workshop for reasons of time). When winning the browser game, the players are given the coordinates of the last Dead drop containing the final file 'Final GMDC' with the winner photo. This project can be seen as a kind of a paper chase (scavenger hunt).

13.3.4.2 The Project 'Shake a Leg'

The game 'Shake a Leg' is a dance battle instead of the often encountered war games. The participants wanted to design a game, in which the players themselves had to act. At the beginning, a self-produced video is shown. The background story of the game is told with the help of video recordings, photographs and drawings. Then, the player can watch a self-developed tutorial. Here, video recordings and audio recordings explain how the game has to be played and who the winner of the game is. On a self-designed dance floor, a self-developed dance video is projected onto the wall by a beamer. Two player groups have to dance as it is shown on the video. With a decibel app started on an iPad near the dance floor, the winner is determined by the applause of the audience. The game is characterized by competition.

13.3.4.3 The Project 'The Last Big Thing'

The game 'The Last Big Thing' is about a bank robbery. At the beginning of the game, the player is given a laptop and a photo of the Dead drop 'Z'. This Dead drop has to be found by the player. There, the player can connect his laptop. The Dead drop contains a self-developed audio file simulating a phone call. The work order and the objective of the game are explained. The player has to solve various riddles (e.g. poem) and to move through the ZKM. At various works of arts, he is given new hints regarding the location of the final action. There, a safe is located, which is connected to a notebook via Makey Makey. When the safe is opened slowly, a video file starts on the connected notebook. This file shows the explosion of a safe (self-cut video). A self-developed stop-motion video production shows how the safe opens and what is contained in the safe. The objective is reached, and the safe is opened (Fig. 13.5).

13.3.5 Portfolio Documentation and Reflection

Portfolios usually are considered, and used as, collections of originals, such as sketches, drawings, and other documents, or as combinations of methods, processes or options for action. Aims and objectives of portfolios are self-management, documentation and reflection as activation of the learner(s) (Häcker 2007; Schwarz et al.

Fig. 13.5 Testing the interactive safe based on Arduino Makey Makey technology

2008; Reimann 2014). The specific MediaArt@Edu portfolio[4] design goes beyond the tool idea. It serves as a means to support self-managed learning, imagination, representation, visualization, documentation and reflection.

The portfolio consists of several parts. Firstly, it serves as a poster, including the structure of the games, which is presented in the exhibition. It follows the idea of visualizing and documenting the processes, to support the reflection about one's own acting, designing and thinking.

Secondly, the portfolio contains an online questionnaire and feedback session with the student mentor. Thirdly, the digital version of the portfolio is an explanation video as well as a blog, developed and realized by the participants themselves. In the explanation videos, they present the final project and the development and design processes (Fig. 13.6).

13.3.6 Final Exhibition as a Didactic Concept of Dialogue

A major element of the didactic concept was a public exhibition of the games at the ZKM museum. The exhibition was aimed at presenting the participants' work in the context of the museum and describing the process of game development. The

---

[4]The MediaArt@Edu research project portfolio refers to preparatory work tried at universities within the framework of the 'Aesthetic Research Book' portfolio variant and the 'Artistic Research Book' (Reimann and Biazus 2007) portfolio variants.

Fig. 13.6 Final portfolio
including the structure of the
game 'Shake a Leg'

work phases were documented by portfolio posters, sketches, photos and by the explanation videos. The participants also used the posters for presenting and explaining their game concepts to the spectators. In this way, the visitors were given the opportunity to discuss the work with the makers at the stations in the museum. Posters also presented those games that could not be developed to maturity due to reasons of time.

In the course of the exhibition, the participants were confronted with ideas, associations and new contents of the games expressed by the visitors, which resulted in an extensive exchange between designer and visitor. The possibility to present the games in a museum led to a high appreciation and relevance of the own-developed games and enhanced the self-confidence of the participants in their own skills. The exhibition is a concept opening up the opportunity for the participants' self-presentation.

The researchers as well as the student mentors observed that all groups presented and discussed their projects in a highly self-confident manner.

13.4 Lessons Learned

In the project, the evaluation is still ongoing. In the following, we sum up the first findings which will be underpinned by single quotes of the participating actors such as young people and student mentors. All quoted comments are translated from the qualitative group interviews.

The workshops were perceived very positively by the participants. This was also reflected and visible through their high motivation, their regular presence and high commitment. Most of the participants would like the workshop to be repeated and the workshop duration to be extended as we came up with in the interviews:

Participant: *'Well, if I had had one or two weeks more [in the workshop], I would have developed something more complex'.*

The pedagogical approach with its open definition of the task and the free creative and experimental work along the own-developed idea was rated highly positively by the participants who are used to more instructed learning situations in a teacher-centred classroom. The participants stressed in the interview that they perceived their usual school learning as predetermined. They used the metaphor of 'labyrinth' to describe it as opposed to the learning happening in the workshop:

Interviewer: *'Would you prefer to work that free [and self-determined]?'*
Participant 1:   *'Yes, [...]. It is more fun than to work only in one direction. One can say ... like in a labyrinth if you have more narrow-instructed tasks. But if you can work free, then you have more fun, you can use your own things. [...] it is like you are captured in a labyrinth. You can't get out. And if you can do what you want, then you have more fun. You can decide and make another decision [on your own] ...if it [the project] is not working like that, then we [the team] make it in a different way... [...] I like that [freedom of decision]'.*
Participant 2:   *'Generally, I like to work free [because] it opens up more opportunities for my work as the usual tasks [given and perceived in different education contexts]. Normally, the working tasks are very trivial, [for example], you have to do things that look useless to you if you do it according to the instructed manner [given by the teacher] or to realize it [the task] at all. [If the task is more open], then it is possible to work more creative and to put a lot into it and you are involved differently'.*

The exhibition and presentation of the games enhanced the self-confidence and self-esteem of the participants. In this way, they were given the opportunity to train their appearance and presentation skills:

Mentor: *'[I]t was K. (participant) [...] as it was visible on the presentation [at the exhibition]. He is 100 % proud of what we [the group] have had developed ... [...] he was completely enthusiastic and [...] he got self-confidence from the game [development]. For example, he [the participant]* said: *"This is mine [game]. I have worked on it in the team". [...] He presented the game and its functionality at the exhibition on his own to a group of people, without me being around. I kept an eye on him from distance. And I think it is great what he has achieved. It is [...]. I only know him from the first day of this workshop and then he wasn't like that. And ... I think all the three guys of the group [participants] developed especially self-confidence'.*

The participants are not necessarily aware of what they experience during the workshop and which competencies were trained and applied. Furthermore, they have little experience in managing working tasks and time frames. They quickly invent a variety of complex game ideas, but they are rather not used in dealing with realistic project planning according to the given time. This is where the mentor comes in. He/she plays an important role to provide support when participants reflect the workshop and especially their own working manner and capacities:

Mentor: *'In my group, one [mentor] had to tell it to them. [...] That was during the feedback session ... then I have told it to them. It was like "Oh, really?" [They reacted rather surprised]. I had to point it out to all the three of them, in what they were good at'.*

The mentor is also required in the phase of free project work, which initially overstrains the participants if they work on their own. As soon as a structure has been defined, the mentors can withdraw:

Mentor: *'At the beginning, when the participants have to find an idea, well, I think, if you don't guide them a little bit and if you don't take care that they get to the point to have an idea, and everyone agreed with this idea, and it is mainly a realizable idea. If [the mentor doesn't intervene], I think they would simply sit there and discuss the whole day what was possible to do. And they would become obsessed [e.g.] into dimensions with up to 20 levels and who knows what else. This is a real task of the mentor, to intervene and to say: "We only have three days, play it cool"'.*

Interviewer: *'You mean the feasibility?'*

Mentor: *'Yes, a little bit simpler, so that it is producible. And if this is done, one can add something more, something more difficult'.*

As we found, portfolio practice often is perceived by the participants as an additional task to be fulfilled in the workshops. That's especially the case when they develop artefacts such as interactive light object (Reimann and Bekk 2014a, b) or robots (Reimann 2014) which attract attention rather than the portfolio work. Usually, portfolio work is introduced in long-term scenarios rather than in 3-day workshops. However, single cases have shown that the participants who have participated for the second time self-initiatedly developed the portfolio without any requests:

Mentor: '*Because J. [participant] already knew [the portfolio procedure because he already participated in the previous workshop] [...] we designed the Portfolio [of the game workshop] like in the other light installation workshop, that is, one has described what one had thought about, how the idea was developed*'.

If the portfolio is perceived reasonable and useful by the participants, then the portfolio is carried out accurate and is taken seriously:

Interviewer: '*That is very similar to the compulsory 'apprenticeship report port-folio'[5] in an apprenticeship*'.

Participant 1: '*Exactly, that is supposed to simulate this, like in an apprenticeship*'.

Interviewer: '*But you don't like it [to fill it in]?*'

Participant 1: '*It is useless*'.

Interviewer: '*And what about this portfolio in this workshop? How have you designed it? [...] Why have you designed it?*'

Participant 2: '*Because in this workshop, it makes sense [to me]*'.

Participant 1: '*Because we work on something in the workshop and create some-thing. And you [the researcher] want to see what we have done*'.

Participant 2: '*Also that we have a reference point for us, what we have worked on*'.

Participant 2: '*Of course. There are some differences. [...] That is a different story as if one says [to you]: "You have to write it down, so that if you are controlled by us [the teacher of the vocational prepa-ration provider] [...], you can prove it". Because of this reason, they [the vocational preparation measures] request us to do it. [For example], then even things are filled in which they have never happened*'.

Interviewer: '*[...] And in this case [in the game workshop]? What do you think is the reason for you having to do it? You just said before: 'In this workshop it makes sense.'[...]*'.

Participant 2: '*The portfolio has the this very sense, that [...] one can illustrate what one has done, one can explain it, one has examples. One really can explain it to people, who did not attend the whole pro-cess, who are just interested [in the project] or who want to know what really [had happened]. [...] It works well. ... It's descriptive. And these are the reasons why one actually works with it [the portfolio]*'.

In order to initiate a portfolio culture on the long run which is reasonable for the participants, it has not only to be embedded into the didactic concept of the work-shop, but it also has to be integrated into the project planning and realization process from the very beginning.

---

[5] In Germany, the 'Berichtsheft' is a compulsory regular task in the framework of the dual system of vocational education and training and has to be controlled by the trainer.

Acknowledgements This chapter is based on the research project MediaArt@Edu – funded by the Research Planning and Education. Further, we would like to thank the (GMK), an incorporate society concerned with media education and communication culture, to support the idea of MediaArtLab@School. We would like to thank the BMBF, Federal Ministry of Education and Research and the DLR as well as the project partners Agentur für Arbeit Karlsruhe (agency for employment Karlsruhe) and their collaboration partners USS and AAW. We further thank the participants of the vocational preparation measures (BVB) of the year 2013/2014 of the Agency of Employment Karlsruhe, department BVB as well as the referee Thorsten Belzer of the department Museum Communications (Head: Janine Burger) and Banu Beyer at ZKM, the Center for Art and Media Karlsruhe. Further, we thank the students of KIT, the members of the project team, namely, Sabine Bauer, Raphaela Pelliccia, Nicole Widmann, Christian Schneider, Carolin Uller as well as Tobias Brauchler who worked as student assistants and mentors in the module GamesLab ON/OFF and who supported the evaluation of the project.

References

Engeström Y (1987) Learning by expanding: an activity theoretical approach to development research. Orienta Konsultit Oy, Helsinki

Häcker T (2007) Portfolio: ein Entwicklungsinstrument für selbstbestimmtes Ler-nen. Eine explorative Studie zur Arbeit mit Portfolios in der Sekundarstufe I. Baltmannswei-ler

Jenkins H (2009) Confronting the challenges of participatory culture. MIT Press https://mitpress. mit.edu/sites/default/files/titles/free_download/9780262513623_Confronting_the_ Challenges.pdf, p XIV

Kafai Y (1995) Minds in play: computer game design as a context for children's learning. Lawrence Erlbaum, Mahwah

Reimann D (2006) Ästhetisch-informatische Medienbildung mit Kindern und Jugendli-chen. Grundlagen, Szenarien und Empfehlungen für Gestaltungsprozesse in Mixed Reality-Lernräumen, Oberhausen, 2006 (ATHENA)

Reimann D (2014) Digital media in creative processes with young people in vocational preparation, paper for the international symposium on "Youth as Visual Culture Pro-ducers: Artistic Skills and Knowledge in Secondary Education", Public University of Navarra, Pamplona/ Spain, 22–23 November 2013

Reimann D, Bekk S (2014a) Introducing artistic processes with digital me-dia in vocational preparation. In: Leonardo Electronic Almanac, issue: the culture of digital education: innovation in art, design, science and technology practices, Senior Editors for this volume: Lanfranco Aceti, Nina Czegledy and Oliver Grau, in review/to appear 2014

Reimann D, Bekk S (2014b) Künstlerisch geleitete Medienbildung mit Port-folios: Potenziale für Jugendliche in berufsvorbereitenden Bildungsmaßnahmen. Herausfor-derungen beim Übergang Schule – Beruf und das Konzept der berufsbiografischen Gestal-tungskompetenz. In Medienimpulse. Potenziale digitaler Medienkunst. 02.2014. http://medienimpulse.at/articles/ view/659

Reimann D, Biazus MC (2007) Augmented virtual 3D-Community spaces as an intercultural inter-face for higher media art education. In: Koschke R, Otthein H, Rödiger K-H, Ronthaler M (Hrsg.) Informatik 2007, Informatik trifft Logistik, Beiträ-ge der 37. Jahrestagung der Gesellschaft für Informatik e.V. (GI), 24.-28.9.2007 in Bremen, Bd. 1. (pp 528–534). Köllen, Bonn, p 531

Reimann D, Blohm M (2007) The concept of MediaArtLab@School as a didactic tool to integrate digital media, Interactive Systems and Arts in Education. Ped-agogika, Journal, University of Vilnius, pp 68–74

Robinson K (2001) Out of our minds: learning to be creative. Capstone, Chichester

Schwarz J, Volkwein KW, Felix (Hrsg.) (2008) Portfolio im Unter-richt. 13 Unterrichtseinheiten mit Portfolio. Kallmeyer, Seelze-Velber, p 22

Author Biographies

Simone Bekk, MA, is a researcher in the project "MediaArt@Edu" and PhD student at the Karlsruhe Institute of Technology's Institute of Vocational and General Education. She studied Vocational Education and General Pedagogics with focus on General Pedagogics at the Karlsruhe Institute of Technology (KIT) as well as at the University of Cádiz, Campus Rio San Pedro, Spain, from 2005 to 2011. She completed with the academic degree Master of Arts. In 2008, she received a scholarship from the Heinrich-Hertz-Gesellschaft for her degree Bachelor of Arts in Vocational and General Education. Since 2011, she is accepted as a PhD student at the Faculty for Humanities and Social Science at the Institute for Vocational and General Education at KIT. Her PhD thesis focuses on theater pedagogy. Since October 2013, she is an academic staff at the Institute for Vocational and General Education in the project "MediaArt@Edu."

Vlada Botoric received his MSc in Marketing, PR, and Multimedia Communications. At Aarhus University in Denmark, he became interested in the intersections between business models and participatory culture. Currently, in his PhD project, he examines aspects of interactions between fans and corporations, trying to indicate how the most heterogeneous participants and business practices are blended together in the value cocreation process. In his research, Vlada focuses on LEGO fandom, as one of the most active fan communities in the world.

Pedro Branco is a professor in the Department of Information Systems at the University of Minho and cochairs the research group engageLab. He worked as researcher at the Fraunhofer Center for Research in Computer Graphics and later at iMedia in Providence, RI, USA, in the areas of human-computer interaction. He received his doctorate degree in Information Systems from the University of Minho in 2006 on facial expression analysis for assessing user experience. His research interests spans several areas of human-computer interaction such as interaction design, novel interfaces, and the intersection of those with interactive art. He is

© Springer-Verlag London 2015
N. Zagalo, P. Branco (eds.), *Creativity in the Digital Age*,
Springer Series on Cultural Computing, DOI 10.1007/978-1-4471-6681-8

currently the director of the Master Course in Technology and Digital Art at the University of Minho. He works closely with students from a wide range of backgrounds developing interactive systems that explore a synergy of technology and aesthetics, exploring future directions for our interaction with technology.

Andy M. Connor is a Senior Lecturer at Colab, the "collaboratory" at Auckland University of Technology in New Zealand. His undergraduate training is in mechanical engineering and he holds a PhD in mechatronics. He has worked at the Engineering Design Centres at both the University of Bath and the University of Cambridge in the UK. Following a number of years of commercial experience as a software engineer and a systems engineering consultant, Andy migrated to New Zealand and took up a number of roles in software engineering and computer science at Auckland University of Technology prior to joining Colab in 2012. Andy has a broad range of research interests that include automated design, computational creativity, education, evolutionary computation, machine learning and software engineering.

Leandro Costalonga is a professor at the Department of Computing and Electronics of the Federal University of Espírito Santo (UFES), in Brazil. He is the head of NESCoM – Núcleo Espírito-Santense de Computação Musical, a research group in creative technologies. He received his PhD in Computing at the University of Plymouth, UK, in 2009, and his master's degree in Computer Science at UFRGS in 2005. Since 2003, he has been researching at computer music-related topics, with special interest at programming language for music, expressive performance modeling, and ubiquitous music.

Clara Coutinho, PhD in Educational Technology, is an assistant professor at the Institute of Education, Minho University, Braga, Portugal. She develops research in the development of digital resources for education, teacher education, and research methods in the social sciences and published more than 100 papers in proceedings and specialized journals as well as three books.

Nicholas Davis is a PhD candidate in Human-Centered Computing at the Georgia Institute of Technology. He received his BA in Cognitive Science from Case Western Reserve University (2009). His research focuses on understanding and developing software systems that can collaborate with humans in creative domains. He is a member of the Adaptive Digital Media (ADAM) Lab led by Brian Magerko and the Creative Machine Environments (ACME) Lab led by Ellen Yi-Luen Do. Outside of the academia, Nicholas has worked in Adobe's Creative Technologies Labs developing creativity support tools and as a user experience (UX) researcher at Google working on Google TV. Most recently, he joined the UX team at YouTube to help define a vision for supporting the creative community on YouTube.

Maria Helena de Lima is a teacher and researcher from the Music Education Area from the Application College of UFRGS – Federal University of Rio Grande do Sul (2004) – with a PhD in Education in the same institution. She acts in the field on basic education, school education (children and teenagers), popular education, popular culture, education and community, learning music, musical semantics, music education, and information and communication technologies and emphasizes on multidisciplinary educational/research perspective. She is a member and researcher of the Ubiquitous Music Group (g-ubimus) and the CTA/UFRGS – Academic Technology Center. She is the founder of the NGO Music and Citizenship (2000).

Gloria Gómez Diago is a PhD candidate at the Rey Juan Carlos University. She obtained a BS in Advertising and Public Relations from University of Vigo, where she also received a Master of Advanced Studies with a thesis entitled "Proposal of criteria to evaluate the quality of the Web Communication." At the University of Vigo, she also received a master in pedagogy, specialty in business organization. Her research is aimed at developing communication research methodologies and to identify virtual communication utterance. Her latest publications include "Emancipative Technology in Formal Education: The Case for 'Free and Open Source Software (FOSS)'"; in Stocchetti, M. (Ed.), "Media and Education in the Digital Age" (2014); "Cyberspace and Cyberculture"; and in Kosut et al. (Eds.), "Encyclopedia of Gender in Media" (2012).

María Ruth Garcia is Assistant Professor of Audiovisual Communication and Research Fellow at the University of Alcalá. She is a member of the research group Grupo Imágenes Palabras e Ideas (GIPI) (Images, Words and Ideas Group). She works on video games, new technologies and audiovisual narratives. Her current research on the topic of computer games and narratives is supported by the Spanish Ministry of Culture and Education. She has been a visiting scholar at the Department of Media and Culture Studies – Media and Performance Studies, Utrecht University.

David Gauntlett is a professor in the Faculty of Media, Arts and Design and codirector of the Communications and Media Research Institute, at the University of Westminster, UK. He is the author of several books, including *Creative Explorations* (2007), *Making is Connecting* (2011), and *Making Media Studies: The Creativity Turn in Media and Communications Studies* (2015). He has worked with a number of the world's leading creative organizations, including the BBC, the British Library, and Tate. For almost a decade, he has worked with LEGO on innovation in creativity, play, and learning.

Sara Cortés-Gómez is Assistant Professor in Audiovisual Communication at the University of Alcalá, Spain. Sara is interested in the role of new technologies and video games as cultural tools aimed to develop new literacies in a global world. The main lines are focused on analyzing the creation of new educational spaces where new technologies become literacy practices and the construction of one's identity when children and youngsters play with video games or use social media. She has been a visiting scholar at LCMI (University of Luxembourg) and GLS at the University of Madison. In addition, she works as the coordinator and web designer of www.aprendeyjuegaconea.com.

Stefano Gualeni is first and foremost an individual human being. When asked to talk about himself in third person, he customarily starts by stating that he was born on the shores of a northern Italian lake in 1978 and that he worked on his first commercial videogame at the age of 16. Stefano obtained his PhD in Philosophy at the Erasmus University of Rotterdam. He currently lectures and researches in the fields of game design, game studies, and philosophy of technology at the University of Malta. His upcoming book is titled 'Virtual Worlds as Philosophical Tools' (Palgrave/McMillan) and it will be available from the summer of 2015 [stefano.guale-ni.com].

Chih-Pin Hsiao is a PhD candidate specializing in Human-Computer Interaction and Design Computing at Georgia Institute of Technology. His research focus is on interaction and creativity in the following fields: CAAD, Information Visualization, Tangible User Interfaces, and Sketch and Gesture Interactions. He is an active member of Creative Machine Environments (ACME) Labs under the GVU Research Center at Georgia Tech. Besides academic activities, he has also worked in the software industry and contributed software projects in various roles.

Marcelo Johann (Member of IEEE, AES, ICMA) received his bachelor (5 years), masters and the Ph.D. degrees in Computer Science from the Federal University of Rio Grande do Sul (UFRGS), at Porto Alegre, Brazil, in 1992, 1994 and 2001, respectively, having spent 6 months as a visiting student at UCLA, USA, in 1997. He worked as a professor at the Catholic University of Rio Grande do Sul (PUCRS) from 2000 to 2002, and is a full-time professor at UFRGS since 2003. His research interests include algorithms for placement, routing, discrete gate sizing, combinatorial optimization, and his activities include also teaching digital design, compilers, operating systems and computer music.

Damián Keller (DMA, Stanford University, 2004; MFA, Simon Fraser University, 1999) is an associate professor at the Federal University of Acre, Brazil, where he coordinates the Amazon Center for Music Research (NAP, Núcleo Amazônico de Pesquisa Musical). As a member and founder of the Ubiquitous Music Group (g-ubimus), his research focuses on ecologically grounded creative practice and ubiquitous music. His artistic works include tape pieces and music for theater, film, and installations. For more information, see http://ccrma.stanford.edu/~dkeller.

Pilar Lacasa is Professor of Audiovisual Communication. Researcher at the Faculty of Humanities at the University of Alcalá, she coordinates the *Images, Words and Ideas Research Group* since 1998. She loves video games, new emerging communication technologies and classic European and American movies. Her research work has been developed from a socio-cultural approach. She has been a visiting researcher at the University of Utah, at the Comparative Media Studies program (MIT) and at the University of Southern California, Annenberg Innovation Lab. Pilar is the author of *Learning in Virtual and Real Worlds* (2013) edited by Palgrave.

Victor Lazzarini is a senior lecturer in Music and the dean of Arts, Celtic Studies, and Philosophy at Maynooth University in Ireland. A graduate of the Universidade Estadual de Campinas (UNICAMP) in Brazil, where he was awarded a BMus in Composition, he completed his doctorate at the University of Nottingham, UK. His research interests include musical signal processing and sound synthesis; computer music languages; electroacoustic and instrumental composition.

Brian Magerko is an associate professor of Digital Media and the head of the Adaptive Digital Media (ADAM) Lab at Georgia Tech. He received his BS in Cognitive Science from Carnegie Mellon (1999) and his MSc and PhD in Computer Science and Engineering from the University of Michigan (2001, 2006). His research explores the intersection of creativity, cognition, and computing. This interdisciplinary work leads to studying creativity and human cognition, building artificial intelligence systems that can creatively collaborate with human users, and exploring the use of human creativity as a gateway to better understand how to effectively teach computing skills.

Stefan Marks is a Lecturer at Colab, the "collaboratory" at Auckland University of Technology in New Zealand. He has several years of industry experience as a hardware and software developer, a diploma in microinformatics, a master's degree in human-computer interaction, and a PhD from the University of Auckland for research combining virtual environments, serious games, and image processing into a medical teamwork simulation. His research interests include virtual and interactive environments, 3D data visualization, human-computer interaction, simulation of physical processes, serious games, robotics and electronics, image processing, and computer science education. In his spare time, he enjoys photography, preferably while exploring beautiful New Zealand's outdoors.

Nuno Otero is a senior lecturer at the Department of Media Technology, Linnaeus University, Sweden, and is interested in theories and conceptual frameworks in HCI, from more traditional approaches taking a user-centered perspective to more recent trends focusing on the user's experiences with technologies. In a nutshell, the question driving his research concerns the understanding of how the properties of distinct devices and embedded external representations impact people's activities (from work-related activities to educational and ludic contexts). Furthermore, he is also keen on understanding how distinct methodologies suit the investigation of different issues along the artifact design cycle and how the design solutions can the documented and reused by the design team.

Marcelo Soares Pimenta is an associate professor at the Institute of Informatics from the Federal University of Rio Grande do Sul (UFRGS), in Brazil. He is the head of the Computer Music Lab (LCM), also at UFRGS. He received his PhD in Informatique at Université Toulouse 1, France, in 1997, and bachelor and master's degree in Computer Science at UFRGS in 1988 and 1991, respectively. Since 1998, he is a member of a multidisciplinary research group at UFRGS working with topics in Human-Computer Interaction, Software Engineering, and Computer Music, with emphasis in the integration of these areas. Currently, his research is focused on collaborative design, adaptive interfaces, networked music, ubiquitous music, and user-centered software engineering.

Yanna Popova has studied linguistics, literature, and philosophy and received her PhD from the University of Oxford, UK. She was one of the founding members of the Department of Cognitive Science at Case Western Reserve University, USA. Her main areas of research include narrative as a fundamental cognitive process, the implications of the embodied/enactive paradigm for the study of language and art, and the intersubjective nature of social cognition. Her book *Narrativity and Enaction* is forthcoming from Routledge in 2015.

Daniela Reimann's PhD thesis looked at integrated arts and computer science in children and young people education, based on the German model project "ArtDeCom." She teaches and undertakes her postdoc research in the field of didactics of artistic processes in the digital media, exploring the overlap between arts, design, media culture, technology, computer science, and engineering in education at the university and school level. She is the coordinator of the research project "MediaArt@Edu" at the Karlsruhe Institute of Technology's Institute of Vocational and General Education which focuses on artistic approaches to media skills, funded by the German Federal Ministry of Education and Research (BMBF).

María T. Soto-Sanfiel is an associate professor at the Audiovisual Communication and Advertising Department at the *Universitat Autònoma de Barcelona*. Her main research interests are media psychology, narratives, interactivity, cross-cultural reception, science communication, and voice/audio reception. Until 2014, she has published 37 articles in scientific publications. In 2004, she received the National Research Award on Mass Communication by the Catalonian Government. Dr. Soto-Sanfiel directs inscience.tv (http://inscience.tv) and c-radio.org (http://c-radio.org), an IP television and IP radio for the dissemination of science.

Cristina Sylla has a PhD in Educational Technology, and she is currently involved in the design, development, and evaluation of innovative pedagogic materials that promote the young children's experimental, participatory, and active involvement with technology, focusing on the intersection of traditional games and playful activities and the new interactive technological solutions.

Joshua G. Tanenbaum is an assistant professor in the Department of Informatics at the Donald Bren School of Information and Computer Sciences at the University of California-Irvine. His research interests include digital games and storytelling, with an emphasis on the pleasures of agency and transformation in digital narratives. His work draws on theories from theater and dance to explore the connections between performance and play.

Karen Tanenbaum received her PhD in Interactive Arts and Technology from Simon Fraser University and does research on game design, artificial intelligence, tangible and ubiquitous computing, and maker culture. She is a project scientist at the Transformative Play Lab in the Department of Informatics at the University of California, Irvine.

Charles Walker studied engineering and painting before qualifying as an architect at Edinburgh College of Art. He has an MSc from the Faculty of Business, University of Strathclyde, Glasgow, and a PhD in architecture from the University of Auckland. He is a founding director of Colab, a future-focused center for research, development, and industry partnerships in design and emerging technologies, based at Auckland University of Technology.

Nelson Zagalo is professor of Interactive Media at the University of Minho, Portugal. He is the director of the Master of Interactive Media degree program on the board of the Master on Technology and Digital Art degree program. He cochairs the research group engageLab and was a founder member of the Portuguese Society of Videogame Sciences. He is the author of the books *Interactive Emotions, from Film to Videogames* (2009) and *Videogames in Portugal: History, Technology and Art* (2013) and the editor-coeditor of the books *Interactive Storytelling* (2009) and *Virtual Worlds and Metaverse Platforms: New Communication and Identity Paradigms* (2011).